RURAL FIJI

RURAL
FIJI

Institute of Pacific Studies
University of the South Pacific
Suva

1988

USP Library Cataloguing-in-Publication Data

Rural Fiji / (edited by John Overton
with assistance from Barbara Banks. —
Suva (Fiji) : Institute of Pacific
Studies, University of the South
Pacific, 1988.

xii, 230 p. ; 21 cm.
Bibliography : p. 209-225.
ISBN 982-02-0045-8

1. Fiji — Rural conditions 2. Fiji —
Economic conditions 3. Fiji —
Social conditions I. Overton, John
II. Banks, Barbara

HN 936 .A8 R8   330.9'9611

Published by the
Institute of Pacific Studies
of the University of the South Pacific

Cover Designed by Nigel Duffey
Photographs by Margaret Chung, Setareki Delana, John Overton,
and Fiji Ministry of Information
Typeset by the Department of Human Geography,
Research School of Pacific Studies, Australian National University
Printed by Star Printery Ltd., Suva

AUTHORS

Imam Ali
Tim Bayliss-Smith
Joseph Chung
Margaret Chung
Setareki Delana
Charles Eaton
Patrick Haynes
Jiten Mangal
John Overton
Asesela Ravuvu
R.R. Thaman
Mesake Tukai

Edited by:

John Overton

with assistance from
Barbara Banks

CONTENTS

PREFACE

During the course of a temporary lectureship at the University of the South Pacific in 1985, I was impressed by much of the work completed by final year undergraduate geography students. It often, though not always, lacked the polish of the better student work in other countries, but some had qualities of insight and original thought that were novel. Pacific students, it seemed, were applying theories or international comparisons to their own situations at the village or community level that increased our understanding of these societies and economies in a way that many academics were not able to do. They deserved wider readership. I was interested then either in producing a collection of this work or reviving the former 'Basic Research in Pacific Islands Geography' series, which was a past outlet for some student papers. I was encouraged in this aim by Bill Clarke, Rajesh Chandra, Randy Thaman and David Routledge.

However, after leaving USP, the difficulties of editing a collection of papers from afar soon became apparent and, unfortunately, several of the student papers that were to be included, but which required extra work, had to be dropped as contact was lost with the authors. Only those of Mesake Tukai, Jiten Mangal and Setareki Delana *et al.* remain. I decided to continue but to include other examples of recent research, each with their own 'flavour'. There are chapters based on MA research (Margaret Chung, Imam Ali and Charles Eaton); one from consultancy work (Tim Bayliss-Smith/Patrick Haynes); one from a former agricultural officer (Joe Chung); and three from present and former USP staff (Randy Thaman, Asesela Ravuvu and John Overton). Together they give a cross-section, if not completely representative, of recent research in rural Fiji.

The production of this book owes much to a number of people. Foremost amongst them, Barbara Banks undertook the lengthy and thankless task of proof-reading, standardising, and correcting our errors of grammar, spelling, and expression. In addition, the Cartography Unit of the Research School of Pacific Studies at ANU produced the maps and diagrams; Judith Robson, Norma Chin and Karen Manning were able typists; photographs were culled and reproduced from the collections of Margaret and Joe Chung, Setareki Delana, and John Overton, with the help of Merv Commons; Michael Bourke at ANU kept a watchful eye on our use of botanical names; and the Institute of Pacific Studies at USP encouraged and supported the publication of the book. To all are due our thanks.

John Overton
Department of Human Geography
Australian National University
Canberra

ABBREVIATIONS USED

ADP	Agricultural Development Programme
ALTA	Agricultural Landlord and Tenant Act
CPI	Consumer Price Index
CSR	Colonial Sugar Refining Company
DP7 (8,9)	Development Plan 7 (8,9)
EEC	European Economic Community
FBA	Farm Basic Allowance
FDB	Fiji Development Bank
FSC	Fiji Sugar Corporation
GDP	Gross Domestic Product
LDA	Land Development Authority
MPI	Ministry of Primary Industries
NLC	Native Lands Commission
NLTB	Native Land Trust Board
NMA	National Marketing Authority
SDC	Southern Development Company
UNESCO	United Nations Educational, Scientific and Cultural Organization
UNFAO	United Nations Food and Agriculture Organisation
UNFPA	United Nations Fund for Population Activities
UsP	University of the South Pacific

1

THE STUDY OF RURAL FIJI

John Overton

Rural Fiji has been much studied but, in some cases, poorly understood. The coups and political crises of 1987 took many observers, especially those outside Fiji, by surprise. Despite the generation and more that has passed since detailed research by social scientists began in earnest, many were at a loss to describe and explain the changes, conflicts and frustrations within Fiji as a whole, and the rural areas in particular, that came to a head in 1987. The reasons for this lack of understanding have been many, but uppermost have been the adoption of either inappropriate theoretical frameworks, such as modernisation, or facile social and ethnic stereotypes. Also, the pace of change in the Fijian countryside has been such as to overtake many of the conclusions reached twenty or more years ago.

We lack more recent and detailed analyses of rural societies and economies, especially those taking account of continuing, even increasing, disparities; of the partial failure, and occasional successes, of rural development programmes; of regional contrasts; and of the centrality of land issues. Generally, this involves eschewing discredited theoretical approaches either for greater empiricism or for a search for new theories.

Yet the volume of research in and on rural Fiji *has* increased markedly in the 1980s. This has developed out of academic interests, especially out of research programmes at the University of the South Pacific, and from consultancy reports, mostly for the Fiji Government. Unfortunately, much of this work is dissipated or left unpublished. This volume is an attempt to bring some of this recent work together. The papers here share no common focus, beyond the fact that they are about different aspects of the economy, society and geography of the Fijian countryside. They all stem from independent research projects and none attempt to address 'big' issues, such as the causes of political crisis or social change. However, when read together, they do amount to a coverage, albeit somewhat patchy, of many facets of change in

1

rural Fiji and it is hoped that they increase our understanding of some of the processes of transformation, preservation and differentiation.

STUDYING TRADITIONS AND TRADITIONS OF STUDY

Fijian Society

Rural Fiji has been studied often and in depth in the past forty years. There has been work stimulated by theoretical concerns and a range of practical interests. The first topic to interest researchers was traditional Fijian society and that has remained perhaps the most central theme in studies of rural Fiji.

Anthropologists have taken the lead. Foreign researchers, from Thompson (1940), through Roth (1953), Sahlins (1962) and Belshaw (1964), to Rutz (1976, 1978a, 1987) worked extensively in Fijian societies. The local contribution has been equally important, with Nayacakalou (1975, 1978)[1] and, more recently, Ravuvu (1983, 1987) adding new insight. From all this work, there has evolved a fairly complete understanding of what constitutes indigenous Fijian society and culture, its regional variants, and its economic characteristics.

Extending this basic research, a number of academics have focused on the elements of change in traditional society under the influence of colonialism and capitalism. Thus, the evolution of a colonial land tenure system which protected and preserved Fijian customary rights, was examined, amongst others, by France (1969), Chapelle (1978) and Lloyd (1982). Similarly, Belshaw (1964) and Rutz (1976, 1977, 1978b) have monitored the impacts of cash cropping on traditional economies. So anthropologists have been at the forefront of research, focusing on the features of traditional Fijian society but also on its capacity to adapt[2].

Modernisation theory

Whilst such work placed the research spotlight on traditional society, and saw change as evolving out of that context, a second tradition of study viewed change from the opposite end, from the perspective of an ideal or modern society that Fiji appeared to be heading towards or, some felt, *ought* to be heading towards. These were the 'modernisers'. Some, such as Watters

---

1   Though most of Nayacakalou's work was not published until the late 1970s, his basic field research was conducted in the mid 1950s, and his work was well-known.

2   Though nearly all of this work has involved indigenous Fijian society, there have been a few similar efforts to understand the immigrant and locally adapted Indian society (for example, Mayer 1961, Jayawardena 1971).

(1969a, 1969b), were directly influenced by modernisation theory, whilst others, if less theoretically inclined, nonetheless echoed many of its recommendations: a change from communalism to individualism, the development of a secular materialist society, and the monetisation of economic relations. The Spate (1959) and Burns *et al.* (1960) reports were in this mould, whilst the rural survey work of Ward (1960, 1964, 1965), Frazer (1961, 1964, 1973) and Anderson (1969, 1974) seemed to concentrate on the new processes of socio-economic transformation.

All these researchers were interested in, and excited by, what they recognised as the rapid changes in indigenous Fijian society. Belshaw's[3] 'emergent Fijian enterprise' phrase summed up the plethora of new activities taking place: *galala* individualism, promising cooperative ventures, new forms of leadership and capital formation, improved education levels, urbanisation and, seemingly, rising standards of living. These were all transforming the way Fijians lived and worked. Despite noting some elements of social economic malaise, most were optimistic. It was a time of change; a time when the colonial government, and even some of the chiefly Fijian elite, seemed responsive to the changes.

The consultants

A surprisingly large volume of research on rural Fiji has been carried out in the course of consultancy work for government. This began during the late colonial period with the largely impressionistic reports of Shephard (1944) and Clay (1955) on agriculture and Stannar (1953) and Burns *et al.* (1960) on the economy as a whole[4]. Spate's report (1959), however, drew on primary research. It was aimed specifically at the 'Fijian people' and, by implication, at the situation in the villages. After travelling widely throughout the country, speaking to many Fijians, and using the research data of Nayacakalou, Frazer, Ward others, he made strong recommendations in favour of *galala* individualism.

Later consultancies, however, have been much more technical and specific and have attempted to meet the need of the independent government for practical solutions to rural development needs. Thus, the United Nations Regional Planning Project recommended decentralisation and more planning of Fiji's rural and regional sectors[5] and the UNESCO/UNFPA 'Population and Environment Project in the Eastern Islands of Fiji'[6] was an impressive

---

3   Belshaw, though an anthropologist, also seems to have been interested in the theoretical aspects of social transformation and modernisation.

4   These reports were policy-oriented and based on often subjective impressions and little or no primary research. They reflected contemporary colonial neglect for Fijian rural development.

5   For example, Titley, 1976. Gunasekera continued this work locally: Gunasekera 1982, Chandra and Gunasekera 1984).

6   The research findings were published in a variety of forms. The main report

attempt at integrated rural research and did much not only to describe in detail the economies of the island periphery of Fiji but also commented on themes such as regional planning, migration, transport and environmental constraints. It represented the largest concerted and detailed micro-level research in Fiji since the early 1960s.

Consultancy studies have appeared often in Fiji in recent years. The independent government's concern for rural development and import substitution has led to three major reports on the rice industry (UNFAO/Fiji Ministry of Agriculture and Fisheries 1982, Australian Agricultural Consulting and Management Company n.d., 1982. In 1985, they were complemented when the Ministry of Primary Industries published a series of 'commodity profiles', being important nation-wide surveys of crops, detailing their levels of production, distribution and prospects for future development (for example, Fiji Ministry of Primary Industries 1985). As well as these agricultural surveys, there was a further impetus for research in the regional development initiative set out in the eighth development plan. This gave rise to three 'integrated regional plans' by foreign consultancy teams on Western Vanua Levu (Atkins 1983), Vunidawa (McLennan Magasanik 1984), and the Sigatoka Valley. Perhaps the most important major study in recent years, though, has been the Fiji Employment and Development Mission (Bienefeld 1984)[7]. This involved, again, the use of consultants to conduct basic research and review general topics such as land use, employment generation and key sectors of the economy.

Local initiatives

In the mid 1970s, there were signs of academic independence and a move away from the heavy reliance on research by non-Fijian residents. This largely followed the founding of the University of the South Pacific and the encouragement of more research by 'locals'. Since then, there has been a large volume of research, not all published, that has added much to the understanding of changes occurring within Fiji.

Examples of such work by Fijian citizens include that of Satish Chandra (1981, 1983) on agronomy, and Rajesh Chandra (1980) on Indo-Fijians, Low's (1985) analysis of off-farm labour, Sharma's (1985, 1986) discussion of the efficiency of different types of farming, and Tubuna's (1985) account

---

(UNESCO/UNFPA 1977) was submitted as 'information for decision makers', there were a multitude of working papers, and some of the more theoretical spin-offs from the project are still appearing (Bayliss-Smith *et al.* 1988).

7   Although most of the working papers for this remained unpublished, those by Brookfield, Ellis and Ward (1985), and Ellis (1983a, 1983b), were given a wider audience. The papers and the report say much about recent trends in the rural economy and suggest that there are serious limits to the extension of agriculture and to the labour absorptive capacity of the villages.

of Fijian migration patterns. Similarly, the collection of papers on ethnic Fijian urbanisation edited by Griffin and Davis (1986), was important in bringing forward the research and ideas of a number of Fijian social scientists.

One of the recent trends in some of the published work emanating from USP scholars is the use of a Marxist political economy approach. However, this has been apparent in work of a more general or historical nature (for example Narayan 1984, Sutherland 1984) rather than on specifically 'rural' topics. This theoretical perspective stresses increasing socio-economic differentiation — 'proletarianisation' and 'peasantisation' — and it sees rural societies as being exploited, whether through control of wages or cane prices, or through 'colonial conservation'.

Research by 'foreigners' has also continued alongside this upsurge in local work. Much of this was in individual research projects, some of which were for doctoral dissertations[8]. Added to these has been important new work by Ward on land and village agriculture (1985, 1986, 1987), Brookfield on the coconut industry (1985, 1987), and Connell on migration (1985).

So there have been many 'traditions' in the study of rural Fiji. The early concern for traditional society moved to greater interest in transformation and modernisation and, latterly, there has been some influence from the Marxist political economy approach. Yet perhaps of more significance in research has been not these theoretical frameworks but more basic practical needs, principally the collection and analysis of data to inform and advise government policy. That has been a constant theme in rural research in Fiji and has parallelled the more academic pursuits. Only in the past few years, however, has the overall quantity and quality of research being carried out on topics in rural Fiji begun to match, monitor and interpret the pace of change occurring so evidently throughout the countryside. Unfortunately, though, many of these later studies have been confined to reviews of literature or analysis of official aggregate statistics and it is also difficult to discern common themes in many of the individual field studies. More work is required, not just to add further detail to our knowledge of rural Fiji, but also to integrate some of the recent research around general themes or problems.

THIS VOLUME

This volume presents a collection of studies, covering a cross-section of recent research undertaken by geographers and others in related disciplines. There has been no attempt to impose a theoretical or thematic perspective, the chapters having been brought together after research was conducted on

---

[8] Examples of such work include that by Evans on Seaqaqa (1982a, 1982b), Britton on tourism and Fiji's spatial economy (1980, 1983), Sofer on peripheral economies (1985, 1987), and Knapman's analysis of Fiji's colonial economic history (1976, 1987).

separate projects for a variety of purposes, including consultancy reports, university theses, and academic papers. The book is an attempt to present a 'flavour' of some of the work that has marked a recent upsurge of interest in rural Fiji.

A variety of authors is involved. Three of the chapters, those by Mangal, Delana *et al.*, and Tukai began as undergraduate research projects in geography at the University of the South Pacific. These have a special character and value, for, whilst the authors were applying research methods and writing research reports often for the first time, they were able to draw upon first-hand experiences of rural Fiji, from their villages, families or everyday lives. As such, they give insights that the foreign or academic researcher may be blind to. Similarly, the three chapters drawing on research carried out for masters dissertations, those by Imam Ali, Charles Eaton and Margaret Chung, also benefit from experiences outside the university environment. Eaton and Ali completed their theses in geography at the University of the South Pacific, whilst Chung completed her dissertation at the University of Hawaii. All three are either Fijian citizens or long-time residents and have worked as teachers, farmers and managers throughout the country. Thaman is the only example here of work by a member of the teaching staff at USP, a major source of recent research[9]. The contributions by Bayliss-Smith, Haynes, and Overton, are representative of what constitutes perhaps the largest body of published research carried out on rural Fiji, that by foreign academics. Though still important, this source is becoming relatively less so, as more studies by 'locals' are completed. Finally, this volume presents, though under-represents, the work of non-geographers and people who have had both long practical experience in Fijian rural change and participation in consultancy teams. Joseph Chung is able to draw on his training in agriculture, his years as an Agricultural Officer throughout Fiji, and his recent involvement in projects on ginger, rural development communication and disaster rehabilitation. Similarly, Ravuvu, an anthropologist, is able to combine both a deep understanding of the 'development' experiences of rural Fijians and the detached perspective of an academic.

By including these latter two chapters, and noting the contribution of the agronomist Haynes, it is clear that there is considerable scope for more dialogue between researchers working in different disciplines but with a common interest in agricultural change and rural societies. Perspectives may be different but the problems addressed are common — be they rural-urban income disparities, social inequalities, land shortages, or monetisation of economic relations.

---

[9]   Ali and Ravuvu are also current members of staff, though Ali's chapter is based on work for his MA thesis, before he joined USP, and Ravuvu, now Director of the Institute of Pacific Studies, is less involved in teaching. Much of Overton's research, too, was conducted when he was at USP.

Despite the lack of a common theme in these chapters, there is a broad division between two main concerns. Both focus on change, though one set of research is concerned with the adaptation of traditional crops, established methods of cultivation, or customary modes of production (chapters 2 to 7). Thus activities, such as the growing of *yaqona*, fishing, or the cultivation of traditional root crops, are being adapted to meet new, principally commercial, opportunities. Similarly, it is noted that communal forms of organisation or customary forms of land tenure are being modified and mobilised to deal with institutional constraints or monetary needs. In short, there is no simple sweeping aside of the old in the transformation of rural Fiji in recent generations and, in custom and established skills there are valuable, often unrecognised, resources for meeting and exploiting change.

The second set of studies (chapters 8 to 12), though far from ignoring the old, concentrates on new features of the rural economy, on roads, specialised cash cropping, new forms of agriculture and on government efforts to induce rural change. In effect, these are mainly 'impact studies', noting in part how successful or otherwise these processes have been, but more, investigating how they have affected existing ways of life and well-being. Also, there is a notable interest in how new features of the rural economy have not been adopted in full, but rather significantly adapted to fit local resources and requirements.

As well as these two main divisions, however, it is possible to discern a number of commonalities in the studies that are worth noting, for they do distinguish these and other recent research as exploring new concerns from those highlighted two or more decades ago. There is first a fairly marked spatial focus for the studies (Figure 1). All but one of the chapters presents work on a field area in Viti Levu and the remaining chapter is on Vanua Levu. Much previous work by geographers and anthropologists looked at remote areas and traditional societies. The reason was clear: these were areas that were experiencing very rapid change as a result of their incorporation into larger economic, social and political systems in the past fifty years . Many tried to describe and analyse 'traditional' systems (even though these may have experienced several generations of colonialism and Western contact) and detail the important processes of change such as cash cropping, migration, and monetisation. More recently, interest in rural-urban and core-periphery disparities have given rise to research on peripheral economies and resources and possible means for development.

The chapters in this volume, however, place the focus on rural areas that are relatively close to the main economic 'cores' of the country and which have undergone a long period of incorporation and transformation. It puts the emphasis back on the main rural areas, on the centres of agriculture and on the regions that have undergone most in the way of socio-economic transformation. The themes of 'marginalisation', even 'peripheralisation', are still apparent for some, though the real interest is in understanding the complexity of change and the emergence of new modes of production. These

Figure 1
Fiji and the Study Areas

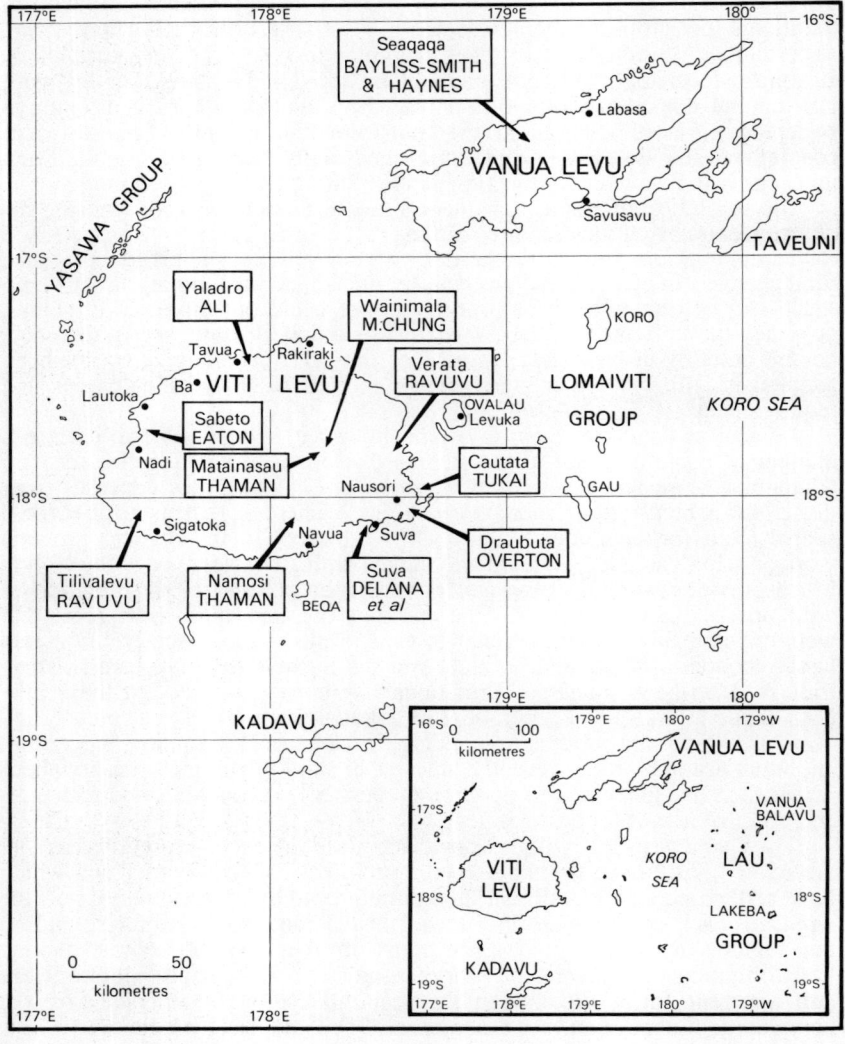

are places that are linked to urban areas by roads, well-developed marketing infrastructures, and (in some cases) daily migration. In many ways, the communities are indistinguishable from the traditional social and economic systems (whether Fijian communalism, or CSR plantation capitalism) that once governed every aspect of daily life. But many elements of these systems do remain, and maintain central positions in rural life.

A related theme that can be drawn from the studies is the difficulty in dealing with the old rural/urban dichotomy. In the days of strong village society, of colonial regulations restricting Fijian exemption from village obligations, or of indentured labour on the sugar plantations, a distinction between towns (such as they were) and the countryside was easy to draw. Today that division is less easy to discern, empirically or theoretically. Not only are there now complex structures of marketing, communications and migration that reach deep into the countryside, but also, in villages such as Cautata, the boundary between rural and urban is indistinct. That village, and others, have become virtual commuter suburbs, with a high proportion of households dependent on urban wage labour and few reliant solely on cultivating village land. There may be common sense justification for using the terms 'urban' and 'rural' (as we do here), but increasingly, they lack empirical validation as normative categories.

A third theme, again closely related to the earlier point about the shift in geographical focus, is the view of change. Most early studies examined processes of change as they occurred, often for the first time. Money, radios, crops were novel and their impacts only recently noticed. The studies in this volume, perhaps with the exception of Margaret Chung's work on the Monasavu road, look at change after a generation or more of experience. It has been over twenty years since many of the late colonial development programmes were initiated and nearly twenty years since Fiji gained independence. Many of the young people growing up in rural Fiji have experienced little of life before modern roads, corrugated iron, or paraquat; some even will not be able to remember a time before electricity, videos and frozen chickens. It is this more worldly and Western way of life that is becoming more typical of rural Fiji than thatched *bures* or shifting cultivation. These studies recognise that change.

Yet, by way of a contradiction, they also recognise the survival and value of traditional crops, methods and social relations. This is not just evident in the first six studies, but throughout. Change in rural Fiji has not been even, inevitable or, in some cases, desirable. And producers are actively and deliberately exploiting customary methods to obtain land or labour, and are developing long-established crops and cropping techniques. In a parallel way, urban consumers continue to demand established products, be it fresh fish, *yaqona, ota*, or *dalo*. As long as these consumer preferences remain strong, and there are few signs of them abating, then there will be a basis for the continuation and development of established agricultural crops and systems. These are as worthy of study as the new, because they constitute an alternative or complementary basis for rural development.

Another common concern of the chapters, and one that arises from their focus on the impact of recent changes, is the role of the state. Any researcher working in rural Fiji cannot but be struck by the pervasive influence of the state in almost every rural area of the country. Whether it is welfare provision (in the form of schools or health clinics), communications (roads, radio-telephones, shipping services), or agricultural change (with the work in the field of officers from the MPI, FDB, NMA or NLTB), the government of Fiji has taken a very active role in encouraging economic growth and improving social welfare. However, the development experiences detailed in this book point to the fact that state efforts are not entirely neutral or benign in their impacts. True, there are successes. In many respects, schemes, such as Seaqaqa, have achieved their targets and improved the well-being of rural people. But in other respects, the results of state action have not been entirely successful nor predictable: achievements in one area have been at the expense of others; development spread effects have not been sustained over time; and, importantly, the impacts (good and bad) have not been experienced evenly, in both social and regional respects. Part of the reason for this unevenness is recognised as the differential reaction of rural people to state policy. People are not merely passive recipients of state action: they react in different ways, they adapt the new and the old, and they act often outside the purview of the state. Lastly, it is shown that state intervention is not a necessary condition for regional development. The case of the *yaqona* industry points to success without state involvement.

The final common element in these studies is the value placed on empirical research. The chapters that follow draw on material gathered from field surveys, interviews, or long experience with rural development. Whilst there is a place for analysis based on aggregate statistics gathered at the national level, we argue that it must be balanced by village-level or regional-level studies that can illuminate the unevenness of change and, significantly, which can present the real experiences, ideas and problems of people. There is much to be learned, for example, about the government's programme for the import substitution of beef by talking to Fijian farmers who have had a generation of unfulfilled expectations on the Verata cattle scheme. Rural people, those affected by government rural development projects, those resisting change, those innovating, and those falling further behind, are put on centre stage.

WAYS FORWARD?

There are common elements and concerns in the studies presented here. Though these features are not unique, they do, to some degree, distinguish present work from much previous research. There is a need, also, to look forward, to extend these new directions and to identify ways in which research on rural Fiji might proceed in the future. Although far from exhaustive, three areas of concern are suggested.

First, there is a need to move from a study of the impacts of past policy to recommendations for new policy. It is relatively easy to point to past failings, somewhat more difficult to suggest how those might be rectified. Similarly, there is the challenge of putting forward possible strategies that do not involve expensive government schemes or foreign aid. There is enough to suggest, in these studies at least, that there is scope for much local mobilisation of resources and ideas, as in the use of *vakavanua* land tenure, marketing crops, such as *yaqona*, or using traditional root crops rather than imported food for disaster relief. Sometimes these involve a low level of state involvement, more facilitative than directive.

A second direction, also beyond impact studies, is to concentrate more clearly on the differential effects of state policy. Because the state does not operate evenly in space, or across different levels of society, more needs to be known about how and why policy is formulated and how it is directed. Similarly, the effects, intended and unintended, are not being monitored sufficiently well at present. Only when these processes and patterns are better known, can the implications for wider social and economic change in Fiji be better understood.

Finally, given the complexity of Fiji's rural economy, there is enough in the following chapters to suggest that future studies will not be well served by former frameworks which stress dichotomies such as Fijian/Indian, core/periphery, traditional/modern, capitalist/non-capitalist or individualism/communalism[10]. Whilst elements of such divisions do still have some validity, in terms of basic models of society, they are appropriate only at the very broad level. They do not inform research sufficiently, their use can impose frameworks that are too simplistic and rigid and, furthermore, the studies below indicate that the organisation and interactions within the Fijian rural sector are much more complex than indicated by such crude social, ethnic or regional classes. To move forward, research in Fiji, whether in human geography, anthropology or sociology, must recognise commonalities of experience, as well as the differences, and the importance of inter-relationships across social, spatial and racial divisions.

---

10 Overton (1988) has critically examined the continued usefulness of *'galala'* (and, by implication, of individualism) as a category for analysing Fijian rural society.

A newly-settled *galala* household in Serua

Yaqona being loaded onto mule for transport to market

2

MODERNISATION THEORY AND A FIJIAN VILLAGE[1]

Mesake Tukai

MODERNISATION

Modernisation theory developed in the 1950s and 1960s as a means of explaining the relative backwardness and poverty of Third World countries. It was popular within the social sciences, particularly sociology and political science, and it came to influence many academics, planners and politicians. The main assumption behind the theory was that there was a dichotomy between traditional societies and the modern nation states. The two were distinct and they possessed certain characteristics which identified one from the other. However, there were policy implications: traditional societies could be mobilised and modernised to follow the path of the West towards social and economic development.

In explaining the slowness of the Third World to develop, modernisation theory placed the focus on 'internal' factors, on constraints to change. These were many but included the following: traditional and fragmented social and political institutions (including tribalism and ascribed social status), conservatism, exchange through reciprocity and barter, poor communications, and a low level of economic differentiation and specialisation. Conversely, modernisation could be achieved by dispensing with these traditional ways of life and adopting new forms: mass media, better transport, greater social mobility with wider and more numerous social linkages, large and secular

---

1   This chapter was first written as an undergraduate essay in geography at the University of the South Pacific. Mesake Tukai is from Cautata village.

political units, the use of money exchange, and a move from communalism to individualism[2].

Modernisation theory may have been of little importance for Fiji had not several academics who worked in the country come to apply, or at least been influenced by, some aspects of the theory. Watters (1969a, 1969b) applied modernisation ideas, more than any other, in his study of six Fijian villages. He suggested that there was a form of development continuum across them. At one extreme there were very traditional villages that remained isolated, were still dominated by subsistence production, and clung to communal modes of production. At the other pole were the 'modern' villages, ones that were heavily engaged in cash cropping, had higher standards of living, and were characterised by numbers of individual *galala* farmers. Watters' ideas were criticised (Crocombe 1971) and probably had little impact on policy but, earlier, the report of Professor Spate (1959) was very influential. Although he did not use modernisation theory, Spate's recommendations bear many similarities to what modernisation theorists may have suggested. He criticised the heavy role of the chiefs and, above all, he was strongly in favour of *galala* individualism and a move away from the old communal forms of organisation. Since 1960, many of these suggestions seem to have been put into practice, with more *galala*, a reform of Fijian administration, and encouragement of cash-cropping.

It has now been many years since these ideas were forwarded. Because life in Fiji has changed so much since then, it is now possible to test how correct those assumptions and suggestions have proved. The main hypothesis of this paper is that 'internal factors' are, in fact, not barriers to modernisation but can be mobilised to promote modernisation. In this application of modernisation theory, it will be suggested that: traditional society does not necessarily involve fewer external social and economic linkages; new forms of organisation are not imperative; and modernisation does not mean destroying traditional social units such as *tokatoka* and *mataqali*.

CAUTATA SOCIETY

This chapter is based upon interviews conducted in Cautata village in 1985. Cautata village is located on the south eastern coast of Viti Levu, on a hill overlooking Bau Island, 35 kilometres from Nausori. Traditionally, like any other Fijian village, Cautata was more or less self-sufficient except for a little barter involving articles such as earthenware pots, tapa cloth, mats, *lali*

---

2   Modernisation theory was adopted by a number of geographers including Gould (1970), Soja (1968) and Riddell (1968). They discussed many of these general features of both traditional and modern societies.

(Fijian drums) and canoes. There was some specialisation of labour, such as by carpenters, fishermen and warriors, and their services were rewarded in particular ways. As there was no money, exchange was limited. Accumulation of wealth, too, was limited because 'wealth' consisted of non-durable goods such as mats or *masi*, and these were constantly being passed around in expression of established social relations. This web of relations was a source of assistance from which one could draw in times of need. Thus, in a way, the lack or absence of a money economy was compensated for by this pool of assistance which was readily available. The economic system, therefore, had to draw upon these social relationships to a very great extent and it also formed the basis for organising activities in other spheres of life. One could say that the economic process was part and parcel of the social process.

At the core of this organisation and the processes, kinship was the coordinating principle. Cautata society, like that in any other village in the Fijian archipelago, is organised for the most part on patrilineal descent principles. The village comprises a number, perhaps three or four, major divisions, or *mataqali*, each of them made up of a similar number of minor divisions. The minor divisions, or *tokatoka*, will contain members who are closely related on the male line. These *tokatoka* are the basic units in which the accumulation of food, the entertainment of visitors or community work is done. Land ownership is also secured here. While the members have equal rights to the use of land for cultivation or for collection of wild produce, none of them has the right to dispose of it in any way without consulting the other members. Thus, in the process of village life, these minor and major divisions of the village are cooperating social groups whose identity is strongly emphasised because of their special position in the organisation of the village as a whole.

Cautata comprises about 600 people, not counting those in urban areas and other parts of Fiji. There are four *mataqali*: Gusuna, Nakula, Koroni and Koroisovivi. Within these *mataqali* there are subunits or *tokatoka*. Traditionally, the chiefly *tokatoka* is protected by another socially related *tokatoka,* the warriors. The present chief is a member of the *mataqali* Gusuna. However, the chief may also be appointed from *mataqali* Koroni, and there is also the possibility of appointing a member of *tokatoka* Nauluvatu, a subunit of *mataqali* Nakula. Other *tokatoka* have traditional functions which they are required to carry out from time to time when their services are needed. The *mataqali* Koroisovivi are the *mata-ni-vanua* or heralds, the representatives of the chief, who take messages and receive other representations on his behalf. The fourth *mataqali*, Nakula, are traditionally those who communicate with the spirits or gods to determine whether activities, such as wars, can be carried out. Today this has been abolished, as Christianity has replaced the old religions.

Concerning land tenure, land is held communally by the *tokatoka* and the *mataqali*, and, economically, resources for labour are drawn from this communal pool of labour, either the *tokatoka* or *mataqali*. Sometimes the whole village is called upon for traditional tasks concerning the welfare of the village. The term '*soso*' refers to one of the main communal forms of work and is used by the *tokatoka* to help in clearing land, planting crops, building houses and for life-cycle functions.

Today, as in the past, this web of social relations is still intact but is under more and more pressure from the economic changes currently facing Fijians, especially the establishment of individual enterprises. The village chief is still in power and the decisions made by the elders or village council are still abided by and enforced. Land tenure also is still in the hands of the *tokatoka* and the *mataqali*, and subsistence cultivation is practised, though few households depend solely on these gardens for their welfare.

MODERNISING SOCIETY

Modernisation theory often assumed that traditional society involved few economic linkages outside the social unit and that customs act to impede the development of such linkages. But, in Cautata, this has not been the case as village social organisation has been used to encourage economic development and wider economic relations.

During the Second World War, the Nausori-Bau road (which passes near Cautata) was upgraded by the Americans and, in 1958, the Cautata Bus Company was started. Today it is a thriving business with modern coaches, repair garages and offices. It employs a large number of villagers on both a full- and part-time basis. About the same time as the bus company started, a village cooperative store was opened. Both enterprises came about because village society was still strong. At first, there was some resistance to the idea of forming the bus company, with some villagers suspicious of such Western businesses and ideas. However, there were others who won the day. Many villagers, including the better educated, were working in town and these, along with the early manager of the company, persuaded the village to support the bus scheme, by stressing the importance and likely benefits to be gained from better transportation.

It was decided then that the company would be managed by the village council while the day to day running would be under the control of a committee. The benefits of the company would be for the village as a whole. As the venture is village-owned, the employees are all from Cautata, though advice was sought from the Fijian Affairs Board. The finance needed to start the company was raised within the village. A call was made for the *soli-vaka vanua* (donations) and, in subsequent years, there have been two or three such meetings of the villagers to donate and help the bus company. This method has proved successful and much was forthcoming even from *yasa*, people from Cautata who had left to work in the towns. This is a fine example of the traditional social and economic organisations boosting economic development.

16

CONCLUSION

As a result of the establishment and operation of the Cautata Bus Company, there have been a number of new economic linkages forged or strengthened. Profits from the company are used for village projects and, in the past, have helped in the educational advancement of children from the village. Some of these have now established small businesses of their own in urban centres. One has a taxi business, another a clothing shop. In other cases, the provision of cheap transport to Suva and Nausori has meant that villagers can commute to city jobs yet still reside in the village and strengthen its economy. Thus, traditional society has been able to survive and encourage greater economic interaction between the village and the city.

As can be seen, the proposition that new forms of organisations are imperative is proved wrong, with modern-day business ideas and the traditional organisation intertwining perfectly. New forms of organisation, including the management committee for the company, as well as 'nuclear' families, which are now dependent on urban wages for their livelihood, have developed, but they have not displaced older social units. All have been modified in order to incorporate the others.

Finally, it is clear that modernisation does not necessarily mean the destruction of traditional ethnic compartmentalisation (traditional Fijian social units). The village social structure is still intact with the chief making decisions after matters are discussed at length in the village council where every man can give his views. The village has retained control over the new enterprise.

It is concluded, therefore, that, in this micro-scale of a Fijian village, modernisation can be achieved to a large degree, and that modernisation theory needs be critically reviewed in the Fijian case. Internal 'barriers' have a spontaneous capacity to adapt to, and merge with, modern ideas and can be experimented with successfully.

Yaqona for sale at Labasa market

3

VAKAVANUA LAND TENURE AND TOBACCO FARMING[1]

Charles Eaton

Throughout history, patterns of landownership have shaped
patterns of human relations in nearly all societies. They
have also helped determine the possibility and pace of
economic change. In agrarian societies, land is the primary
productive asset, the tangible expression of economic and
hence political power. (Eckholm 1980:55)

Land use patterns are determined not only by the natural environment but
also by the nature of ownership and, in feudal and tribal societies, by the form
of customary land use arrangements. It has been suggested by Eckholm
(1980) that land shortage and lack of land reform are perhaps the major
obstacles to equitable agricultural development, and that the poorest of the
poor are those with the least secure tenure to land. As agriculture is the major
economic activity in most developing countries, it is these rural landless
people who might greatly increase their nation's capacity to produce if they
had the incentives and access to land. This is often said to be the case in Fiji,
where a complex land ownership system, designed to protect the land
holdings of the indigenous population, is sometimes seen as a deterrent to
agricultural expansion (Burns *et al.* 1960:6, Spate 1959:1-2, Fiji Institute of
Agricultural Science 1985, Chandra 1983:21).

This system increasingly is responsible for insecurity of tenure and
landlessness among Indo-Fijians in particular and, recently, also indigenous

---

[1]   The author gratefully acknowledges the assistance of Bill Clarke and Randy Thaman of
      USP; Andrew McGregor of the East-West Center, Hawaii; John Overton of ANU; Mitieli
      Bulanauca of the NLTB, Lautoka; and Brian Hardaker of the University of New England,
      Armidale. All gave advice, helpful comments and constructive criticism in the preparation
      of this paper.

Fijians, as the 'commercial imperative' puts pressure on arable areas (Tudge 1977). For Fiji's farmers to survive and the agricultural sector to develop, the country needs to intensify its farming to make maximum use of all arable land. This puts the focus squarely on land tenure and tenure reform.

As elsewhere in the world, this issue is vital to the advancement of the country's rural communities both as landowners and users. Fiji's unique situation of having a large, mainly agrarian, immigrant population which cannot own most of the land, has complicated the problem and created social and political tension. The land tenure system in Fiji is often subject to criticism and analysis, but there has not been much change.

This paper looks briefly at the system in .Fiji and focuses on the experiences of a smallholder farming operation to highlight the positive advantages and constraints of the *vakavanua* system. The effect of the internal contradictions of Fiji's land tenure system is illustrated in the case study of farmers growing tobacco in the Sabeto valley, south-west Viti Levu, for the Southern Development Company (SDC), the only company involved in the production of Virginia tobacco in Fiji.

THE FIJIAN LAND TENURE SYSTEM

All land in Fiji was originally owned under a descent group structure of the traditional tribal hierarchy and the most striking aspect of tenure in modern Fiji its persistence within the dualist system created by the former colonial government: alienated areas, which include both freehold and Crown lands (17 per cent of total land area) on one side, and traditional native and native reserve land (83 per cent) on the other. It is generally accepted that all land, apart from that which is freehold or Crown, belongs integrally and in perpetuity to indigenous Fijians. Although native land can be leased, to Indians, Chinese or ethnic Fijians, native reserve land is designated for the use only of Fijians.

The bulk of Fiji's prime agricultural land is freehold, Crown or leased — at least that most involved in commercial agriculture — while native reserve lands are devoted largely to subsistence or semi-subsistence agriculture. However, substantial market-oriented production has developed in the past few decades on reserve and non-leased native land, usually near urban areas or within the sugar cane growing regions.

Side by side with the legally accepted and formal lease system there is also an extra-legal tenure practice known as *vakavanua* ('the way of the land' or customary), whereby the controlling owners make a direct arrangement with a cultivator for payment in cash or kind, sometimes both, for a plot over a set period. Normally, the money is in excess of the formal rental and is unencumbered from normal deductions and taxes. This practice circumvents the usual leasing channels and allows the tenant immediate access for the cultivation of a short-term cash crop without the expense of purchasing or the long and, in most cases, time consuming process of formally leasing communally owned land.

The Native Lands Commission

Prior to Cession in 1874, a considerable portion of the best arable land was alienated to European planters and speculators through purchase and barter. After further alienation was prohibited soon after cession, and the European land claims investigated, the new colonial government took steps to identify and protect customary land. The Native Lands Commission (NLC) was created and commenced the identification of customary owners and the demarcation of the physical boundaries in Fiji of some 6000 *mataqali* holdings. These units can consist of a single person or several hundred, and the areas involved range from one under hectare to several thousand. The final delineations of this massive undertaking were completed in the late 1960s, after almost ninety years of sensitive investigation. The result has been that the majority of Fijian land has been defined and mapped, the owners recorded, and a division made between native reserve and land available for leasing to all races.

The Native Land Trust Board

In 1946, the Native Land Trust Board (NLTB) was established to manage native land and act as an estate agency for native landowners. The NLTB was accepted by owners mainly because of their trust in the Fijian statesman and founding father of the NLTB, Ratu Sir Lala Sukuna. To the 1936 meeting of the Great Council of Chiefs he stated that the NLTB system

> ... is the only way in which native lands can be made of general use and benefit — and all without storing up troubles for ourselves ... [It is] in the best interests of the native race that all lands not required for the maintenance of the Fijian owners be opened for settlement .. and that all land (including leases) not so required be handed over to the Government to lease on behalf of the Fijians ... more land will become available for cultivation. And as the leasing will be under better control, we shall receive more rent, for there will be no waste land. We will live peacefully with our neighbours, men who have taken up their homes in this country. (NLTB 1986)

In essence, the NLTB was seen as a formal leasing agency which would ensure Fijians due recompense for use of their land and also give others tenure for long-term development. It was hoped that it would administer and improve the existing and somewhat haphazard methods of leasing native areas operating at the time of its establishment (Ward 1965:129). Its prime aim remains to ensure that unused land is opened up to Fijians and non-Fijians alike, taking into account the wishes of the owners and the ambitions of tenants, while fulfilling the policy of the government in developing the country's agricultural base. There are five main lease classifications of native land: agricultural, residential, commercial, industrial and special — each with its own particular lease arrangements.

Lessees are charged rent at the rate of up to 6 per cent per annum on the unimproved value of the land, of which 25 per cent of lease income and 10 per cent of any royalties are retained by the NLTB to cover their costs, and the remainder is returned to the owners, being distributed amongst members according to the chiefly hierarchy.

Areas leased for agricultural use covers 193,000 hectares, or 12.6 per cent of all native land, forming a major segment of the sugar cane growing area of western Viti Levu (NLTB 1984:19). Since 1966 agricultural leases have been issued for a maximum of thirty years, giving more security to lessee farmers, Indians in particular, and increased incentive to develop the land responsibly.

The NLTB Act has been supplemented by legislation which protects the rights of tenants. The Agricultural Landlord and Tenant Act (ALTA) was introduced in the mid 1960s and aimed to give tenants a stronger feeling of security and the incentive to increase productivity.

However, this official land tenure system has been the subject of recent criticism. The large areas of unused land which are unavailable for legal leasing and the lack of tenure security have been cited as major constraints to productivity (Yarrow 1986). Furthermore, the NLTB has been accused of being too rigid and ineffective, with consequent administrative delays, and legal and financial problems stifling agricultural production (Overton 1987).

Native reserve land

Native reserve land, 28 per cent of Fiji's total land area (Chandra 1983:19), is proclaimed as reserved entirely for the use of the owners who can lend it as *vakavanua* to any race or formally lease it to other Fijians only through the NLTB. The philosophy behind the 1940 legislation which created the 'native reserve' category was that the owners retained land they required for the foreseeable future, leaving the rest for leasing. In theory, the idea was a practical means of achieving equitable distribution and tenure. However, there is a growing tendency for owners, particularly in the sugar cane areas, to make informal *vakavanua* arrangements with non-Fijians, especially Indians, thus avoiding the legal obligations of the native land legislation. This growing phenomenon has been confirmed elsewhere by Overton (1987).

Native leases and traditional arrangements

The various types of tenure and occupation rights found on native land include traditional users (*'wasewase'*[2]), formal intra-*mataqali* leases, formal extra-*mataqali* leases, and *vakavanua* extra-legal arrangements with both Fijians and non-Fijians.

Traditional users, normally members of the land owning unit, the *mataqali*, have usufruct rights to subsistence shifting cultivation or establish semi-permanent garden plots, graze domestic animals and, in the fallow or wildland areas often found in forests at higher elevations, hunt and gather wild foods. These usufruct rights include seasonal cultivation of *mataqali* land by members for short-term cash crops, such as market vegetables and tobacco, and longer-term crops, such as *yaqona*, cocoa and coconuts.

Land formally leased through the NLTB by *mataqali* members is normally occupied by individual settlers or *galala*, who establish cash crops, such as sugar cane, *yaqona*, coconuts, or small dairy and beef farms, though sometimes the land may be used for subsistence cropping only. Although such leases contain a termination factor, renewal is usually automatic unless there are strong objections from fellow *mataqali* members. Agricultural land leased through the NLTB to Indians or other Fijians (not members of the landowning *mataqali*) comprises the majority of agriculturally profitable land in Fiji. Again a variety of agriculture may be carried out but, in this case, renewals may be more problematic.

Vakavanua arrangements

Traditionally, agreements on the use or 'borrowing' of another's land (*vakavanua*), is a long-standing custom in Fiji and is a well entrenched facet of Fijian land tenure, despite not having any legal status. However, it is not encouraged as government prefers that all transactions be channelled through the NLTB, thus preventing sharecropping or leasing by *vakavanua* arrangements particularly to non-Fijians, and facilitating the regulation of other abuses. In fact, the opposite appears to be happening, with more owners bypassing NLTB — and its sometimes lengthy processes — in preference of immediate, cash-in-hand profits.

Vakavanua can best be described as an agreement where a farmer requests permission from a Fijian owner or land 'controller'[3] to plant a crop for a

---

2   *Wasewase* means both the traditional process of dividing and that which is divided. In this case it is taken to mean the parcels of land which are divided in the customary manner to members of a *mataqali* or *i tokatoka* and Fijian use of their own land on a usufruct basis.

3   The 'controller' of land may be a *mataqali* member who is an individual or *i tokatoka* head with long established customary rights to a well-defined area of land. Though legal ownership is vested in the *mataqali*, *de facto* control often rests in the hands of such individuals or small sub-groups. France (1969:173) believes that the *i tokatoka* (or, in the west, *bito*) are the more definitive landowners. The author has found that, in some

specified period. The request is normally made by a ceremonial presentation of *sevusevu* (gift), *yaqona* , or *tabua* (whale's tooth) but the modern trend is to supplement the traditional offerings with cash. Indeed, some landowners demand rates well above the normal offerings, often as much as ten times in excess of NLTB rents (see below). However, *vakavanua* allows the cultivator immediate access to land for short-term cash crops such as tobacco and vegetables and provides the individual owner/controller a reasonable and instant income. If leased through the legal system at a rate perhaps four to five times lower, the end result is insignificant after 25 per cent is deducted by the NLTB for costs, another 30 per cent for leaders of the *vanua, yavusa* and *mataqali*, leaving only 45 per cent amongst sometimes scores of *mataqali* members. One observer noted, "it is hardly surprising that, in household surveys, no one considered income from rents large enough to mention" (Overton 1987:146).

While there appears to be an established history of *vakavanua* dealings between Fijian landowners and newly-arrived Indian migrants as long ago as 1884 (Anderson 1974:18), the concept of sharefarming under *vakavanua* arrangements is rapidly growing and encourages instant cash crop agriculture. This phenomenon is common in western Viti Levu and also in the eastern parts of the island where, in another variant of *vakavanua*, non-Fijians and Lauans settled on Fijian owned land, later to become a government-sponsored resettlement scheme (Overton 1986).

In short, *vakavanua* practices are good for the landowners, because they get more money from rents and more direct control over tenants and their land, and good for the tenants, because they get access to land that, probably, would otherwise be closed to them. However, while there are immediate benefits for both the owner and the cultivator, the long-term effects of this generally transitory farming are, in many cases, detrimental to both the soil and the promotion of permanent agriculture.

Land tenure and agricultural development

There is a belief that Fijian landowners have an excess of rich, arable land only waiting to be opened up for rural settlement, but this belief is more fantasy than fact and only serves to mask the essential problems facing Fiji's agricultural future. In a study of land, land use and land availability, Ward (1985) showed that Fiji's hitherto expanding land frontier had begun to close. On Viti Levu, the area of land used increased by 233 per cent between 1958 and 1978 (1985:44). Expansion had occurred onto more marginal areas, and, as a result, farmers had to have larger holdings to maintain income levels. He also warned that if not leased, most usable native land was committed and none would be available in the 1990s. He concluded (1985:38):

---

thousands of *vakavanua* arrangements of which he has experience, none was negotiated on a *mataqali* basis and none came to grief due to *mataqali* interference.

Clearly, there is a great deal of inequality in access to land, the distribution of monetary benefits which accrue from it, and marked segmentation of the land market.

A sad social consequence of the competition between users for the diminishing land resource is the many intravillage, intervillage and lessor/lessee disputes. Both litigation and illegal actions are being taken, some leading to violence, all leading to loss of production and social segmentation. Ward (1985: 39-40) attributes intravillage disputes to the introduction of cash crops, which require more *mataqali* land. Land is often under long-term crops, or livestock farming, which lock up the large areas for many years. The cash society has precluded land loans through customary mechanisms and created a desire to keep land for potential personal use.

Perhaps the single largest factor controlling land use today is money. This has led to owners being unwilling to lease their land, particularly on long-term lease as required by NLTB and ALTA legislation. The areas either remain unutilised or underutilised as subsistence gardens until the landowner has the incentive to develop, often depriving other, more efficient and productive farmers from benefiting from the land.

Another factor which controls the leasing to outsiders and distribution of land within the landowning unit is the imbalance of ownership throughout Fiji. It is common to have some *mataqali* with a surplus quite beyond their immediate ability to use or develop, while many others have little or no land to cultivate even at a subsistence level. In reality, many Fijians, as individuals as well as extended families, have little or no land of any commercial consequence. They are commonly faced with problems of co-ownership of plots of land in the mountainous interior or on distant outer islands, or have only fleeting usufruct rights to another *mataqali*'s land.

Given that there is an increasing lack of arable land available, the expiry of NLTB leases over the next twenty years could cause major agricultural and social upheaval. The leases have already been extended once, under ALTA, but will start to expire in the mid-1990s. A cohesive plan must be instigated soon to accommodate the redistribution and allocation of both land and farmers necessary to avoid a national crisis. One illustration of the need for extreme care and diplomacy in this matter was the return to Fijian occupancy of cane lands at Koronubu, Ba, in the mid-1960s. Poorly selected *mataqali* members repossessed the productive land and flagrantly squandered capital development funds allocated for the improvement of their farms[4]. An unpublished NLTB report in 1987 showed that, of the ninety-five original Fijian settlers, forty-nine had transferred their leases back to 'other races', some of whom were the original leasees prior to 1966. They had continued as sharecroppers on a *vakavanua* basis in the interim period (personal communication, NLTB Lautoka).

---

4   The author has had personal experience in the area and had seen it degenerate into a rural slum.

The tobacco growing area has had a similar experience. In the early 1980s, a few dozen Indian farmers, including some growing tobacco, lost prime land on long-term NLTB leases when the original owners resumed a large area of disputed land. After a government-sponsored compromise was reached, the majority and best part of the disputed land was being farmed by the original Indian lessees, who had made *vakavanua* arrangements with the repossessors. This example, and that of Koronubu above, demonstrate the 'pendulum effect' of land tenure and use.

A CASE STUDY OF *VAKAVANUA* LAND TENURE: TOBACCO FARMING IN THE SABETO VALLEY[5]

Fiji's local tobacco requirements are met through the Southern Development Company, which directs some 433 smallholder farmers to produce a quality crop for very high returns (Eaton 1986). It is based in southwest Viti Levu, where the climate and soils are ideal for tobacco cultivation. Because tobacco is grown ideally on alluvial soil between the levee and river bank, this land is usually classed as 'native reserve' because the native/ Crown/ freehold land tenure boundaries commence at the high levee mark, therefore most of the tobacco crop is grown on native reserve land, which cannot be legally leased to non-Fijians. As a consequence, it is highly sought after for *vakavanua* leasing. In fact, 75 per cent of SDC's total tobacco crop is grown on Fijian land, of which approximately 80 per cent is on native reserve (Table 1). Furthermore, Table 2 below indicates that *vakavanua* arrangements by both Indian and Fijian tobacco farmers in the Sabeto growing area constitutes 72.4 per cent of all tenure in that sector.

This case study was based on data gathered over a six-year period, involving some 690 sample studies. The land tenure issue was considered a major factor affecting the productivity of tobacco farming, but, as will be shown, not in terms of land availability, but in economic considerations. The rather surprising conclusion was that *vakavanua* leases were marginally more productive than the secure NLTB leases.

Preliminary investigations had indicated that land shortage might be the major constraint to higher tobacco productivity in the Sabeto Valley (Eaton 1986:3), but it appears this is only valid in terms of high tobacco quotas (which reflect high cigarette sales) when all suitable tobacco-growing soils not already under sugarcane, vegetable cash crops or subsistence gardens are in demand. Over the study period (1980-1985), only 7.6 per cent of the

---

5   This section is, in part, extracts from a larger thesis on the constraints and advantages of directed smallholder agriculture, particularly pertaining to the productivity levels in tobacco cultivation (Eaton 1988).

Table 1
Land Tenure Status of Virginia Tobacco Holdings
Growing for the SDC in Fiji, 1987

	Freehold		Crown		Native[a]		Total	
	no.	ha	no.	ha	no.	ha	no.	ha
Nadi								
Fijian	-	-	-	-	147	38.0	147	38.0
Indian	2	0.3	-	-	74	17.0	76	17.3
Sigatoka								
Fijian	-	-	-	-	138	32.5	138	32.5
Indian	77	35.0	2	0.3	' 69	19.0	148	54.3
Total	79	35.3	2	0.3	428	106.5	509	142.1
	(24.8%)		(0.2%)		(75.0%)		(100.0%)	

[a] includes native reserve
no. refers to number of sample studies

Source: SDC records (unpublished).

farmers failed to find land, despite having to renegotiate *vakavanua* arrangements annually.

Actual land shortage does not seem to be as much of a constraint as the form and amount of payment demanded by the 'controllers' or 'landlords' of *vakavanua* leases. Although it circumvents established native land legislation, SDC introduced rental advances in 1982 to regularise *vakavanua* agreements, thus giving increased security to both farmers and landowners and minimising the role of land tenure as a determinant of productivity. Unfortunately, despite such advances, or perhaps because of them, landowners began to demand higher and higher payments for tobacco land, thus deterring some farmers from planting. One Fijian landowner demanded as much as 33 per cent of the farmer's mean net income ($667 per hectare equivalent), even from his fellow villagers. After negotiations with the company, however, an advance payment ceiling of $200 per hectare (10 per cent of the estimated net return) was accepted by most landowners, although they also expected the traditionnal *sevusevu*. Although SDC attempts to regularise and formalise such 'informal' tenure arrangements, landowners still demand additional *ex-gratia* payments, which are given directly by the farmer and so avoid the company's formal 'extra-legal' agreement. Thus, it seems that *vakavanua* land tenure can also be a constraint by increasing farmers' obligations, lowering their net returns and making farming a less viable proposition.

Investigation of one Indian *vakavanua* farmer planting tobacco and vegetable cash crops showed he rented first class arable land on a *vakavanua* basis at around $350 per hectare while paying only $35 per hectare for arable sugar cane land under a formal NLTB lease[6]. As so much of the tobacco crop is grown under *vakavanua* tenure, the viability of continuing tobacco production will depend on an economic and equitable accommodation between the land controllers, farmers and the company. Furthermore, an in-depth study probably would confirm that *vakavanua* accords between Indian cultivators and Fijian landowners are much more widespread than officially acknowledged, affecting other industries, such as sugar, the whole land market and, thereby, the nation's economy.

Table 2 outlines productivity by ethnicity of tobacco farmers and the three tenure systems in operation within the Sabeto tobacco growing area: *wasewase*; *vakavanua*; and NLTB lease. The overall picture is complicated by ethnicity, for Indian growers, on average, produce higher yields than their ethnic Fijian counterparts. As the two groups are not spread evenly amongst the tenure groups, it is difficult to draw unqualified conclusions. Yet some

Table 2
Annual Productivity by Land Tenure and Ethnicity
for Sabeto Tobacco Farmers, 1980-1985

Tenure Class	Fijian kg/ha	no.	Indian kg/ha	no.	Total kg/ha	no.
Wasewase	1,805	157	-	-	1,805	157
Vakavanua	1,820	323	2,128	174	1,927	497
NLTB lease	-	-	1,983	36	1,983	36
Total	1,815	480	2,103	210	1,902	690

Source: SDC records (unpublished).

---

6   This shows that NLTB rents are by no means excessive in a commercial sense.

comparisons are significant. Those on *vakavanua* land show 1.3 per cent higher productivity than the total mean. In the case of Fijians on *vakavanua*, productivity was marginally, although probably not significantly, higher than Fijians on *wasewase* (with mean yields of 1820 and 1805 kilograms per hectare respectively). Indian farmers on *vakavanua* even proved 7 per cent more productive than their counterparts on NLTB land. In brief, *vakavanua* tenure is not shown to be correlated with low yields and this temporary tenure arrangement has not proved a disincentive to tobacco productivity.

CONCLUSIONS: A TRADITIONAL ALTERNATIVE?

Many authors have recommended the encouragement of smallholder agriculture and highlighted the need for a 'basic needs' approach focusing on reforms in land allocation and security of tenure (Eckholm 1980:58). These themes are well illustrated in the Sabeto tobacco area. A major conclusion arrived at from the case study was the important influence *vakavanua* land tenure arrangements have on tobacco cultivation. Although the practice is technically illegal, it appears to be working for the mutual benefit of the land controllers, the tobacco growers and the SDC. The company, as director of small farmers, has provided them with land security to a greater extent than they could have themselves, by facilitating land tenure arrangements through direct negotiation with the land controllers. By guaranteeing the owners a fair rent, the SDC gives financial security to both lessee and lessor and has, in fact, created a locally accepted *modus operandi*. However, any restrictions or bans on *vakavanua* land usage would spell the demise of tobacco growing in the Sabeto Valley and impose severe restrictions on other areas.

In so far as the tobacco and other annual short-term crops are concerned, the main recommendation is for greater stability of *vakavanua* tenure, through a legally recognised agreement regarding rental rates which would give a fair and equitable rental and be of mutual benefit to both the landowner and the farmer. In a broader sense, *vakavanua* should be assessed for its long-term role in Fiji's economic, social and political future, particularly at this time, when there is agitation by some political groups for a return to traditional fundamentalism, involving greater use of Fijian customs and traditional social relations.

Interestingly, the *vakavanua* agreements between the two racial groups remained quite unaffected by the political turmoils of 1987. This fact, coupled with the 'pendulum effect', perhaps proves that the commercial imperative overcomes political pressures and the landlords' frequently stated desire to farm the land themselves. The major constraint and deterrent facing *vakavanua* tenure is that, whilst it is conducive to short-term subsistence and cash crops, it offers no long-term security and there is no responsibility on the part of the cultivator for protecting and conserving land.

As it now stands, *vakavanua* tenure has no legal status, but the practice is well entrenched and acknowledged at a customary and grass roots level. Consideration should be given to its legal acceptance as a possible means of resolving Fiji's land dilemmas and as a way for the owners to negotiate the use of their own land for the betterment of the rural community in particular and the nation in general. Official recognition also could ensure that landowners would have direct control over land misuse, overgrazing and burning. Due to a lack of policing, the existing land use conservation laws have failed to do this.

The majority of the legal NLTB leases under ALTA will expire following 1996 and a solution must be found to accommodate both landusers and landowners. The regularisation of *vakavanua* tenure on a more legal basis would help to sustain and support Fiji's future smallholders. Sharecropping and more direct relation between landowners and tenants, through *vakavanua*, could be part solutions. If no accommodation is reached, there is a very real possibility that a rural gypsy community of both races will emerge, moving from one *vakavanua* 'lease' to another and enlarging the mushrooming squatter settlements which are to be found Fiji-wide. That scenario would not only jeopardise the stability of commodity supply, but also increase social and economic inequalities that would have serious long-term political repercussions.

4

FIJIAN AGROFORESTRY: TREES, PEOPLE AND SUSTAINABLE POLYCULTURAL DEVELOPMENT[1]

R.R. Thaman

Agroforestry, the planting and protection of trees as integral components of a polycultural agricultural system, has always been central to the economic, cultural and ecological stability of Fijian society. This chapter focuses on trees as symbols of stability and cultural well-being; sources of a diverse range of subsistence and commercial products; and ecologically important components of agricultural systems which, if lost, would lead to irreversible environmental degradation and cultural deterioration. Two interior villages of Viti Levu serve as case studies of Fijian village-level agroforestry, which is addressed rarely in any detail in studies of Fijian 'agriculture'. It is suggested that the planting and protection of trees within existing agricultural systems is of paramount importance in the promotion of monocultural agricultural and forestry development currently favoured by Fiji's development planners and managerial elite.

TREES AS SYMBOLS OF ECOLOGICAL AND CULTURAL STABILITY

Despite being symbols of ecological and cultural stability, forests are rapidly disappearing. Thaman and Clarke (1983) have argued that, although

---

[1]   The author acknowledges the help, hospitality and insight provided by the people of Namosi and Matainasau, particularly Prof. Asesela Ravuvu, Adre Suinaika, Ratu Serevi Nakutaoro, Tomasi Nacagilaba, Enosi and Petero, and the late Tui Namosi, Ro Simione Matanitobua.

there are short-term benefits in replacing long-lived trees in mixed stands by shorter-lived, or in the complete removal of trees, these practices severely debilitate the human habitat. Oedekoven (1962:55) stresses:

> In the course of history, civilizations have flourished and disappeared with a resultant depletion of trees and plants, leaving only steppe and desert behind. Only in recent centuries has man begun to realise that he was cutting off the branch that he was sitting on.

Thaman (1986) argues that the protection of trees may well be one of the most important preconditions for conflict resolution and the peaceful co-existence of humankind.

DEFORESTATION IN THE PACIFIC ISLANDS

Although precious tropical forests remain on some of the larger Pacific islands, and small areas of mangrove and ubiquitous strand forest have been preserved on others, deforestation in the Pacific is proceeding at a frightening rate. Forests, both primary and secondary, continue to be transformed into degraded savannas and fern-grasslands; mangroves into housing and industrial estates; polycultural tree-studded traditional agroforested gardens into monocultural plantations; and urban areas divested of their remaining trees to make way for industrial, commercial, and residential developments or as fuel for the squatter housing of low-income families. The trends are the same from the high continental islands of Melanesia to the smallest atoll islets of Polynesia and Micronesia (Thaman and Clarke 1983).

Severe erosion has occurred in Wallis and Futuna, the Cook Islands, French Polynesia and Hawaii, where most of the indigenous forest has been removed, leaving degraded fernlands and grasslands no longer suitable for agriculture (Kirch 1982:4). Flenley and King (1984) suggest that deforestation was responsible for the collapse of the pre-European megalithic culture on Easter Island, a view supported by McCoy (1976:145), who argues that the "radical reduction of forest, shrub, and grassland communities, following over-exploitation and misuse by man", was responsible for a change from open-field cultivation to protected stone garden enclosures (*manavai*). Similarly, drastic deforestation of the central plateau on the Hawaiian island of Kahoʻolawe, due to shifting cultivation and increasing population pressure between AD 1375 and 1600, reputedly led to a major fall in population and the total abandonment of the interior of the island by 1700 (Kirch 1982). Although, today, some countries have conservation legislation and forestry ordinances, trees are still felled and forest products continue to be exported at low prices to Japan, South Korea, China and other countries, who continue to protect their own forest resources and implement major reafforestation efforts (Richardson 1981).

The situation is similar in Fiji, where extensive highly-degraded and highly-laterised *talasiga* grasslands are evidence of pre-European contact environmental deterioration. Unfortunately, such trends continue unabated today; agricultural expansion has spread further into steep forested areas and exports have accelerated rapidly since the two military coups and the resultant economic crisis of 1987. Clarke and Morrison (1987) report dangerously high rates of soil erosion due to deforestation; Thaman and Ba (1979) state that the widespread removal of coastal strand species and mangroves for fuel has exacerbated coastal erosion in many areas; and 'agrodeforestation' — the removal, neglect, or the failure to replant trees — persists, almost unheeded by policy makers in the agricultural and forestry sectors. As Chambers (1983) argues, trees and tree planting as traditional components of agricultural systems have been ignored in institutionalised rural development because they 'fall into the gaps' between the traditional sectoral responsibilities of 'agriculture' and 'forestry'.

AGRODEFORESTATION AS AN ISSUE

Although deforestation has received most attention globally, probably of greater importance is 'agrodeforestation' in the forms of both declining tree planting and the elimination of trees. Trees that, for generations, have provided food, timber, firewood, medicines and served other important cultural and ecological functions, increasingly are *not* being replaced or protected by the present generation. Although some countries have more forest reserves, conservation areas, or national parks, few, if any, have legislation prohibiting the felling, or promoting the replanting, of important or endangered tree species as part of agricultural or other modern-sector development. Thus, agrodeforestation continues, with little or no official recognition or resistance.

The situation is not yet beyond hope — as it appears to be in some areas of the world — because most traditional agroforestry strategies of the Pacific Islands have been preserved, if only in relict form. Nonetheless, monocultural expansion, of both commercial export crops and low-labour-input crops, such as cassava (Thaman and Thomas 1982, 1985), together with commercial livestock production, rapid population growth, demands for fuel, continued urbanisation, and the 'commercial imperative' (Tudge 1977), are the dominant trends that will be reversed only by deliberate planning and action.

THE NATURE OF TRADITIONAL AGROFORESTRY IN THE PACIFIC ISLANDS

In traditional Pacific Island 'development', forestry, agriculture, housing, medicine, and the production of a wide range of material goods were not compartmentalised into 'sectors'; rather they were part of integrated agroforestry systems or strategies tailored to the environmental and societal needs of each island ecosystem. Trees, of course, were major components of such systems (Thaman and Clarke 1983).

In terms of composition and spatial organisation, all traditional agroforestry systems, from the highlands of Papua New Guinea to the smallest atolls, exhibit a high degree of interspecies diversity, incorporating a wide variety of cultivated and protected indigenous and exotic species. These range from some 75 species commonly encountered on atolls, which have among the poorest floras on earth, to over 300 species in the larger-island agroforestry systems of Fiji, Vanuatu, Solomon Islands, and Papua New Guinea. Species include traditional staple tree crops, such as coconuts, breadfruit, and bananas intercropped with staple and supplementary ground crops, as well as a wide range of fruit and nut trees and other useful trees and plants, which are either deliberately planted, encouraged and protected in the regeneration of fallow regrowth, or spared when clearing new garden plots.

Moreover, for most traditional tree cultigens, non-tree understorey cultigens, recently-introduced cultigens, and a lesser number of indigenous species found in Pacific island agroforestry systems, there is also a high degree of intraspecies diversity. These are well-known and recognised locally. Within a given species, these cultivars have variable yield characteristics and seasonality, thus spreading yield distribution and seasonal surpluses more evenly. Similarly, as has been found true in other parts of the world, different cultivars have shown varying resistance to pests and diseases and to tropical cyclone damage, saltwater incursion, salt spray or drought. Different ecological tolerances cover varying soil types, shade conditions and hydrological regimes, and may result in a range of uses being possible[2].

Also seen as integral components of the broader village agroforestry systems are: secondary or fallow forest areas, indigenous stands of tropical rainforest, and mangrove or coastal strand forest which border or fall within the matrix of active garden or fallow areas; permanent, often sacred, groves of, primarily planted, useful trees in garden areas or surrounding villages; and trees planted in home gardens in nucleated villages or around isolated dwellings.

Together these diverse arboreal resources present an image of agroforestry very different from, and far more polycultural and utilitarian than, the

---

[2] For example, some coconut cultivars are used purely as drinking nuts, some for the flesh, and some for the large shells or the coir which can be used for vessels or for rope respectively.

predominant view of 'modern' agroforesters. Agroforestry is commonly seen as constituting the intercropping of export cash crops, such as cocoa, coconuts, coffee or bananas, with selected ground or shade crops; cattle under coconuts; fuelwood plantations; or the intercropping of exotic forest species with export or subsistence ground crops. No mention is made of the hundreds of other useful plants and wild animals that are integral to the traditional systems which are being replaced.

In terms of the utilitarian attributes of individual Pacific agroforestry systems, Table 1 attempts to show the multi-functional nature, as well as the value, of the individual arboreal components. Although modern agroforesters and horticulturalists may see native forests; silvicultural tree plantings; coconut, oil palm, cocoa, coffee, or banana plantations; or orange, avocado or macadamia orchards in terms of their economic value, or, possibly, even in terms of their ecological, recreational, or nutritional values, it is clear the Pacific Island agroforesters perceive arboreal resources to be far more multi-purpose.

In terms of the ecological value of trees, shade, for example, is critically important to humans, plants, and animals, especially in open savanna lands, in highly reflective low-lying coral island and lagoons, and in villages and urban areas. Damage from wind, erosion, and flood are increased when forests are removed; and mangrove and coastal strand forests stabilise tidal-zone soils and reduce the impact of storm surges. Soil improvement is another area where trees are of critical importance, especially given the high cost and detrimental impact of fossil-fuel-dependent inorganic fertilisers. The value of forests and trees as habitats for plants and animals, many of which are of considerable subsistence and commercial value, cannot be overstated (Thaman and Clarke 1983). Destruction of the habitats of beneficial insect, bird, and other vertebrate predators severely limits the implementation of integrated pest management programmes designed to minimise reliance on dangerous herbicides and pesticides.

Timber is important in local construction throughout the Pacific, as well as being among the top generators of foreign exchange in Papua New Guinea, the Solomon Islands, Fiji, and Western Samoa. Also, trees are significant in the informal sector in most countries for house construction, fencing, boatbuilding, toolmaking, weaponry, making containers, fishing gear, cooking equipment, and handicrafts (Table 1).

Foods from trees are of immense value, whether as staples, supplementary sources, or occasional snacks and famine foods. The nutritional importance of dominant staple tree crops, such as coconut, breadfruit, bananas, sago palm, and pandanus[3] and the wide range of fruit and nut trees found

---

3   See Appendix 1 for the Latin botanical names of species mentioned. In general, the common and vernacular names are given in the text, except where local names are not available or when the species are not included in Appendix 1.

Table 1
Ecological and Cultural Functions and Uses of Trees in Agroforestry Systems in the Pacific Islands

Ecological

Shade	Soil Improvement	Animal/Plant Habitats
Erosion Control	Frost Protection	Flood/Runoff Control
Wind Protection	Wild Animal Food	Weed/Disease Control

Cultural/Economic

Timber(commercial)	Broom	Prop or Nurse Plants
Timber(subsistence)	Parcelisation/Wrapping	Staple foods
Fuelwood	Abrasive	Supplementary Foods
Boatbuilding(canoes)	Illumination/Torches	Wild/Snack/Emergency
Sails	Insulation	Foods
Tools	Decoration	Spices/Sauces
Weapons/Hunting	Body Ornamentation	Teas/Coffee
Containers	Cordage/Lashing	Non-alcoholic Beverages
Woodcarving	Glues/Adhesives	Alcoholic Beverages
Handicrafts	Caulking	Stimulants
Fishing Equipment	Fibre/Fabric	Narcotics
Floats	Dyes	Masticants
Toys	Plaited Ware	Meat Tenderiser
Switch for Children/	Hats	Preservatives
Discipline	Mats	Medicines
Brush/Paint Brush	Baskets	Aphrodisiacs
Musical Instruments	Commercial/Export	Fertility Control
Cages/Roosts	Products	Abortificants
Tannin	Ritual Exchange	Scents/Perfumes
Rubber	Poisons	Recreation
Oils	Insect Repellents	Magico-religious
Toothbrush	Deodorants	Totems
Toilet Paper	Embalming Corpses	Subjects of Mythology
Fire Making	Dancing Grounds	Secret Meeting Sites

Source: Adapted from Thaman and Clarke (1983). Based on fieldwork in Papua New Guinea, Solomon Islands, Fiji, Tonga, Western Samoa, Kiribati, and Nauru.

throughout the Pacific have been widely stressed elsewhere (Parkinson 1982; Coyne 1984; Thaman 1979, 1982a,b, 1983b, 1985; Yen 1980a,b). Supplementary foods and snacks are described by Thaman (1976, 1976/77, 1982a,b) for Tonga, Fiji and other Pacific Islands, and by Clarke (1965, 1977) for a highland Papua New Guinean community. Powell (1976) provides a comprehensive coverage of wild food use and other important aspects of ethnobotany for the entire island of New Guinea.

It should be stressed, however, that although many tree foods are energy-rich in carbohydrates and/or vegetable fats, it is in other nutritional essentials, such as vitamins and minerals and fibre, that they often excel in comparison with the ubiquitous root crop staples and other annual non-arboreal plants. For example, mango, papaya and some pandanus are excellent sources of provitamin A; *Canarium* spp., Tahitian chestnut and avocado of B-complex vitamins; guava, mango, papaya, and citrus of vitamin C and most seeds or green leaves[4] are good sources of plant protein and a range of other micronutrients necessary for optimum health (Thaman and Clarke 1983; Thaman 1983b). Spices and sauces from tree products can also be of nutritional value.

Wild foods, which contribute significantly to the dietary well-being of many Pacific islanders, particularly in the interior of large continental islands, are also lost when the plants and animals that supplied them disappear along with the forest that served as their habitat (Clarke 1965, 1977; Thaman 1982a). Deforestation has severely restricted the habitats for wallabies and the valued cassowary bird of Papua New Guinea. The destruction of mangrove forests is of particular concern because of their importance in marine and estuarine food chains, as well as being favoured habitats or nurseries for a wide range of fin-fish, molluscs, and crustaceans (Thaman 1982a).

Trees are also valuable sources of food and fodder for domesticated animals. *Pisonia grandis* leaves, for example, are used as pig feed in Tonga; leucaena leaves and pods are used widely for goats, pigs, and cattle; and coconuts and papaya are important animal foods throughout most of the Pacific.

In terms of other uses, the arboreal pharmacopoeia is widely known and valued by modern science and industry as well as by local inhabitants, with all parts of the Pacific possessing medicine-producing trees and plants. Wrapping materials include coconut, breadfruit, banana, and *vau* leaves and other leaves (notably *Ficus* spp.) serve as effective abrasives. Dyes are derived from many sources, amongst them *Bischofia javanica* (a major red-brown dye for tapa), *Bruguiera* spp. and *Aleurites moluccana* (black), *Morinda citrifolia* (yellow), and *Bixa orellana* (red).

Perfumes, such as sandalwood, are well known outside of the Pacific, while less cosmopolitan fragrances are derived from *makosoi* and other scenting agents that are put into coconut oil from trees such as *Pimenta*, frangipani, and pandanus[5]. In Tonga, for example, there are over 50 species of sacred or fragrant plants, known as '*akau kakala*, which are central to the spiritual and economic fabric of Tongan society and which are planted or protected as integral components of Tongan agroforestry (Thaman 1986, 1987).

---

4   For instance, from *Moringa oleifera, Ficus* spp., and *Gnetum gnemon* (which also provides edible seeds).

5   Other sources of scents that are often used include *Gardenia* spp., *Parinari glaberrima, Aglaia saltatorum, Fagraea erteriana*, and *Calophyllum inophyllum* (Thaman and Clarke 1983).

These few examples, show the utilitarian diversity and the economic and cultural value derived from trees and agroforestry in the Pacific, values that are rarely acknowledged in planning or project documents, but that would be extremely difficult or impossible to replace with imported substitutes. The elimination of such utilitarian and cultural diversity can only serve to lock Pacific societies more tightly into the vicious circle of economic and cultural dependency.

FIJIAN AGROFORESTRY AT NAMOSI AND MATAINASAU

The in-depth case studies of the agroforestry systems of Namosi and Matainasau Villages in Fiji, conducted from 1979 to 1988, similarly underline the critical economic, cultural and ecological importance of agroforestry to the future of the Fijian people.

Namosi and Matainasau villages are located in the interior wet zone of Viti Levu, some 56 and 95 kilometres respectively from of Suva. The village lands extend from elevations of about 150 to 1000 metres, with much of the land in slopes in excess of 50 per cent, which makes accessibility difficult. Rainfall ranges form 2500 to 5000mm per year, although it can be as high as 9000mm. Both villages are situated on major rivers, Namosi on the upper Waidina River and Matainasau on the Wainimala River. Both have access to sizeable areas of alluvial land and extensive areas of more mountainous agricultural and forest land. The humic latosols which predominate in the upland areas are characterised by stony clay, stony sandy clay and stony silt to 60cm in depth. Although prone to erosion, these soils have relatively high fertility and are particularly suited for short-term root crops, *yaqona*, and long-term tree crops. The alluvial sandy loams and sandy soils of the alluvial flats and colluvial areas have relatively high fertility when drained (Groom *et al.* 1981). In the early 1980s, it was estimated that there were some forty-five households in Namosi, with a total population of approximately 250 (Rizer *et al.* 1982). The population of Matainasau is slightly less, with some thirty households in the mid-1980s.

As stressed by Ravuvu (1983:70), the Fijian term for land, *vanua*, "has physical, social and cultural dimensions which are interrelated" and includes the vegetation and animal life, as well as the social and cultural system. As such, the agroforestry systems of the Fijians include not just those trees planted on their agricultural lands, but would include all trees that are integral to the success of the wider agricultural system, including trees in fallow areas and forest stands bordering and protecting agricultural areas, as well as living fences, tree groves near villages, and trees planted or protected in and around villages. In this context, the major agroforestry land use zones would include: the village site (*koro*); the areas surrounding the village (*bili ni koro*); the agricultural lands (*qele ni teitei*), including active gardens (*vei were*) and fallow areas (*raki*) on the alluvial flats (*buca*); agricultural lands (*qele ni teitei*), including active gardens (*vei were*) and associated fallow areas (*raki*) on rolling colluvial and mountain soils (*vei delana*); secondary forest areas (*veikau*) on both alluvial flat and upland areas; the dense primary forest (*lekutu or veikau loa*); scattered fenced beef cattle pastures (*loma ni ba* or *ba ni bulumakau*); and riparian areas (*bati ni wai*).

Trees in all zones provide a matrix for ground cropping, grazing, residences, a wide range of food and other resources. Appendix 1 lists over one hundred trees or tree-like species that were encountered in surveys of agroforestry areas surrounding Namosi and Matainasau villages, with particular focus on existing agricultural areas[6]. Although primarily restricted in distribution to forest areas (and not listed in Appendix 1), some tree species are occasionally found as protected individuals in recently cleared upland garden sites. Moreover, although these species are technically 'forest', rather than 'agroforest', species, *veikau* areas are seen by Fijians as integral components of the wider *vanua* and agricultural land use system, and were generally used by the entire community to supply materials for construction and firewood, as well as for hunting and foraging. Although the pressure for commercial logging in such areas has made communal use of forest lands more restrictive, access to more distant forest areas is still very much open, as long as a member of the community is extracting resources for personal or communal use, rather than for commercial sale or export (Ravuvu 1983:74).

The more than one hundred tree or tree-like species found within the more active agricultural areas and surrounding villages are listed in Appendix 1 in the approximate order of their agroforestry importance or abundance. They include important widely-cultivated food and non-food species, species that are protected or preserved when clearing garden areas, and species which are protected upon spontaneous generation. The most common species are a wide range of bananas, kava, *bele*, citrus, breadfruit, *duruka*, sugarcane, papaya, coconut, *kavika*, *wi*, *soursop*, *vutu kana*, guava, cocoa, *vutu*, jakfruit, palms[7], and *waciwaci*. All are commonly planted or protected in active garden areas, fallow areas, and in tree groves around villages, although, as Ravuvu (1983:73) reports, they are "usually grown in small patches away from the land used for root crops". The mango and the avocado are found infrequently because they seem to bear few fruit in wet inland areas, but are common,

---

6   Accordingly, not included in the table are a majority of those species commonly found in surrounding primary forest stands, where the major species include *yaka* (*Dacrydium nidulum*), *dakua makadre* (*Agathis vitiensis*), *dakua salusalu* (*Decussocarpus vitiensis*), *asi* (*Podocarpus affinis*), *kuasi* (*Podocarpus neriifolius*), *lekutu* or *kauvula* (*Endospermum macrophyllum*), *kaudamu* (*Myristica* spp. and *Phaleria acuminata*), *damanu* (*Calophyllum vitiense*), *damanu dilodilo* (*Calophyllum cerasiferum* and *C. neo-ebudicum*), *roga* or *mavota* (*Gonystylus punctatus*), *sacau* (*Palaquium hornei*), *bauvudi* (*Palaquium fidjiense* and *P. stehlinii*), *buabua* (*Fagraea gracilipes*), *laubu* (*Garcinia myrtifolia*), *rogi* (*Heritiera ornithocephala*), *yasiyasi* (*Cleistocalyx eugeniodes*), and *kaunigai* (*Haplolobus floribundus*) (Parham 1972; Groom *et al.* 1981).

7   Two of the most important are *Veitchia joannis* and *Prichardia pacifica* — now found more often growing wild.

especially in the case of the mango, in drier coastal agricultural areas. Palms and *waciwaci* were more common in the past, but are only occasionally planted today.

In active garden areas, these species are generally found interspersed with staple food crops in gardens, as well as remaining throughout fallow periods, which traditionally ranged from five to fifteen years. Cropping periods on the poorer upland soils were from two to seven years, depending on whether kava was planted, though on the richer alluvial and colluvial soils nearer the villages, longer cropping periods and shorter fallows were possible. Although burning of debris cleared from new garden patches is practiced widely in Fiji, including Namosi, the practice has been traditionally discouraged at Matainasau because it was believed to have deleterious effects on soil and arboreal regeneration.

In the upland garden areas, taro (*Colcasia esculenta*) and cassava (*manihot esculenta*) are the dominant ground crops, taro generally being planted after clearing and intercropped with kava. Cassava is planted next, sometimes up to three or more times in succession. Less common crops or intercrops in these gardens include yams (*Dioscorea alata*), wild yams (*D. nummularia*) (which are both cultivated and grow wild in fallow and secondary forest areas), tannia (*Xanthosoma sagittifolium*), giant taro (*Alocasia macrorrhiza*), and giant swamp taro (*Cyrtosperma chamissonis*)[8]. It must be stressed that one factor responsible for decreasing fallow periods and increasing cropping periods and associated agrodeforestation has been the propensity of Fijians to abandon more labour-intensive and less-nutritional traditional crops, such as yams and taro, in favour of cassava, which is less often intercropped and which requires little or no fallow between successive plantings (Thaman and Thomas 1982, 1985).

The same crops are also found in alluvial gardens, although kava is less commonly planted there, with sweet potatoes (*Ipomoea batatas*) growing particularly well in the sandy soils. Some non-traditional vegetables and fruits, such as Chinese cabbage (*Brassica chinensis*), tomatoes (*Lycopersicon esculentum*), long beans (*Vigna sequipedalis*), corn (*Zea mays*), and eggplant (*Solanum melongena*), are increasingly intercropped between staple root crops during the early stages of gardens, particularly on the alluvial flats near villages, where water for short-term seed crops is readily available. Pineapple (*Ananas comosus*) is also increasingly common.

Of the tree crops listed in Appendix 1, banana cultivars (especially *jaina* and *vudi*) are probably of greatest economic and subsistence importance. A range of *vudi* is found in most gardens and is an important staple. It is estimated that the *vudi* cultivars scattered throughout garden areas, could constitute as much as 5 per cent of total food-crop area, and, as perennials, they continue bearing without replanting for ten years or more if kept disease- and weed-free. The common banana of commerce, or *jaina*, which was

---

8   The latter is occasionally found growing wild, although it was probably originally planted, along small streams and poorly-drained areas bordering the garden areas.

formerly an important export crop for both villages, is still numerous in gardens, especially on alluvial and colluvial soils, and remains an important local cash crop in Matainasau Village. Although bananas are susceptible to black-leaf-streak fungal and bunchy-top viral diseases, widely dispersed plantings and intercropping seem to control damage from disease[9]. Other banana cultivars include the *liga ni marama* or lady's finger banana; the *bata* or blue Java plantain; the *viavialevu*, *qamure* or horn plantain — all of which are occasionally found in garden or recent fallow areas — and the *sowaqa* or wild banana, which is sometimes cultivated and found in old secondary vegetation. It was widely cultivated in the past.

Yaqona is currently the most important cash crop in both areas, being planted both as a monocrop, but it is more commonly intercropped with taro and other crops, which are harvested first, leaving the kava to mature over its four-to-seven-year optimum yield cycle. Because new kava gardens have been extended into new, more distant, upland areas, with the opening of improved road transport, these gardens often have fewer deliberately cultivated kava plants, as is the case in the more traditional gardens closer to the villages. As with bananas, there is considerable intraspecies diversity, with at least six recognised kava cultivars in the Namosi area. Being relatively shade resistant, small plantings of kava are commonly found in tree-dominated gardens near settlements.

Although technically a shrub, *bele* (*vauvau — Abelmoschus manihot*) is a perennial which, under good conditions, can grow to over three metres in height. Along with taro-leaf spinach (*rourou*) and a wide range of wild ferns found throughout garden and fallow areas, *bele* is one of the main green vegetables of both villages. It is reputedly one of the most nutritious green vegetables, being very high in vitamins A and C, and iron, and having 12 per cent protein by dry weight (Standal *et al.* 1974). Moreover, it is easily propagated from cuttings, easy to cultivate, relatively disease-resistant, is highly desired as a vegetable, and even is considered to be of medicinal value. It is widely planted either along borders of gardens or as an intercrop throughout gardens, thus enhancing the three-dimensional and temporal yield structure of gardens.

The wide range of citrus species — cultivated and protected as volunteers throughout gardens, fallow areas and around villages — are a major economic resource, particularly in Namosi, which is renowned for its oranges. Species include the sweet orange, or *moli Taiti* (literally Tahitian orange), and the mandarin orange or *moli madarini*, which are sold in the thousands at the Suva Municipal Market (Thaman 1976/77) and provide a major seasonal source of cash as well as a very nutritious snack food. The rough lemon, or *moli karokaro*, is also common, especially in fallow areas and is widely used to marinate raw fish or squeezed on a wide range of foods. It constitutes one of the main ingredients, along with coconut cream, chillies, onions, and salt,

---

9   These diseases proved to be the death knell of banana monocropping and the export trade to New Zealand and Japan in the mid-1960s.

of the sauce known as *miti*. The young leaves are also used to make tea (*drau ni moli*). The sour orange (*moli kula*, kalamantsi, or *moli witiwiti*) and the pummelo (shaddock, or *moli kana*) are also frequently cultivated or protected, and are used for eating, making drinks, squeezing on food, or, occasionally, sale at the market.

Coconut and breadfruit, although both important and common in garden areas and around villages, especially on the alluvial flats, are not as dominant here as in coastal areas. Nevertheless, the coconut remains a very important supplementary staple in both areas, the expressed cream from the flesh of the endosperm of mature nuts being widely used in cooking, the green nuts for drinking, and the mature nuts commonly fed to poultry and pigs. Similarly, breadfruit also constitutes an important seasonal staple. There are at least five recognised coconut and three breadfruit cultivars in Namosi. Needless to say, the coconut palm, the Pacific's 'tree of life' has countless other uses, and, because of its small crown structure, is the perfect arboreal intercrop[10].

Unlike commercial sugarcane cultivation, where the entire crop is taken at each harvest, traditional aboriginally-introduced chewing cultivars are kept in tree-like clumps, often growing to over three metres in height. They are continually harvested as an energy- and fibre-rich natural snack food. As such, sugarcane, which is widespread in most gardens, constitutes an important 'agroforestry' species. The closely related cane inflorescence or *duruka* (known locally as 'Fiji asparagus') is also found in a cultivated or almost wild state throughout garden areas, especially in poorly drained alluvial sites. In Namosi, where it is an important seasonal food and source of cash income, some nine cultivars are recognised.

Also of very considerable collective economic and subsistence importance are a range of other traditional and more recently-introduced fruit trees which are found planted and protected. The traditional, possibly aboriginally introduced trees, such as the *kavika* and *wi*, which are common in both Namosi and Matainasau, and the *vutu kana*, which is common in areas around Namosi, all provide seasonal flushes of fruit, some of which is sold. Of the recent introductions, papaya is particularly widespread and an excellent non-seasonal vitamin- and mineral-rich fruit. *Seremaia* is also common in both gardens and around villages, and the jakfruit increasingly is to be seen. The guava, which is generally found growing wild, but occasionally planted or protected, is a common and very important seasonal crop, especially in areas where livestock have been grazed or tethered. The mango, which is believed to be a post-European contact introduction to Fiji, and the avocado are only occasionally found and bear little in the cold, wet conditions of Namosi and Matainasau.

Senile experimental plantings of cocoa and coffee (*Coffea* sp.) are found at Namosi, with scattered trees found at Matainasau. No cocoa or coffee is

---

10   Two other palms with edible seeds and useful fronds, the *saqiwa* and the *sakiki*, although more common in other areas of Fiji, are found only occasionally, often growing wild, but reportedly planted more widely in the past.

produced, although the ripe cocoa fruit pulp is consumed as a snack food and occasionally sold. Cocoa, however, is becoming a more important commercial crop in some areas, such as the nearby Wainibuka Valley, and does offer some prospect for agroforestry cash cropping.

Also of considerable cultural importance are a number of cultivated non-food plants. Principal amongst these are pandanus (*voivoi*), of which there are a range of cultivars used in the production of plaited ware, such as ceremonial mats, rough mats, baskets, and hats; and the ti plant (*vasili*), of which there a number of cultivars planted as ornamentals in villages, providing the most commonly used leaves in traditional dance costumes. The bright red ti plant is planted also as a 'protective' plant in gardens to ward off evil spirits and to insure good yields, while the larger dark-green variety, *vasili ni Toga*, was formerly an important famine food and source of sugar[11]. Other non-food plants include *danidani* (panax), a common ornamental hedge, living fence, boundary marker, source of medicine and ornamental plant; *kalabuci*, also a common ornamental and hedge plant; frangipani (*bua ni Vavalagi*), widely planted as an ornamental and for the use of its fragrant flowers in garlands; *banidaki (wiriwiri* or physic nut), of medicinal value and planted as living fencing; *vauvau* (*vauvau ni Vavalagi* or kapok), occasionally planted as a source of fibre to fill mattresses and pillows; *uci*, a shrub of medicinal value with pungent flowers and leaves used in garlands and to scent coconut oil; *vasa damu*, an attractive rust-red coloured tree-like shrub which is planted as a protective plant to ward off evil spirits and to insure good yields; and *soga* or sago palm, which provides a favoured thatching for roofs. A number of other shrubby ornamentals, such as dracaena, bougainvillea, caricature plant or false eranthemum, are also often planted in and around villages.

Non-cultivated multi-purpose food trees such as *dawa, ivi, lolo, tavola, vini, kabi,* and *sukau,* are commonly protected in garden areas, around villages, and in forest stands within or surrounding garden areas. Other less commonly used wild food sources, which were reportedly more widely used and available in the past, include *vava*, the flower bracts of which are baked or roasted; *losilosi*, the leaves and fruit of which are eaten and used medicinally; and *waciwaci*, the edible seeds of which were roasted or fried in the past over open fires.

Of major economic, ecological and cultural importance is the host of other important non-cultivated species that are frequently found, often as dominants, in agroforestry areas. They are valued for their timber, fuel, medicines, fibre, perfumes and dyes, and they are used for shade, erosion control, soil improvement, and wildlife habitat maintenance. Some also have considerable spiritual importance. In terms of medicinal value, for example, field surveys and Weiner's (1984) study of Fijian medicinal plants indicate that almost 50 per cent (47 of 101) of the plants listed in Appendix 1 have some medicinal use.

---

11   Sugar was extracted from the root which was baked in an earthen oven for four days.

These non-cultivated species include very common indigenous trees, though in some cases they were possibly aboriginally introduced[12]. Examples include *koka*, a favoured water-resistant housepost, medicinal and dye plant, source of firewood, and an indicator of soil fertility; beach hibiscus (*vau*), used medicinally and in house construction, and the inner bark of which provides fibre used in rope making, dancing skirts, and for straining kava; and the coral tree (*drala*), a common boundary marker, medicinal plant, and indicator of the yam-planting season. Others are *bitu* (or 'true' bamboo), found in fallow areas and secondary vegetation, and very important in house and raft construction, as well as being used for torches, fish traps and knives; *drou*; tree fern (*balabala*); *gadoa* and *mavu*; *yaro*; *molau*; *vesida* or *sasawira*; *kuluva*; *sama*; *makita*; *kura*; *bua* or *bua ni Viti*; *bo nokonoko* or *boloa*; *vobo*; *bo*; *mokosoi*; *lekutu*; *midra*; *mako*; *samaloa*; *waiwai*, candlenut (*lauci*); *doi*; *sorua* or *bulei*; *baka*; *tadau*; *isusu*; *sakelo* or *dava*; *ai masi*; *tirivanua*; *sa*; *sisisi*; *salato*; sandalwood (*yasi*); and *kaukaro*. All of these are found in garden and fallow areas. Associated with these species are a wide range of other species, including non-arboreal understorey species, which are also seen as integral to the maintenance of traditional agroforestry stability.

Although most of the above are generally found growing naturally, some such as *vau, drala, yaro*, and *kuluva* are commonly planted as living fencing, and others, such as *makita* and *lekutu* (also called *lekuti or kauvula*) are particularly valued and often planted around villages. Trees which are sacred totems (or *i cavuti*) of the various descent groups, or *mataqali*, of Namosi include *mako*, *bua*, *bitu*, and *niu*.

Exotic trees of widespread importance for agroforestry include *yaqona ni Onolulu*; common bamboo; and two species referred to as *vaivai ni Vavalagi* — leucaena and the raintree or monkeypod. *Yaqona ni Onolulu* is a weedy large shrub to small tree which is abundant throughout garden and fallow areas, often being coppiced as a readily available source of fuelwood. Common bamboo, or *bitu ni Vavalagi*, is sometimes cultivated, but usually found wild and protected in large stands on the alluvial flats and occasionally in upland garden areas. It provides a ready source for construction materials of wide utility[13] and is a good source of fuel, especially on rainy days, when other sources are wet. Leucaena is important, especially in grazing areas, and is commonly used for fencing, the construction of pig pens and as a source of firewood and fodder. The raintree is often planted or protected around villages or in grazing areas as a shade tree, and is particularly common on the alluvial garden flats near Matainasau, where it is an important source of timber, fuelwood and wood for carving.

---

12 Examples of species that were probably of aboriginal introduction include *koka, vau, mokosoi* and *waiwai*.

13 One of the main uses of bamboo in the past was in the building of bamboo rafts or *bilibili*. These were the main means of transporting agricultural produce before road access to urban markets became available in the past ten years or so.

Also of importance for agroforestry are the relatively dense groves of mature trees which are found around the boundaries of villages, particularly Namosi Village. These include a wide range of primarily cultivated trees which are very useful and easily accessible to villagers. The main species surrounding Namosi include sweet oranges, mandarin oranges, rough lemon, breadfruit, jakfruit, coconut, bananas, Tahitian chestnut, Pacific lychee, coral tree, and the ti tree. Such communal groves are also found next to Kumi Village in Tailevu Province, and in Ra Province where they are known as *drukudruku*. Fruit trees and trees of medicinal or spiritual importance, such as those used in ceremonial garlands or for scenting coconut oil, known as *saluaki*, are most commonly found in such groves.

Widely used in inland Fijian villages are the great diversity of non-arboreal wild foodstuffs, medicines and other useful products found within agroforestry systems. If agrodeforestation continues, these sources will be considerably impoverished (Thaman 1982a). Most notable among these are an almost baffling diversity of wild yams[14] and ferns[15]. Other wild foods include: black nightshade (*malasou* or *boro* — *Solanum nodiflorum*); *sou* (*Solanum repandum*); spleen amaranth (*moca* or *tubua* — *Amaranthus viridis*); wild chilli pepper (*boro* — *Capsicum frutescens*); cape gooseberry (*kosopeli* — *Physalis peruviana*); kudzu root (*inoka* — *Pueraria lobata*); and a diversity of fungi (*daliga*), which are found on dead trees. It is estimated that these more common species, plus less important species and the previously mentioned tree or tree-like sources of wild food products, number over sixty in the Namosi area alone. When the wide range of edible birds, frogs, snakes, grubs, insects and finfish, eels, freshwater prawns, and other foods that are found within agroforestry zones are included, the significance of wild food resources to mountain villages becomes obvious. Moreover, apart from being nutritionally important — particularly in the cases of seasonal fruits and nuts, wild yams and wild greens, which, at some times of the year, are the most common foods available — these wild products also constitute important low-capital-input, low-risk cash 'crops' which are seasonally abundant at the Suva Municipal Market (Thaman 1976/77).

In summary, the over one hundred trees or tree-like species found in the agroforestry systems of Namosi and Matainasau collectively represent a resource of enormous economic, cultural and ecological importance. The trees, which, along with the many other species found in surrounding forest stands, have been preserved as part of the integral agroforestry system for generations, are now almost totally neglected by most agricultural developers and researchers. Consequently, although the agroforestry systems of both villages remain relatively intact, recent efforts to encourage cash cropping of

---

14 Known as *tivoli, rauva*, and *tikau*. The most important species are *Dioscorea nummularia, D. pentaphylla*, and *D. bulbifera*.

15 These are mostly referred to as *wata* or *ota*, the most commonly consumed species being *Athyrium* spp., *Diplazium* spp., *Tectaria latifolia, Stenochlaena palustris* and *Marattia smithii*.

bananas, cocoa, kava, and root crops, and commercial livestock grazing, have increased the pressure on nearby alluvial areas and led to increasing agrodeforestation. The new generation of farmers, who have become increasingly cash-oriented, have not been educated in the long-term utility of trees, and they neglect many of the important tree species.

POLYCULTURAL AGROFORESTRY AS A BASIS FOR INNOVATION AND STABILITY

As argued by Thaman and Clarke (1983), trees are both a symbol of, and a basis for, stability in agroecosystems and will continue to be essential sustainable development in the Pacific. Their shortcomings, as seen by modern developers, (for example, taking up space, or slow growth rates), which have often led to their being replaced by short-term crops, should be seen as advantageous in a world where biological stability is increasingly precarious. These very qualities provide a permanence in ecosystems that slows misuse and produces a wide range of ecological benefits: diversity of habitat, diversity of species, prevention of accelerated erosion, maintenance of soil fertility and arable soil structure, flood retardation, and wind protection. The culinary, nutritional, and medicinal value of trees and their contribution to welfare must be stressed in the light of the rapidly declining health and nutrition in the Pacific. This decline has led to high incidences of disorders, such as iron-deficiency anaemia, obesity, general micro-nutrient deficiency, cardio-vascular problems, hypertension, diabetes, cancer, hyperuricaemia and gout, dental disease, and alcoholism (Coyne 1984; Thaman 1979, 1982b, 1983b, 1985).

Increasing population and urbanisation, together with an official emphasis on monocultural production for export, and the neglect of traditional agroforestry-based food systems, is creating a scarcity of local staple foods and, consequently, greater levels of food dependency. Moreover, further agrodeforestation can only cause more reliance on foreign sources of fuel, fertiliser, medicines, perfumes, and other material goods. Similarly, ingenious and time-tested strategies for wild food acquisition, food processing, storage, and preservation have been all but forgotten and are in danger of disappearing (Massal and Barrau 1956; Barrau 1958, 1961; Yen, 1980a,b; Klee 1980; Parkinson 1982; Thaman 1982b, 1985).

In addition to their immense cultural and economic value, trees require less labour than do short-term crops and provide a reserve food supply should the latter fail. Yields may even be higher than monoculture crops, when trees and annuals are combined in a two-storey structure (Thaman 1983b).

Given their many advantages, polycultural agroforestry systems, such as those of Namosi and Matainasau, would seem to offer ideal bases for further development and innovation. Thaman (1987) suggests that the promotion of 'urban agroforestry' may be a very cost-effective way to solve problems associated with increasing urbanisation in the Pacific islands. Although there is a need for innovation and modification of existing systems, some changes have taken place in response to new ecological conditions, increasing population pressure, shifts in societal aspirations, and exposure to new plant species and agroforestry technologies. Pacific islanders have shown themselves willing to adapt their systems to changing environmental and social conditions and technological options (Thaman and Clarke 1983). It is critical, however, that today's development planners and managerial elite recognise the need to *base* modern agricultural and forestry development on traditional Pacific island agroforestry systems, and to see the planting and preservation of trees within existing agricultural systems as of primary importance. Rather than encouraging thoughtless agrodeforestation and associated helplessness, dependency, and the destruction of a significant part of Fiji's cultural heritage, they should foster development and innovation which would protect trees, people and their agroforestry traditions and promote economic self-reliance and cultural and ecological stability in Fiji.

Appendix 1

Important Tree and Tree-Like Species of Agroforestry Systems of Namosi and Matainasau Villages

(**B** = the common Bauan dialect, used as the Fijian 'Lingua Franca', **N** = Namosi dialect, **M** = Matainasau dialect, and no designation = common English or other widely used vernacular names)

Vernacular Names	Latin Name	Notes
vudi (N,M,B); cooking banana	*Musa* AAB triploid	Abundant in garden areas, in both alluvial flats and hill slopes; common intercrop in almost all gardens; green fruit an important staple, ripe fruit occasionally cooked as a dessert (*vakasoso*); leaves used to wrap food for cooking in the earthen oven and for general food parcelisation; important supplementary cash crop for local sale
yaqona (N,M,B); kava	*Piper methysticum*	Very abundant; most important cash crop in both Namosi and Matainasau; important alkaloid-rich social beverage made from the roots and lower stems; commonly intercropped with taro on rich slope soils; used medicinally
vauvau (N,M); *bele* (B)	*Abelmoschus manihot*	Abundant in gardens and around villages; major leafy green vegetable, very rich in vitamins A and C, iron and plant protein; commonly sold in markets; used medicinally
soco ni Taiti (N); *moli lecau* (M); *moli Taiti* (B); orange, sweet orange	*Citrus sinensis*	Common in garden areas, fallow vegetation, around villages, and in community tree groves, and occasional in secondary forests; ripe fruit eaten and made into drinks; sold as a major seasonal source of cash income; used medicinally

soco madirini (N); *moli madirini* (M,B); mandarin orange, tangerine	*Citrus reticulata*	Common in garden areas, fallow vegetation, around most villages, and in community tree groves, and occasionally in secondary forests; ripe fruit eaten and made into drinks; sold as a major seasonal source of cash income
koka (N,M,B)	*Bischofia javanica*	Abundant in garden and fallow areas, and common on alluvial flats; protected in past when clearing garden lands, but increasingly felled by younger generations; favoured tree for houseposts, good firewood, used medicinally, leaves boiled with pandanus leaves to dye them black; bark formerly used with other ingredients to dye hair red; its presence believed to be a sign of good soil
uto sori (N); *uto* (N,M,B); breadfruit	*Artocarpus altilis*	Common around villages, in garden areas, and in secondary forests and in village tree groves; fruit cooked as an important seasonal staple; leaves used for wrapping food for cooking in earthen oven or boiling; occasionally sold; used medicinally; various cultivars
vadra, voivoi (N,M,B); pandanus, screwpine	*Pandanus* spp.	Commonly planted in garden areas and in and around villages, often along fence-lines or garden boundaries; leaves treated and dyed for use in a wide range of plaited ware including ceremonial and rough mats, baskets, hats, and lashings; used as a fuel; proproots used medicinally; fruit and fibre used in garlands
dovu (N,M,B); sugarcane	*Saccharum officinarum*	Common intercrop in garden areas and around villages; stems an important snack food; used medicinally, leaves of some varieties occasionally used for thatching
duruka (N,M,B); Fiji asparagus	*Saccharum edule*	Common crop in garden and fallow areas, especially in moist alluvial areas; planted and protected in a somewhat naturalised state; internal inflorescence an important seasonal food and cash crop
jaina (N,M,B); banana, Cavendish banana	*Musa* AAA Group	Common intercrop in garden areas, especially on alluvial flats; important cash crop for local sale and eaten green as a supplementary staple and ripe as a fruit; leaves used to wrap food for cooking and for general food parcelisation

uto, uto maoli (N); *weleti* (M,B); papaya, pawpaw	*Carica papaya*	Common in garden and fallow areas and around villages, both planted and wild; ripe fruit eaten raw; green fruit occasionally cooked or mixed with meat as a tenderiser; used medicinally
vasili (N,M,B); ti plant	*Cordyline fruticosa*	Abundant in villages, common in garden areas, and occasional as an escape in fallow areas; a wide variety of cultivars exist; bright red varieties commonly planted as 'protector' plants to ward off evil spirits and to bring good luck to gardens and as ornamentals in villages; large roots of green varieties (*vasili ni Toga*) cooked in earthen oven in the past as a food, now only as a famine food; leaves of many varieties used in ceremonial skirts and other ornamental attire; used medicinally
dawa (N,M,B); Pacific lychee	*Pometia pinnata*	Common in garden areas, fallow areas and secondary forest; usually protected when clearing garden lands; ripe fruit eaten; leaves and bark used medicinally; good firewood and good timber
niu (N,M,B); coconut palm	*Cocos nucifera*	Occasional in garden areas and more common on alluvial flats and surrounding villages; a minor food plant in the interior, unlike in coastal areas where it is a major source of vegetable fat and energy in cooking, a poultry and pig feed, and used in an endless variety of ways; still an important intercrop, but more important in the past; the totem (*i cavuti*) of the Natuvora *mataqali* of Namosi; used medicinally
ivi (N,M,B); Tahitian chestnut	*Inocarpus fagifer*	Common in poorly drained areas, along rivers, and in tree groves and occasional in alluvial and some upland garden areas and around villages; seed cooked as a supplementary staple; leaves used to cover food in earthen oven; good fuelwood; used medicinally; sold occasionally
vau (N,M,B); beach hibiscus tree	*Hibiscus tiliaceus*	Common in fallow and garden areas, and around villages; commonly planted as living fences and pig pens; wood used in walling for houses, inner bark as fibre for skirts, for straining *yaqona*, and house and canoe lashings; leaves used medicinally

drala (N,M,B); coral tree, dadap	*Erythrina variegata*	Common in garden areas and around villages; commonly planted as property markers, living fences, or pig pens; flowering indicates the onset of the yam planting season; used medicinally
onolulu (N), *qonaqona* (M), *yaqona ni Onolulu* (B)	*Piper aduncum*	Common in fallow areas and protected in garden areas; coppiced as a very accessible and renewable firewood source; used a shade in active garden areas
kavika (N,M,B); Malay apple, mountain apple	*Syzygium malaccense*	Commonly planted or protected in garden areas, around villages, and in village tree groves; leaves and bark used medicinally, fruit eaten green and ripe, leaves cooked in the past
wi (N,M,B); Polynesian vi-apple, hog plum	*Spondias dulcis*	Commonly planted or protected in garden areas, around villages, and in village tree groves; ripe and green fruit eaten and occasionally sold at markets; leaves boiled with fatty food, particularly pork
drou (N,M,B)	*Trema orientalis*	Common pioneer species in fallow areas, secondary vegetation, and disturbed ruderal sites, particularly along road cuts
seremaia (N,M,B); soursop	*Annona muricata*	Common around villages, and occasional in garden areas; ripe fruit eaten and made into drinks
bitu, bitu dina (N,M,B); bamboo	*Schizostachyum glaucifolium*	Common in garden areas and in open secondary forest in hilly areas; large stems used for general construction purposes, in the construction of light rafts (*bilibili*), for piping, and for cooking food, especially freshwater prawns in the earthen oven or over an open fire; the totem (*i cavuti*) of the Soloira *mataqali* of Namosi; used medicinally
bitu ni Vavalagi (N,M,B); common bamboo	*Bambusa vulgaris*	Common in garden areas, fallow and secondary forest areas, and around villages; large stems used for housing, other construction purposes, for construction of bamboo rafts (*bilibili*), for ladders, and smaller sections for steaming food in the earthen oven or over open fires

balabala (N,M,B); tree fern	*Cyathea* spp.	Common in fallow areas and secondary forest and occasional in garden areas; trunks used in house construction and occasionally used, or sold to ornamental gardeners for use as orchid supports; when dry, used to carry fire long distances before matches were available
moli karokaro (N,M,B); *soco ni Vavalagi* (N)	*Citrus hystrix*	Common in garden and fallow areas and occasional in secondary forests and village tree groves; juice of fruit used to marinate raw fish and to flavour foods, young leaves used to make tea; used medicinally; occasionally sold; good fuelwood
gadoa (N,M)	*Macaranga harveyana*	Common in fallow areas and secondary forest and occasional in garden areas; wood used in construction and for firewood; used medicinally
mavu (N,M); *davo* (B)	*Macaranga graeffeana*	Common in garden and fallow areas, and as a pioneering species in secondary forests; wood used for construction and for firewood; used medicinally
yaro (N,M,B)	*Premna obtusifolia*	Common in garden and fallow areas and secondary forest and surrounding villages; commonly planted as living fencing; leaves and bark used medicinally
molau (N,M,B)	*Glochidion* spp.	Common in fallow vegetation and occasional in garden areas and secondary forests; leaves used medicinally; one of most widely used medicinal plants
vesida (N); *sasawira* (M); *sasauira* (B)	*Dysoxylum richii*	Common in secondary forests and occasional in garden areas; timber used in construction and for firewood
kuluva (N,M,B)	*Dillenia biflora*	Occasional in garden lands and around villages, common in secondary forests; planted as living fencing, pig pens, and bath house walls
sama (M)	*Commersonia bartramia*	Common in garden and fallow areas and secondary forests and along road frontages; good fuelwood; inner bark used for string and lashings; used medicinally

makita (N,M,B)	*Parinari glaberrima*	Occasional in garden and fallow areas, secondary forest and around villages; timber used for construction and small straight rods used for spears; seed used for dying hair and scenting coconut oil; leaves used for thatching houses
moli kula (M,B); *kula* (N); sour orange	*Citrus aurantium*	Occasional in garden and fallow areas and around *soco* villages; fruit used to make drinks, to squeeze on food and occasionally sold
kura (N,M,B)	*Morinda citrifolia*	Occasional in garden and fallow areas, secondary forest and around villages; used medicinally; pungent fruit eaten in the past
bua, bua ni Viti (N,M,B); *bua tokaikau* (N)	*Fagraea berteriana*	Occasional in garden and fallow areas and secondary forests and around villages; fragrant flowers used in garlands and for scenting coconut oil; the totem (*i cavuti*) of the Nasilime *mataqali* of Namosi; used medicinally
lolo (N,M)	*Ficus vitiensis*	Occasional in garden and fallow areas and secondary forests; sweet fruits eaten as a snack food; used medicinally
vutu kana, vutu (N,M,B)	*Barringtonia edulis*	Occasional in garden areas on alluvial flats, in tree groves and near or in villages; seeds eaten raw as a snack food; occasionally sold
bo nokonoko (N); *boloa* (N,M)	*Neubergia corynocarpa*	Occasional in garden and fallow areas and secondary forests; timber used in house construction
vobo (N,M); *bovu* (B)	*Mussaenda raiateensis*	Common in fallow areas and secondary forest; bark and leaves used medicinally
bo (N,M)	*Neonauclea forsteri*	Occasional in garden areas and secondary forests; wood used in construction
vaivai, vaivai ni Vavalagi (N,M,B); leucaena	*Leucaena leucocephala*	Common locally as a long-introduced inventive in garden areas, around villages, and in some areas where cattle are grazed; good source of firewood, posts for fencing and general construction purposes, such as animal pens; foliage and young pods used a fodder and occasionally eaten

quwawa (N,M,B); guava	*Psidium guajava*	Common in cattle paddocks and occasional in garden areas and around villages; leaves used as a treatment for diarrhoea, fruit a favoured, vitamin-C-rich snack food; good firewood
vaivai, vavai ni Vavalagi (N,M,B); *vu ni kau ni Vavalagi* (M); rain tree, monkeypod	*Samanea saman*	Commonly planted or protected in garden and grazing areas on the alluvial flats and near villages; excellent shade trees, wood favoured for wood carving and firewood
makosoi (N,M,B); perfume flower, ylangylang	*Cananga odorata*	Occasional in garden areas and around villages; leaves used medicinally; fragrant flowers used in garlands and for scenting coconut oil
moli witiwiti (N); kalamantsi (Philippines)	*Citrus microcarpa*	Occasional in garden areas, tree groves, and around villages; ripe fruit used to make drinks and to squeeze on food
koko (N,M,B); cocoa, cacao	*Theobroma cacao*	Occasionally planted in old garden areas; fruit eaten and occasionally harvested to make cocoa; increasingly important cash crop in some nearby areas in the wet zone
lekutu (N); *lekuti* (M); *kauvula* (B)	*Endospermum macrophyllum*	Occasional in secondary forests and protected in garden lands, and common in surrounding forests; wood used in house construction, for dug-out canoes, and for fuelwood; an important timber species for local milling and export
danidani (N,M,B); panax	*Polyscias* spp.	Common in villages and occasional in garden areas; planted as live fencing, hedges and pig pens and ornamentally in villages; leaves used in preparation of attire for traditional dances; used medicinally
kalabuci, kalabuci damu (N,M,B); Joseph's coat, beefsteak plant, copperleaf	*Acalypha wilkesiana*	Common in villages and occasional in garden areas; important planted ornamental and hedge plant; used medicinally
bua ni Vavalagi (N,M,B); frangipani, plumeria	*Plumeria* spp.	Common in villages and occasional in nearby gardens; fragrant flowers used in leis and garlands and to scent coconut oil

bata (N,M,B); blue Java plantain	*Musa* ABB Group	Occasional in garden areas; green fruit cooked as a supplementary staple and eaten ripe occasionally; leaves favoured for parcelisation of foods for earth oven
liga ni marama (N,M,B); lady's finger banana	*Musa* AAB Group	Occasional in garden areas and around villages; ripe fruit eaten, very minor cash crop for local sale; leaves used to wrap food
vava (N,M,B)	*Heliconia indica*	Occasional in garden areas, fallow areas, and secondary forests; flower bracts cooked as a famine food; leaves used to parcel food
midra (N,M)	*Cyrtandra jugalis*	Occasional in garden and fallow areas and secondary forests; timber used for house framing
moli kana(N,M,B); *soco vi kana* (N); pummelo, shaddock	*Citrus maxima*	Occasional in garden and fallow areas, in secondary forests, and surrounding villages; excellent firewood; ripe fruit eaten and occasionally sold; used medicinally
mako (N,M,B)	*Cyathocalyx vitiensis*	Occasional in garden and fallow areas,and secondary and primary forest; totem of the high-ranking Nabukebuke *yavusa* and *mataqali* of Namosi; used for firewood; inner bark occasionally used for string or lashing
samaloa (N)	*Melochia mollipila*	Occasional in fallow areas and secondary forests; good firewood; used medicinally
tavola (N,M,B); beach or Indian almond	*Terminalia catappa*	Occasional in garden areas and around villages; ripe seeds eaten; young leaves and bark used medicinally; the totem of the Navatusila *mataqali* in Namosi
vini (N); *vaivai* (M); lera (B); red-bead tree	*Adenanthera pavonina*	Occasional in garden areas and around villages in tree groves; timber used in house building and for firewood; seeds eaten
lauci (N,M,B);*waiwai* (N); candlenut	*Aleurites moluccana*	Occasional in garden and fallow areas and secondary forests and around villages; seeds used to produce oil beneficial to the skin; used medicinally
doi (N,M,B)	*Alphitonia zizyphoides*	Occasional in garden areas and secondary forests; timber useful; good firewood; used medicinally

kabi (N)	*Elaeocarpus cheloni-morphus*	Occasional in garden and fallow areas and in surrounding secondary forest; seeds eaten as a snack food and favoured food of fruit bats
molau (N,M,B), *molau vuloa* (N)	*Antidesma lassophylum*	Occasional in fallow areas; leaves used medicinally; good fuelwood when thoroughly dried
sorua(N,M); *bulei*(B)	*Alstonia vitiensis*	Occasional in garden areas and dried for chewing gum
baka, baka ni Viti (N,M,B); strangler fig; banyan	*Ficus obliqua*	Occasional in garden areas and common in secondary forest; fruit eaten by birds and fruit bats; used medicinally
tadau (N); *tadanu* (B)	*Homolanthus nutans*	Occasional in fallow areas and secondary vegetation; used for firewood
isusu(N)	*Elattostachys falcata*	Occasional in fallow and secondary forest areas; timber used in construction and for firewood
sakelo (N); *dava* (M)	*Astronidium conferti-florum*	Occasional in secondary forest in garden areas; used as fuelwood
saqiwa (N,M); *niusawa* (B)	*Veitchia joannis*	Infrequent in secondary forests and around villages; planted more in the past; immature seeds eaten as a snack food; the totem of Naqelekautia *mataqali* of Namosi
ai masi (N)	*Ficus fulvo-pilosa*	Occasional in garden and fallow areas and secondary forest; leaves used as sand paper in the past
tirivanua (N)	*Timonius ffinis*	Occasional in fallow areas; used medicinally by women
losilosi (N,M,B)	*Ficus barclayana*	Occasional in garden and fallow areas, secondary forest, and around and in villages; leaves and fruit eaten; leaves used medicinally
banidaki (N,M); *wiriwiri* (B)	*Jatropha curcas*	Occasional in garden areas and around villages; planted as a living fence; used medicinally
uto ni Idia (N,M,B); jakfruit	*Artocarpus heterophyllus*	Occasional around villages in garden lands; fruit eaten and occasionally sold

sukau, bele, sukau (N,M,B)	*Gnetum gnemon*	Occasional in secondary forest and forest areas surrounding garden areas; seeds edible, young leaves cooked as a spinach
uci (N,M,B)	*Euodia hortensis*	Occasionally planted in garden areas and common in and around villages; flowers and leaves used to scent coconut oil, to make garlands (*salusalu*), and commonly worn behind the ear; leaves used medicinally
vasa damu (N,M,B)	*Euphorbia fidjiana*	Shrub occasionally planted as a 'protect' or spiritual plant to protect gardens from evil spirits and to ensure good yields; used medicinally
tulip (M); African tulip tree	*Spathodea campanulata*	Occasional ornamental and living fence around villages, occasional as a naturalised escape in garden areas
vauvau, vauvau ni Vavalagi	*Ceiba pentandra*	Occasionally planted in garden areas and around villages; occasionally planted as living fences; fibres surrounding seeds used to stuff pillows and mattresses
maqo (N,M,B); mango	*Mangifera indica*	Occasional in garden areas and surrounding and in villages; ripe fruit eaten; fruit rarely sets in wet higher elevations
pea (N,M,B); avocado	*Persea americana*	Occasionally planted in garden areas and around villages; ripe fruit eaten, commonly as a butter substitute; does not bear fruit as well in wet higher elevations
dracaena	*Dracaena fragrans*	Common ornamental in villages
bougainvillea	*Bougainvillea* spp.	Common ornamental in villages
soga (N,M,B); sago palm	*Metroxylon itiense*	Occasionally planted along rivers or around villages and gardens; fronds used for thatching houses; maristem sometimes sold to Indians for use in curries; leaf ribs used for brooms
sa (N,M,B)	*Parinari insularum*	Occasional in garden and fallow areas and open forest stands; excellent firewood
sowaqa (N,M,B); fe'i banana, mountain banana	*Musa fehi*	Occasional in secondary forest as relict of former cultivation, or occasional in garden areas; fruit cooked as a staple and occasionally sold at Suva Market

yasi ni wai (N)	*Syzygium seemannianum*	Common along streams and river banks; leaves used medicinally
tokatolu (N)	*Euodia vitiensis*	Infrequent in secondary forests; leaves used medicinally and taken by women after giving birth
sisisi (N)	*Gironniera celtidifolia*	Infrequent in secondary forests and in fallow areas; wood good for digging sticks
salato (N,M,B)	*Dendrocnide harveyi*	Infrequent in fallow areas and secondary forests; used medicinally
waciwaci(N)	*Sterculia vitiensis*	Infrequent in garden areas and secondary forests and occasionally planted around villages; seeds eaten roasted or fried in the past
yasi (M)	*Santalum yasi*	Uncommon in secondary forests; harvested commercially in some areas of Fiji
viavia levu (M); *qamure* (B); cooking banana	*Musa* cultivar	Uncommon banana cultivar in garden areas; green fruit cooked as a staple
sakiki(N,M); *masei* (B); Fiji fan palm	*Prichardia pacifica*	Infrequently planted around villages and gardens; seeds eaten; leaves once used for fans
false eranthemum	*Pseuderanthemum curruthersii*	Occasional ornamental in villages
kaukaro (N)	*Buchania attenuata*	Infrequent in secondary forest areas; used medicinally
caricature plant	*Graptophyllum pictum*	Occasional ornamental in villages

Source: Field surveys by the author, 1979-1988; Weiner, 1982 for some medicinal usages.

5

THE MARKETING OF *YAQONA*[1]

Jiten Mangal

YAQONA IN FIJI'S ECONOMY

Yaqona, kava, or, often, 'grog' (*Piper methysticum*) is grown and drunk in all parts of the Pacific. The beverage is the colour of muddy water and can be prepared by pounding either the roots (*waka*) or the stem (*lawena*) into a powder and then mixing it with water. Traditionally, amongst indigenous Fijians, *yaqona* was drunk as a central part of ceremonial occasions and much of the ritual associated with its preparation and serving is preserved in present-day consumption. Its use has spread to other ethnic groups in Fiji, and, in both the countryside and the towns, it is common at social gatherings, such as marriages, parties or small get-togethers, and is rightly called the 'national drink of Fiji'. The market is large and stable.

Grown mainly for subsistence use in the rural areas of Fiji, it is normally inter-cropped with staples such as *dalo, kumala* and cassava. However, surplus production is sold to get extra income when necessary. Increasingly, *yaqona* is becoming an important cash crop, grown extensively for commercial sale. In some parts of the country it has become the leading cash crop. In the upper Wainimala, certain villages depend on it for up to 85 per cent of their cash incomes (*Fiji Times* 27 March 1975)[2] and Sofer (1985) has noted its increasing significance in peripheral regions such as Kadavu and Lomaiviti. In Kadavu, Sofer showed that *yaqona* was replacing copra as the leading cash crop, mainly because it brings higher and more stable returns to producers. Because of the distance and high cost of transport between the

---

[1]   Thanks are due to Talei Maimanuku and Isimeli Tukana for their assistance with this research. This chapter began as a student research project at the University of the South Pacific in 1985 but has been rewritten since and extra research has been undertaken.

[2]   This is supported by the recent research of Margaret Chung — see chapter 7.

outer islands and the main urban markets in Fiji, and because it is relatively non-perishable, *yaqona* is proving a particularly suitable cash crop for peripheral areas. Other market crops, more perishable, do not reach the urban centres in saleable condition (Sofer 1985:434).

Another advantageous feature of *yaqona* as a cash crop is its flexibility in harvesting. It takes a long time to mature and can be pulled throughout the year either when relatively young (three years or less) or fully-matured (five to seven years). Thus, growers can choose to harvest when market conditions are most favourable or when their need for cash is greatest, or decide to leave the crop in the ground. It has proved very popular throughout the islands but there are some concentrations (Table 1).

Table 1
Distribution of *Yaqona* Production
By Selected Region, 1978

Region	Number of growers	% farms growing *yaqona*	Mean area per farm (ha)
Western Division	1,076	4	0.25
Central Division	1,943	15	0.16
Eastern Division	3,981	65	0.28
Northern Division	2,280	21	0.31
Total Fiji	9,280	16	0.26
Kadavu	1,496	92	0.29
Lomaiviti	1,886	80	0.25
Namosi	327	52	0.12
Cakaudrove	1,465	35	0.39
Lau	583	32	0.37
Naitasiri	942	23	0.21
Bua	414	20	0.16

Source: Rothfield and Kumar (1980: 14-17, 30). The authors noted a slight decrease in the area under *yaqona* between the censuses of 1968 and 1978 but believe this could be attributable to difficulties in data collection, *yaqona* often being grown in remote hillside and bush locations. The total number of farms excludes 'semi-urban' farms.

Table 1 shows that the major *yaqona* producing areas in Fiji, and those with the larger average plantations, are the Eastern and Northern Divisions, where rainfall is high and soils are well-drained. In the Eastern Division, the provinces of Kadavu and Lomaiviti have the largest number of *yaqona* farms, whilst the provinces of Northern and Central Division, though still large producers, have a lower proportion of producing farms. Another feature of the 1978 agricultural census data is that of the total number of growers, 98 per cent are indigenous Fijians cultivating *mataqali* land. Despite its wide usage it has remained, then, an almost exclusively 'Fijian' crop.

Although *yaqona* is primarily a domestic crop, a small quantity is exported and, as Table 2 shows, the amount has increased since 1982. The major buyers were Australia, Canada and both East and West Germany. Australia is the largest single importer, purchasing one-fifth of total exports. From time to time other South Pacific countries also import Fijian kava when their own supplies are short. By mid 1986, total *yaqona* export revenue amounted to about $50,000 per month (*Fiji Sun* 8 July 1986). Unfortunately, foreign demand varies and the prices, too, are not stable. Despite these exports, though, Fiji has had to import kava and, for a number of years prior to 1984, was a net importer.

Table 2
Exports and Imports of *Yaqona*, 1982-1986

	1982	1983	1984	1985	1986[a]
Exports					
tonnes	17.22	21.70	61.44	75.12	33.35
$F	92,991	107,642	377,406	432,226	187,535
$/kg	5.40	4.96	6.14	5.75	5.62
Imports					
tonnes	38.93	51.27	16.61	8.16	na
$F	178,338	265,422	93,239	42,003	na

[a] 1986 figures are only for January to May inclusive
na Data not available

Source: Fiji Bureau of Statistics (1983b, 1984, 1985). Overseas Trade Reports for 1985 and 1986 data are, as yet, unpublished.

On the domestic markets, fluctuations in *yaqona* production are reflected in gluts or shortages. When supply is short, prices soar and imports are required. In 1973, for example, cyclones Bebe and Lottie led to an acute shortage. Local supplies dwindled and imports from Tonga and Western Samoa became necessary (*Fiji Times* 25 January 1974). Again, in 1983, a significant quantity of *yaqona* had to be imported because plants in Taveuni, one of the leading supply regions, were attacked by disease and there was a considerable, though temporary, local shortage (*Fiji Times* 29 June 1983). These variations in local supply and the sometimes wild fluctuations in prices mean that producers have to keep a close eye on the market and adjust their harvest accordingly. If they can harvest and dry *yaqona* in time to reach the market during periods of shortage, rewards can be very high.

To an extent, *yaqona* faces some competition from alcohol, principally beer. Although, as a drink, *yaqona* is still cheaper than beer, the latter is often favoured and if kava prices rise there may be some substitution of alcohol. Normally, beer (that brewed locally by a subsidiary of Carlton Breweries, Australia) is beyond the reach of most people as a regular drink, though recent increasing sales of home-brew kits may lead to greater competition (*Sunday Times* 16 March 1986).

Lately, a large number of commercial growers has begun to emerge, these being both individuals and communal enterprises. Whilst the average area under *yaqona* per 'farm' is about a quarter of a hectare (Table 1), some plantations cover several hectares and the returns can be very large. For example, a substantial housing loan of $246,000, taken out by Nakarabo villagers in Vanua Levu, was to be repaid with revenue earned from the sale of *yaqona* (*Fiji Times* 15 June 1984). Large-scale production is seen to bring a constant cash income, as opposed to the smaller plantations which allow for only limited harvesting and long delays between harvests. Some of the newer large-scale producers are non-Fijians, though in 1978 Indo-Fijian plantations were still smaller on average (0.19 ha) than those of indigenous Fijians (0.27 ha) (Rothfield and Kumar 1980:31).

Thus, *yaqona* has emerged as one of the principal cash crops of Fiji. It earns little or no export income and areas under the crop are small compared to, say, root crops or sugar, but its importance in everyday consumption, its high income earning capabilities and its particular significance in peripheral regions means that it ranks perhaps only behind root crops and, possibly, rice as a 'domestic' crop in Fiji[3].

Yet, despite the undoubted importance of *yaqona* to the rural and national economy, its significance seems to be little understood by the government. Generally, the Fijian government pays little attention to the *yaqona* industry, being more concerned with export crops, such as sugar, copra and ginger, or import-substituting agriculture, such as rice, beef-raising or dairying. The

---

[3]   Rainfed rice is grown by almost on almost the same number of farms (between 9000 and 9500), occupies a larger area (8533 ha compared with 2422 ha for *yaqona*), but probably has a lower net return per unit area than *yaqona* (Rothfield and Kumar 1980:34).

Ministry of Primary Industries in this regard follows the priorities laid out in Fiji's development plans, which stress these latter sectors and have little to say about traditional domestic crops, including *dalo,* cassava, yams or *yaqona.*

Yaqona farmers have complained that they receive little help from government agencies and that they do not know how to prevent diseases and pest attacks[4]. Yet, when the government has become involved with *yaqona,* its role has been one of control rather than encouragement of production.

In April 1973, the government imposed a price freeze on kava after prices escalated when prolonged wet weather delayed harvesting and drying of the crop. The price freeze, backed by the National Marketing Authority (NMA) which was struggling to control marketing channels, was established, according to the government, in order to avoid possible gluts and low market prices at a later date (*Fiji Times* 19 May 1973). However, the decree proved counter-productive. The major suppliers of *yaqona* refused to sell at the controlled prices, insisting that they were too low. Additionally, a number of market vendors closed their stalls and it proved necessary to import kava from Western Samoa. Since then, the government, possibly having learned a lesson, has adopted a 'hands-off' policy with regard to *yaqona,* not controlling the market, but also little engaging in research and extension work.

MARKETING CHANNELS

Because both production and consumption of *yaqona* are so widespread throughout Fiji, there are a large number of marketing channels through which the crop reaches consumers, either in root or powdered form. The main channels are summarised in Figure 1 and each of the main marketing sectors can be examined in turn.

The Fiji Co-operative Association Ltd.

Until 1983, government involvement in *yaqona* marketing was in the hands of the NMA (Baxter 1980:119). It purchased the crop in outlying areas, centralised stocks in its depots, arranged for export and sold locally to middlemen and vendors. However, the general difficulties experienced by the Authority led it to pass the responsibility for *yaqona* marketing to the Fiji

---

4   Fortunately, *yaqona* is more resistant to such problems than other crops, ginger for example — another of its advantages.

Figure 1
Yaqona Marketing Channels

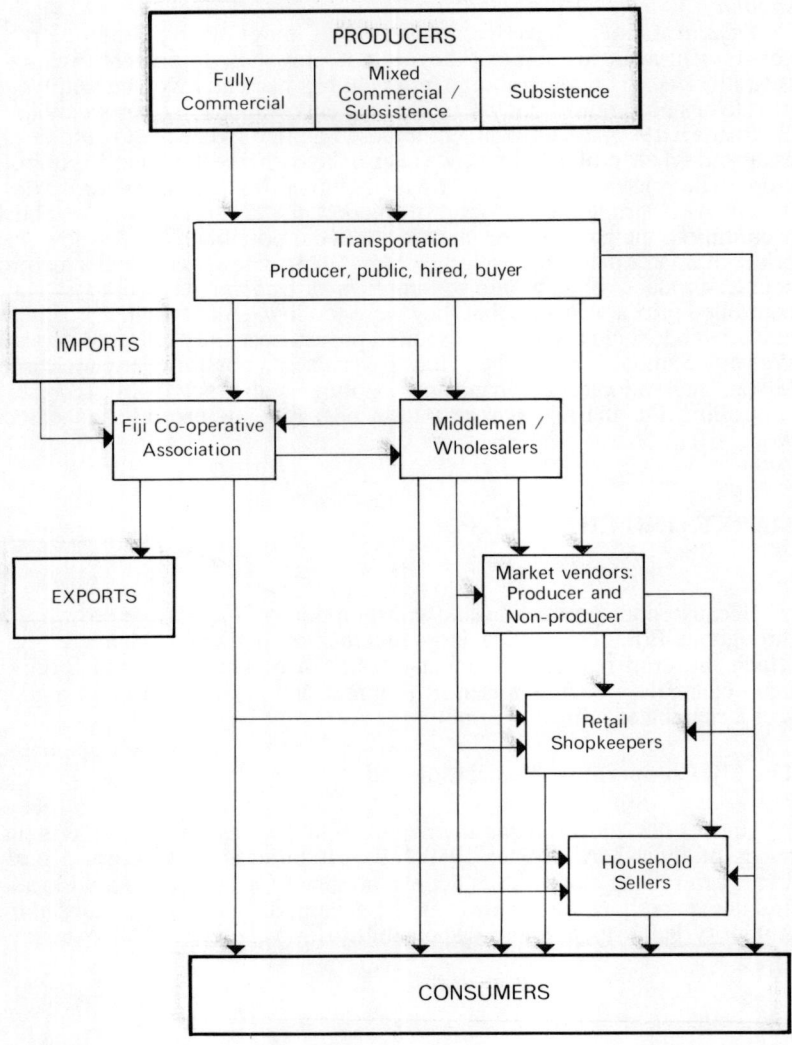

Source: Adapted from Baxter (1980:45).

Co-operative Association in 1983. This body, in receipt of government financial assistance until 1986[5], established its main functions as follows:

> The Fiji Co-operative Association Limited is the tertiary level national apex organisation of all consumer and some marketing co-operatives. Its aims are to import or purchase in bulk and supply the regional wholesale associations which in turn supply the rural based primary co-operatives. At the same time it provides the infrastructure for the flow of some of the products of the many individual small farmers through to a centralized marketing arrangement. This gives the apex the power to negotiate better terms of trade with the buyers of products ... (Fiji Ministry of Co-operatives 1983:18)

It set up buying agents in the major *yaqona* producing areas, such as Vanua Levu and Taveuni, who buy at market prices directly from the producers. They also handle copra and other products. Formerly, the Fiji Co-operative Association used to purchase *yaqona* in the smaller outer islands, such as Koro and Moala, but this was suspended due to fluctuating production levels, occasional poor quality, and subsequent lack of profitability. Purchases may also be made from middlemen or overseas.

The Association also acts as a processing agency. The raw, dried kava is powdered and packed into 100 gram packets which are sold to local retailers or exported. This is the only way in which kava is marketed in a fully processed and packed form. The product is also sold in root form to middlemen, retailers and consumers both in Viti Levu and Lau.

Producer-vendors

Producers who take their kava to urban markets and sell it directly to the public form a major marketing channel, but they are relatively less important, in terms of the number of traders and volume traded, than the non-producer vendors (below). A survey undertaken in the Suva Municipal Market in 1986 revealed that there were only four producer-vendors, or 10 per cent of the total number of those selling kava (Table 3). This figure also fluctuates a great deal from day-to-day, with 'heavy' market days, such as Friday or Saturday seeing relatively more producer-vendors and 'off' days with almost none. It is also interesting to note that, of the four producer vendors, all were 'specialist' *yaqona* sellers, not selling other crops with their kava. Clearly, *yaqona* was worth concentrating upon. In the smaller urban centres,

---

5   Assistance ceased in 1986 and it was then decided that, in future, the Association should operate like a private enterprise (personal communication).

producer-vendors are proportionately more numerous, though, overall, are not found in large numbers.

Table 3
Analysis of Suva *Yaqona* Market Vendors, 1986

	Number	Percentage
Total vendors	42	
Producer	4	10
Non-producer	38	90
Specialist	39	93
Non-specialist	3	7
Producer-specialist	4	10
Producer non-specialist	0	0
Non-producer specialist	35	83
Non-producer non-specialist	3	7

Source: Survey, January 1986. 'Specialist' refers to those vendors selling only *yaqona*.

The reason for the low percentage of producers, probably even less than for, say, root crops or vegetables, is that villagers prefer to take their *yaqona* to the local shop or cooperative store (for sale within the village or locality) or to middle-men who may visit rural areas. Smaller-scale producers tend to sell to the nearest buyer available, especially as most of the commercial *yaqona* is grown in peripheral areas (unlike many market vegetables and root crops) and visits to the Suva or other markets are very costly in terms of time and money, even though the prices received may be considerably higher. The large-scale producers are more likely to sell their own crop but most usually take the *yaqona* to the urban markets to sell to non-producer vendors often under established agreements.

Non-producer vendors

Non-producer vendors are probably the most important outlet for *yaqona*. It can be seen from Table 3 that in the main Suva market, 90 per cent of vendors were non-producers and most of these (83 per cent) dealt only in kava. Such non-producer vendors are also closely related, in a business sense, to middlemen and wholesalers, many individuals performing both functions, or being members of families or partnerships that straddle both. Nearly all are ethnic Indians.

These sellers obtain their supplies from the farm gate, from growers who bring their kava to town, or through agents who purchase *yaqona* in the outer areas and ship it to the markets. Also, middlemen from Viti Levu go far in search of *yaqona*, often to Lau, Lomaiviti and Taveuni. Such long distance trips have been facilitated by the roll-on/roll-off ferry services provided by two local shipping companies. These services are much cheaper and more efficient than that offered by inter-island cutters, for merchants can take their trucks on the ferries, drive to the main producer areas and load the produce directly. Thus, the *yaqona* is not touched again until off-loaded at the market and damage and loss is minimised. When inter-island vessels sail into Suva port, Suva vendors with their trucks and vans are usually to be seen waiting on the wharf ready to buy whatever *yaqona* may be coming in. But many of these may have prior arrangements with the producers.

In Ovalau, shopkeepers from Levuka sometimes go around the villages on the island buying *yaqona*, which is then taken to Suva and sold. As well, Levuka shopkeepers can obtain supplies from villagers visiting town. Two of the shopkeepers are major buyers in Levuka and are agents for some of the larger market vendors in Suva. There is also an agent on Koro island for a vendor in Nausori. Such middlemen have been found to be either immediate relatives or long-standing acquaintances of the Suva merchants. Moreover, it seems that some of the middlemen in Savusavu and Labasa are agents for vendors in Lautoka, Suva and other towns in Viti Levu, where the demand for *yaqona* is high.

Non-producer vendors and middlemen are also involved in limited processing. Whilst much of the *yaqona* is sold in raw form (both *lawena* and *waka*), there is much demand for the powdered form. Many of the sellers machine-pound the grog, thus increasing their mark-up. However, some vendors have been known to adulterate their powdered kava with flour, wood, sand or soil (Duve 1980, Duve and Prasad 1981)[6] and this has become well-known to buyers, thus reducing the demand for the powdered form. Prices charged by market vendors vary but are generally lower than in the suburban

---

6   Duve found that the rate of adulteration with wheat flour was only 0.76 per cent in 1980 and 'under control', but it had been as high as 20 per cent in 1973, a time of shortages and high prices (Duve and Prasad 1981:17). Those who know the product well can often tell if it has been adulterated — 'high grade' *yaqona* that has a whitish hue most likely has wheat flour mixed with it.

shops and stores (Table 4), though not always the cheapest available. In January 1986, *lawena* sold at the rate of $7 per kilogram (it is normally sold in multiples of 100 grams), *waka*, stronger and more prized, for $9. At the same time, the Fiji Co-operative's *yaqona* (*lawena*) was being sold for the equivalent of only $4 per kilogram (in 100 or the larger 500 gram packets), its powdered and packed form not always popular with consumers.

Table 4
Analysis of Nine Raiwaqa *Yaqona* Household Sellers

Ethnicity	Price Charged ($)	Quantity Sold (spoons)	Sources of Supply	Form of Processing
Fijian	1.00	$9^{1}/_{2}$-$10^{1}/_{2}$	Savusavu	hand-pounded
Fijian	1.00	$9^{1}/_{2}$-$10^{1}/_{2}$	Kadavu	hand-pounded
Fijian	1.00	$9^{1}/_{2}$-$10^{1}/_{2}$	Kadavu	hand-pounded
Fijian	0.50	5-$5^{1}/_{2}$	Suva market	machine-pounded
Fijian	0.50	5-$5^{1}/_{2}$	Levuka	hand-pounded
Indian	0.50	5-$5^{1}/_{2}$	Suva market	hand-pounded
Fijian	1.00	$9^{1}/_{2}$-$10^{1}/_{2}$	Koro	hand-pounded
Fijian	1.00	$9^{1}/_{2}$-$10^{1}/_{2}$	Vanua Levu	hand-pounded
Fijian	0.50	5-6	Koro	hand-pounded

Source: Survey, February 1986

Retailers and household sellers

Shopkeepers, particularly those serving small towns and rural areas are important outlets for kava. Many village cooperative stores stock it, being the main local source of supply if villagers have none of their own available (as is often the case). Even in the larger towns, it is a commonly sold item. A survey in January 1986 in Levuka, revealed that half of all shops sold kava.

In suburban areas, away from market centres, household kava sellers have appeared and are now commonplace in many suburbs. Their sources of supply vary, from direct contacts with producers to the purchase of roots and stems at the municipal markets. These sellers normally hand-pound *yaqona*, and advertisements outsides their homes clearly state that their kava is hand-pounded. This is an important selling point, for the rumours about adulterated machine-pounded kava at the markets have led many consumers to trust only a product they can see being processed in an acceptable manner. Another advantage that household sellers can exploit is that they are close to consumers and are often open in the evenings, thus attracting frequent custom from their neighbours.

Whereas most shopkeepers and market vendors are Indians, the household sellers are of both major ethnic groups. The sellers in Table 4 were from Raiwaqa in Suva and all, but one, indigenous Fijians. Yet in other suburbs, such as Vatuwaqa, most would have been Indian.

These sellers sold *yaqona* in packages of a set size, usually $0.50 or $1. Unlike the market vendors, who varied the price according to weight, the household sellers tend to vary the amount sold for a set price. Rarely did they package the grog in packets of more than $1, their main trade being in smaller amounts to satisfy a single informal 'session'. All the Raiwaqa sellers, except one, hand-pounded their kava at the point of sale. The diversity of their sources of supply, directly from the Eastern and Northern Divisions, usually reflected arrangements with relatives in the producing villages. Two relied on secondary supply from the market. One of the suburban sellers interviewed was an interesting example of the links between rural supply and urban marketing. He was an agricultural officer but obtained *yaqona* from his own farm in the islands[7], sold it in Suva, and also exported some to Fijians living in Australia.

So the household sellers, if not the shopkeepers, are a diverse group with linkages to all parts of the kava marketing structure. Such activities represent good opportunities for supplementary income earning in the towns and, at times, they also bring rural producers and their families in close touch with urban marketing.

CONCLUSIONS

Yaqona is a good example of a well-established indigenous crop, the demand for which has increased steadily, and which brought good returns to producers, promoting growth in rural economies, despite government inattention. *Yaqona* is especially important for the economies of many peripheral regions and it has probably replaced copra as the major cash crop in the Eastern and Northern Divisions. Its stability in the market, the flexibility of its cultivation and harvesting, its hardiness in the face of cyclones and disease, and, above all, its good returns, mean that it must be

---

7   This is another peculiarity of *yaqona*, being suitable for absentee farmers because it is long maturing and does not require constant maintenance. Thus, a large plantation can be established (a major task), left under the care of relatives and then harvested as required (though this is also labour-intensive when large lots are pulled).

regarded as perhaps the most suitable of cash crops for Fijian rural dwellers. Given its high and stable domestic demand and continuing urbanisation, *yaqona* will remain an important cash crop and its importance in many rural areas is likely to increase, considering the rise in price of other 'social' beverages and both rural and urban unemployment. Only its popularity, and the possibility over future over-supply, can affect its prospects.

The marketing of *yaqona* reveals a complex structure whereby production and consumption are usually separated (most of the crop reaches consumers through the hands of the Fiji Co-operative Association, middlemen or non-producer vendors), yet family and business relations remain very important and often mean that production and sale are often closer than may first appear. This means, in turn, that returns to producers are often higher than may have been achieved through government or entrepreneurial marketing channels. Also, the apparent increase in the relative importance of household sellers mean that even the rewards to retailing are being spread quite widely. There remains some concern among producers and officials about profiteering by market vendors. No doubt some do well, and some of them are guilty of food adulteration. However, given the highly competitive nature of the trade, the diversity of marketing, and the discerning behaviour of consumers, such problems seem to be held in check.

So far, government has done little to encourage or even assist *yaqona* production. Perhaps it could, in future, perform a more useful role by monitoring adulteration, by conducting more research into pests and diseases, or by disseminating more information to the producing areas about urban and export prices. However, the evidence to date shows that this is one industry that thrives and even regulates itself, without government involvement.

6

SMALL-SCALE COMMERCIAL FISHING

Setareki Delana

with Thelma Raman, Christine Segran, Reynolds Sale,
Savelio Tevaga and Sam Obadiah[1]

DEVELOPING SMALL-SCALE COMMERCIAL FISHING

Fiji has plentiful marine resources. Its territorial waters cover some 1,134,700 square kilometres (Narokobi 1984:372), and, although it lacks a continental shelf, in its shallow fishing grounds Fiji has a great variety of productive marine ecosystems including estuaries, lagoons, reefs, mangrove swamps and rivers. As a source of protein, fish are vitally important for numerous rural communities and urban dwellers. Yet many of the inshore areas, especially those near large urban areas, such as Suva, are being depleted and there is a need to seek fishing grounds in new and deeper waters.

The potential of small-scale fishing

The advantages of developing the small-scale sector are apparent both to government and the fishermen themselves. They can be summarised as follows:

Employment generation. This is encouraged in both urban and rural areas. Because it is flexible in terms of the timing and amount of labour input, rural people can combine agriculture and fishing successfully

---

1 This chapter is based upon a group project carried out by all the authors in 1985 as part of course work for a third year geography paper at the University of the South Pacific on applied rural geography. All contributed to that project, but Delana has been responsible for the rewriting of that paper for inclusion here.

for both domestic and commercial requirements, and fishing can help absorb some surplus rural labour.

Rural development. By encouraging rural employment, the establishment of a fisheries industry is a means of promoting rural development, thus decreasing rural-urban inequalities and arresting rural to urban migration.

Availability of resources. It uses local, usually easily available resources. In more remote areas of Fiji, especially the small islands, land resources are few and the sea is the most important basis for economic activity. At the national level, too, the exploitation of local marine resources can help to lessen the dependence on imported protein and thus save on foreign exchange.

Appropriate technology. Fishing, particularly for subsistence and limited commercial ends, can use and help preserve traditional, low-level technology — an example being *yavi rau*, a traditional fish drive, still used in Beqa. Although more sophisticated equipment, nylon nets, fossil fuels, and larger vessels are being introduced, there is much potential in building on existing skills, including sailing, fish trapping, and knowledge of fishing grounds. These methods, too, can help conserve marine resources (Johannes 1982).

Nutrition. Fish are an important source of protein, particularly in the diets of those living in areas where livestock cannot be reared or where retailing is limited.

National and regional economic growth. Through employment generation and the increase in demand for boats, equipment, fuel and maintenance, a developing small-scale fishing industry can promote both regional and national economic development by stimulating forward and backward linkages with other sectors of the economy.

State development efforts

Recent development plans have stressed the importance of 'rural fisheries' and 'commercial artisanal fisheries' alongside 'industrial fisheries'. Strong government interest developed during the time of the seventh development plan (1976-1980). It is noted that, whilst industrial landings fluctuated around 7000 tonnes per annum between 1979 and 1984 (with a peak of 9800 tonnes in 1981), small-scale production rose steadily during that period from 3000 tonnes to over 5800 tonnes (Fiji Central Planning Office 1985: 69-70). In 1980, fish comprised Fiji's third most important export commodity, after sugar and gold (Fiji Central Planning Office 1980:146). Furthermore, although imports of fish and fish products have been large, exports of canned fish have often been higher in value.

One of the strategies adopted by the government of Fiji to promote rural development and narrow rural-urban disparities has been the promotion of small-scale commercial fishing. This is designed to build upon traditional techniques and utilise existing labour and rights to fishing grounds. The emphasis on smaller-scale fishing, with an eye to the domestic market, has been in conjunction with efforts to expand larger-scale and more capital-intensive fishing aimed at the export market.

The overall objectives of government fisheries policy are to: increase production to satisfy local demand for fish and fish products, both fresh water and marine; increase fish catch and production of fish for export; and increase local value added in the fisheries sector (Fiji Central Planning Office 1980:147).

It is in the first of these that small-scale fishing, both subsistence and commercial, has a major role. Briefly, the nature of state assistance for this sector has revolved around finance, training, marketing, and aquaculture.

Finance and equipment. The Fiji Development Bank (FDB) has come to play an important role in stimulating small-scale fishing through the provision of loans for boats and equipment. FDB loans are provided on the basis of recommendations from officers of the Fisheries Division of the Ministry of Primary Industries (MPI). Some commercial banks are also prepared to lend to fishermen, but with interest rates above 10 per cent in 1985 (compared to the FDB's 5.5 per cent) these did not prove popular. A few individuals seem to have been able to find the purchase price for boats from their own resources and savings.

The main form of capital expenditure is boats. These are built by the government[2] and sold at cost to the selected fishermen. The boats are 8.5 metre multipurpose vessels[3], equipped with a large ice-box, both inshore and offshore gear, an engine and nets. Those undertaking the eleven week training course (below) also get a 5.5 metre punt with an outboard engine. As one appreciative trainee put it in 1985:

> All the above cost only about $6700 and with the current 5.5 per cent interest rate charged by the Fiji Development Bank, I am certainly getting more than what I have to pay for. (Ratu Tevita Veidovi, pers. comm.)

---

2   The boat building programme was forecast to cost some $366,000 during the DP8 period (Fiji Central Planning Office 1980:150).

3   By DP9, these 8.5 metre boats had come to be regarded as expensive to build and a shift was being made to a smaller and deeper vessel (Fiji Central Planning Office 1985:70). The larger boats and their diesel engines also have high maintenance costs, repairs must be carried out by the government and bureaucratic delays are long.

It is not surprising that such provision of boats and equipment proved popular. In 1984, the FDB processed some 281 applications, though during the DP8 period, only 56 of the larger boats were built and sold (Fiji Central Planning Office 1985:70).

Training. Much stress is also placed on training in new fishing techniques. The Fisheries Division of MPI, through a variety of courses (one year, 11 weeks, or *in situ* visits), aims to educate fishermen in boat construction and repair, engine maintenance, use of new fishing gear and techniques, navigation, fish handling, and business management.

To qualify for the 11 week or one year courses, applicants must represent a group venture and must be recommended by extension officers. In the DP8 period, some 340 artisanal fisherman attended such courses, in addition to 500 in the 'rural fisheries' training programme in rural areas (Fiji Central Planning Office 1985:70).

Marketing. The crucial element in any commercial venture is the availability of markets. On the local markets, fish prices have increased dramatically over the past decade with rising urban demand. That trend is likely to continue. However, such opportunities often lie outside the reach of many fishermen in Fiji. Without proper storage and transport facilities, those in more remote areas usually cannot get their catches to market in acceptable condition.

Much of the marketing of commercial fishing on the local market is carried out independently of government. The National Marketing Authority (NMA), however, represents a major effort to assist small-scale fishermen, particularly those in remote areas. Although it buys only selected species and its prices (in Suva at least) are the lowest on offer, the Authority does buy all that is offered (within its species and quality guidelines). For a time, the NMA operated refrigerated ships to remote areas to buy catches there but this proved uneconomical and was scaled down (Baxter 1980:114-127). However, the NMA still operates its Lami depot, buying and selling large quantities of fish, and the government is involved in the outer areas by providing ice-making plants and other marketing assistance (Fiji Central Planning Office 1985:70).

Aquaculture. Whilst most of the above measures target inshore fishing, and, thereby, coastal or small island villagers, programmes to develop fish farming are aimed at people living inland. The Naduruloulou Research Station, established in 1978, has been successful in testing species such as talapia, grass carp, and prawns. Much of this initiative is funded by foreign aid.

Thus, it can be seen that the recent government interest in, and support for, small-scale fishing has been comprehensive. Some of the programme is aimed at subsistence production, but perhaps the most important element of the whole fisheries strategy is the small-scale commercial sector — the so-called artisanal fishermen — for if this sector can develop rapidly, then a whole range of national development objectives can be met including rural employment generation, import substitution, improved nutrition, and regional development. With government efforts having taken place since the DP7 period, it is now possible to assess some of results of the programme.

A SURVEY OF SUVA FISHERMEN

In August 1985, twenty-five fishermen were interviewed in depth about their involvement in fishing ventures. They were interviewed at marketing points in southeast Viti Levu (mostly Suva but also Nausori, Navua and Galoa) and the sample is, therefore biased in favour of those living close to large urban centres. However, some of those interviewed originally came from places such as Beqa, Kadavu, Taveuni, Vanua Levu and even Rotuma, indicating that there is a high degree of mobility in the industry. The sample included both indigenous Fijians and nine Indo-Fijians[4]. Thus, though the sample size is small, it is believed that their responses do give a reasonable indication of the experiences of artisanal fishermen. In addition to the formal survey, a small number of trainees, officials and fishermen were interviewed informally.

It must be noted that those interviewed were fisher*men*. Women are heavily involved in fishing, particularly in meeting subsistence requirements and in undertaking the fishing of mangrove, close inshore, and estuary areas. However, it seems as if the fishing from boats is almost exclusively a male preserve and government development efforts, as in so many other sectors, is directed towards the menfolk.

Questions were asked on many different aspects of the ventures: the background of those involved, labour and capital resources and organisation, fishing grounds, marketing and problems. These were analysed and are discussed below.

Profiles of fishermen

Most of those interviewed were engaged in both inshore and offshore fishing and they employed a variety of techniques including netting, spearing, and rod and line fishing. Relatively little, though, was done in the way of the collection of shellfish or marine vegetation. The fishermen were experienced. Some 40 per cent had been involved in fishing for over ten years, and a further 32 per cent for between five and ten years.

---

4   This ethnic division probably under-represents Indo-Fijians, who proved more reluctant to answer questions.

Most, over two-thirds, turned to fishing from agriculture, being attracted by rising prices for fresh fish and relatively low prices for agricultural produce. Yet few depend solely on fishing for their income and none considered themselves 'full time' fishermen. Because of difficulties with weather (making many days unsuitable or unsafe for fishing) and the need to supplement incomes and diets, most grow some crops and 60 per cent are still rural-based enterprises[5]. Sixty-eight per cent have other sources of income, mostly from agriculture but a few from casual urban employment. The rest are otherwise unemployed.

Organisation of the ventures

Rarely are the fishing ventures in the hands of an individual, though one person may take a leading role. About a third of the sample had the ownership of the venture vested in an individual and nearly all of the rest were under family or clan ownership. This pattern was reflected in the employment of labour (Table 1).

Table 1
Employment of Labour

Labour	Frequency	Percentage
Family/clan members	3	12
Non family/clan members	13	52
Both family and outsiders	9	36
Total	25	100

Source: Interviews, August 1985.

---

5   This figure must be considered an understatement of the balance between rural and urban based fishermen, because the interviews were conducted at urban points of sale. Those who lived in villages, for example, and mostly sold their catches at roadside stalls or within a village, would be under-represented.

Methods of payment varied. In the majority of cases, the group ownership of the venture meant that profits were shared. All the participants, employees and owners also seemed to get some return in the form of part of the catch for their own use.

Where labour was employed, however, as it was in about a quarter of the cases, the payment of cash wages posed a problem. Labour was often on a casual basis, because of the irregularity of trips, but the amount of cash wages was usually determined beforehand. Thus, if the catch was poor, the operators still had to pay and could incur losses. It is not a system that encourages wage employment: labourers dislike the lack of consistent work and employers dislike the payment of wages unrelated to catches. It is hardly surprising that group or family ventures are preferred.

In terms of fishing grounds, all those interviewed were confined to shallower waters as their boats and equipment were not suitable for deep waters. Some were able to exploit traditional rights to fishing grounds, most kept to 'open' waters often in the same locality as up to about ten other boats. The absence of deep water fishing did not prevent occasional quite long trips to fishing grounds far away. In most cases, the fishing trips were daily operations, with an early morning start. But some could be absent for four to six days, if the weather, catches and storage facilities were favourable.

One Kadavu fisherman interviewed informally was an interesting example of the flexible organisation of a fishing operation. This person divides his work, roughly week-about, between agriculture and fishing (the agriculture on village land and the fishing off Kadavu). Once a fortnight he makes the day-long journey to Suva to market both fish and agricultural produce. In this, he has proved very successful, now operating also a well-stocked shop in the village and employing villagers on his 'farm'.

Boats and equipment are the most important aspect of the fishing ventures. All the interviewees owned their own boat, engines, nets and lines. It was apparent that a few others, not interviewed, relied on borrowing engines and/or boats and borrowing was used also when regular equipment was out of operation. Because all the fishermen undertook a variety of net, line and spear fishing, to exploit different grounds, most possessed a fairly wide range of equipment. Not surprisingly, given the cost, not all owned the government-built 8.5 metre vessels, and a number had acquired boats that were smaller, cheaper and, they believed, more suitable.

This perception that the government boats were inappropriate was reflected in the fact that only eight of the sample (about a third) were still paying off their FDB loans. This was not because the others had already cleared their debts, but because they had previously acquired their boats, often some years ago, from private or group savings.

Thus, even within this small sample, diversity in the structure of small-scale commercial fishing around Suva is apparent. Typically, it involves ownership by small groups, they living in rural areas not far from Suva, and moderately well-equipped in terms of boats and gear often purchased with government assistance. And yet outside this norm, it includes others who live in the towns, employ wage labour, or use privately-acquired capital. It is a multifarious sector.

Marketing[6]

A variety of marketing channels has developed over the years, each with particular demand and supply conditions and risks for the commercial operators:

Municipal markets. These places attract high volumes of buyers because of their location in urban areas and the variety of produce for sale. They are located in Suva and smaller centres such as Nausori, Navua, and Sigatoka. However, a major drawback is the market fee charged. In Suva, this amounts to a hefty 32 cents per kilogram which is a major disincentive to the smaller-scale operator. The 11 cents charged at Navua is an improvement but is matched by the smaller volume of buyers.

Shops and supermarkets. Contracts and agreements are often reached between fishermen and these retail outlets. Volumes and prices are predetermined and, for those fortunate enough to be involved and to be able to offer consistent quality and quantity, returns can be high.

Roadside stalls. This method is seen as the most economical as transportation costs and market fees are low or negligible and less time is spent in marketing. One problem with this method is that storage facilities in stalls or boats are often non-existent and the quality can be very poor after fish have been exposed to long periods in the open.

Nabukalou Creek. One of the most popular markets has developed in the heart of Suva at Nabukalou Creek. Here, fishermen bring their catches and tie their boats up to an area that attracts many passing consumers. Trade is brisk and on heavy market days, such as Saturday, the scene is hectic. Market fees do not have to be paid, so returns to the fishermen are higher and competition ensures good prices for the buyers.

---

6   This survey was conducted in 1985. Since then, there have been some major changes. The NMA ceased operation in 1987, following the military coups of that year. In its place, the Army Auxiliary Unit has assumed a major role in marketing. This Unit travels to the outer islands, assists in taking Fijian villagers to fishing grounds, purchases the catches and transports these to Suva. They are sold in army market stalls at Walu Bay, at Vatuwaqa (at the NMA depot) and at the Nasese army camp. Prices are lower but markets are guaranteed for island fishermen. Fijian fishermen, especially those in more remote areas, have benefited most from this much more active state involvement (as rural and regional development are promoted), whilst others seem to have been losers — some of the Indians have lost fishing grounds and cannot sell to the Army Auxiliary Unit.

National Marketing Authority. The NMA depot at Lami, despite the relatively low prices offered and the tight restrictions on species accepted, still attracts many fishermen. The instant sale of any quantity means that time is not wasted selling the catch and a speedy return home can be made.

At the national level, the relative importance of some of these different market outlets have been analysed (Table 2). In all, 76 per cent of the sample sold the bulk of their catches in urban areas, mostly at places such as Nabukalou Creek. The higher prices and constant demand of urban consumers was the main attraction, despite the marketing hassles (competition can be fierce and much time and money can be spent both getting to Suva and selling the fish).

Table 2
Domestic Consumption of Fish and Fish Products, 1976-1980
(tonnes)

Source	1976	1977	1978	1979	1980
Municipal fish sales	872	850	845	840	843
Municipal non-fish sales	na	1,745	1,011	885	956
NMA sales	na	167	99	196	133
Other outlets	na	605	444	623	538
Domestic market production	2,500	3,367	2,399	2,544	3,470
Subsistence production	13,000	13,300	13,500	13,800	14,000

na Data not available

Source: Fiji Ministry of Agriculture and Fisheries (1982).

But rural sales are still important. Selling is easier, even if prices are lower. They include sales within villages, on roadside stalls, and in small 'towns' such as Galoa. Of course, an important element of rural 'marketing' is home consumption. Nearly all retained part of the catch for domestic consumption, this practice being greater in Fijian communities where *kerekere* redistribution through extended families was common. Rural sales also involve sales to middlemen. One village-based fishing group from Vatulele, for example, regularly brings fish from the island to Korolevu on Viti Levu where it is collected and paid for by an Indian, Sigatoka market vendor. The arrangement is regular, convenient and, it seems, profitable, for it saves a long boat trip to the Suva markets.

However, it must not be assumed that all those selling fish in urban areas (even outside the shops and municipal markets) are fishermen. In the course of research, it was noted that some of the 'fishermen' with boats at Nabukalou Creek fished only rarely. In one instance, a vendor purchased frozen fish from the NMA depot at Lami — frozen fish being considerably cheaper to buy than fresh — motored the short distance to Nabukalou Creek with the fish exposed to the sun, and then sold the thawed fish as 'fresh', receiving a good profit in the process! Although most buyers are sufficiently discerning to be able to avoid such tricks, others are not and the quality of fish sold in such circumstances can be suspect.

Government involvement

Despite the emphasis placed by the Government of Fiji on developing small-scale fishing, surprisingly few of the sampled fishermen were directly involved in government programmes. The proportion of those paying off FDB loans, around one-third, was noted above and this relatively low figure is paralleled in participation rates in training and equipment purchase.

Most of the operators (84 per cent) had not undergone formal training, at least in the medium or long courses offered by the Fisheries Division. A few stated that the courses were merely a means of advertising the sale of the expensive government-built boats and subsequent high-cost ventures. Others were sceptical about the quality of government training and advice, believing that field officers knew little about the realities of fishing. Instead, these men placed greater store on traditional knowledge and techniques[7]. Another grievance was that fisheries officers were too confined to urban areas and paid few visits to the villages and more remote locations.

Another reason for the low rates of participation in the government schemes was that the poor could not afford the costs of entering the programmes. Training courses meant time away from income-earning activities and costs, such as the $500 security for FDB loans, were beyond the reach of many. As a result, a common complaint was that the government programmes favoured the more well-off and not the poor, whom it should aim to help.

---

[7]   However, not all were so deprecating about the training programmes. Some, such as the trainee quoted above, were enthusiastic and appreciative.

Problems

By far the most frequent complaint expressed by the interviewees was the lack of profitability of their enterprises. Only 32 per cent believed that their venture had proved financially rewarding[8]. This lack of profitability was a reason for the continued emphasis placed on supplementary income sources such as agriculture. The main component of high costs and therefore, lower profit, was fuel. The high cost of petrol and diesel was incurred not only in fishing trips but also in the, at times lengthy, excursions to Suva to sell fish. If catches were poor or market returns low, these outgoings would be frequently not covered. The fuel cost problem has two aspects. Firstly, it hits those in remote areas more. In Kadavu in 1985, for example, a gallon of outboard motor fuel cost $2.50, compared to $1.60 in Suva — and Kadavu fishermen had to travel much longer distances to sell their fish, even if catches were better than in the depleted waters close to the towns. Secondly, the size of a boat and its engine were critical. The larger government-built boats are higher powered, with 25 or 40 horsepower engines, and consume much diesel. Many, as a result, preferred smaller boats with outboard petrol engines as low powered as 15 horsepower. This was a further reason to avoid the government programme.

In the face of such running costs, operators have tried to cut down on other costs — avoiding taking out loans and using family rather than wage labour. As a result, the small-scale fishing sector faces major constraints to expansion. Although 64 per cent of those interviewed (the response was higher amongst Indo-Fijians) stated that they wished to expand their operations (mainly through the purchase of new nets, boats, and engines and the employment of more people), most believed that they would be unable to do this due to a lack of savings, unavailability of suitable credit, and concern over the uncertainty of prices and catches.

However, it is probable that not all have been struggling in their fishing businesses. When asked about the benefits they had noticed since taking up fishing, many stated that they were now able to meet such costs as education and, in many cases, their standards of living was higher.

Marketing was the second major problem mentioned. As well as the difficulties and cost of transport to the urban markets and uncertain prices, most expressed dissatisfaction with storage facilities. Refrigeration or ice-making plants are rarely available in the remote districts and the potential resources of these more plentiful fishing grounds are not exploited well. Despite the continued importance of domestic fish consumption and some rural marketing, it is urban demand for fresh fish that is the dominant force

---

[8] Detailed data on incomes and expenses were not able to be collected because many were not willing to discuss financial matters. Instead, general comments were noted, though these must be considered suspect in part, because respondents were more willing to complain about low incomes and lack of government assistance than they were to express satisfaction.

for expansion of the industry. Only those fishermen who can profitably reach these markets with good quality catches can benefit.

Improved storage facilities would help but these are usually well beyond the financial resources of the fishermen themselves and government is unable to provide adequate plant in the many scattered rural areas that are in need. As a result, fishermen continue to rely on ice boxes and the purchase of ice[9]. The marketing problem is likely to remain.

A final major problem, but one not expressed strongly by the sample, was depletion of marine resources. With the limited range of the smaller boats, poor storage and heavy urban demand, it is clear that fishing grounds close to the concentrations of urban population are being severely strained. To an extent, the maintenance of traditional fishing rights does limit the exploitation of some areas, but many are facing serious depletion. In addition, destructive and often illegal forms of fishing, such as the use of poisons[10] or explosives, are further dangers.

So, in all, the difficulties being faced by small-scale fishermen are mainly economic. Despite the promise, fishing has not proved a panacea for rural development.

CONCLUSIONS

Fiji's latest development plan summarised the causes of below-expected performance in the rural fisheries development programme as: lack of desire to change from traditional techniques; lack of commitment to commercial operation and business acumen; inadequate maintenance of vessels and equipment; and an absence of adequate fish collection and marketing arrangements (Fiji Central Planning Office 1985:70). All these, except the last, point to the fishermen themselves as the main problem, to their attitudes and lack of skills.

However, this study has shown that there may be good reasons for these failures and that much of the cause for poor performance may lie with the inappropriate design of government programmes, specifically the relatively large and high-cost boats and equipment used. One aspect of the programme, though, that does seem to be creditable is the recognition of group or communal organisation of ventures. Given the high cost of establishing a fishing enterprise and the problem of wage labour, group ownership and participation is likely to continue to be the most important way around capital and labour constraints.

---

9   Rural electrification is rare in fishing areas outside the towns and refrigeration is not common. Ice boxes are not suitable for the preservation of fish for periods longer than a few days.

10 The herbicide, paraquat, has become a notorious instrument for prawn and other types of fishing. The danger to public health is major.

But the problems being faced by the sector are such that government objectives for the industry may not be met. In order to lessen social and regional income disparities, targetted beneficiaries of any fisheries development strategy should include the poor and those in more remote areas. The high entry costs into the government programmes and the subsequent commitment to a high running cost enterprise (with loan repayments and increased fuel bills) have, it seems, meant that poorer individuals and families have not been able to participate and only those with high levels of savings and, often, an established fishing enterprise, derive benefit.

Similarly, in the face of inadequate storage and marketing infrastructures as well as fuel price differentials and higher usage, those in regions far from urban markets are also largely excluded unless they shift their operations closer to the economic core. Pressure on marine resources within a day's sailing from urban markets is thus increased and the abundant resources of the remote rural areas remain under-exploited. Regional and rural-urban disparities are not being dealt with adequately.

Finally, it is clear that, whilst there have been significant benefits to the national economy from fisheries development (mainly in terms of import substitution), any growth in the small-scale fishing sector is not spreading to other economic sectors as hoped. With tight profitability margins, wage employment on the small boats is restricted, the demand for new boats and equipment is diminished, and, with direct marketing by fishermen, fish retailing has not been stimulated, as expected.

Clearly, Fiji must continue to encourage the small-scale fishing sector — it has little choice. National, regional and individual benefits have accrued but there is potential for much more if official policies regarding equipment, credit, storage, marketing and conservation can be brought more closely into line with the real resources and needs of the people involved.

Fresh fish for sale at Nabukalou Creek, Suva

Cyclone damage
(*Photo: Ministry of Information, Suva*)

7

TROPICAL CYCLONES AND DISASTER RELIEF

Joseph Chung

CYCLONES IN FIJI

Of the natural hazards common to Fiji, cyclones are the most frequent, destructive and disruptive. They are initiated within tropical depressions which usually form between 5° and 30° north and south of the Equator. Fiji's location between 12°28' south and 21°20' south thus places it within hurricane zone. Since 1840, over 160 tropical cyclones have been recorded in Fiji. This is an average of slightly more than one per year affecting some part of the Fiji group. During the 147 years that records have been kept, in only 62 of them were no cyclones experienced. In other years several hurricanes have struck Fiji, as in 1985 when cyclones 'Eric' and 'Nigel' followed each other within two days across densely populated parts of the Western Division.

The hurricane season in Fiji is between October and May, with most hurricanes occurring between December and April. Unfortunately for Fiji's farmers and economy, this season coincides with the period when the rates of growth of most tropical crops are at their maximum and is traditionally the growing season for most root crops. When a tropical cyclone causes severe damage to food and commercial crops, considerable hardship is experienced. The provision of food relief to cyclone victims is often considered necessary to prevent serious distress and demonstrate national sympathy for their plight. Unfortunately, the distribution of food relief is highly susceptible to abuse and poor administration. Further, in Fiji, as elsewhere, it has become a highly emotive and political issue. Beyond the obvious problems this creates, it deflects attention from the more serious issue: how can the scarce resources for post-disaster relief and rehabilitation be best used to benefit rural people and reduce their vulnerability to climatic extremes?

This chapter first examines the distribution of food relief following cyclones Eric and Nigel in 1985. It then considers how some of the problems within the relief system have developed, and ways in which this system might be improved.

CYCLONES ERIC AND NIGEL

Cyclone Eric entered the Fiji Group from the west, travelling at 45-55 km/h. The full force of the cyclone hit the Yasawa Group and the Western Division between Nadi and Ba at the predicted time of 1700 hours on 17 January, 1985. Winds of over 140 km/h, gusting up to 220 km/h, streaked through the cities of Lautoka and Nadi and surrounding rural areas, before exiting through eastern Viti Levu, Lomaiviti and Southern Lau in the early hours of the morning of January 18.

Figure 1
Paths of Tropical Cyclones in Fiji, 1985

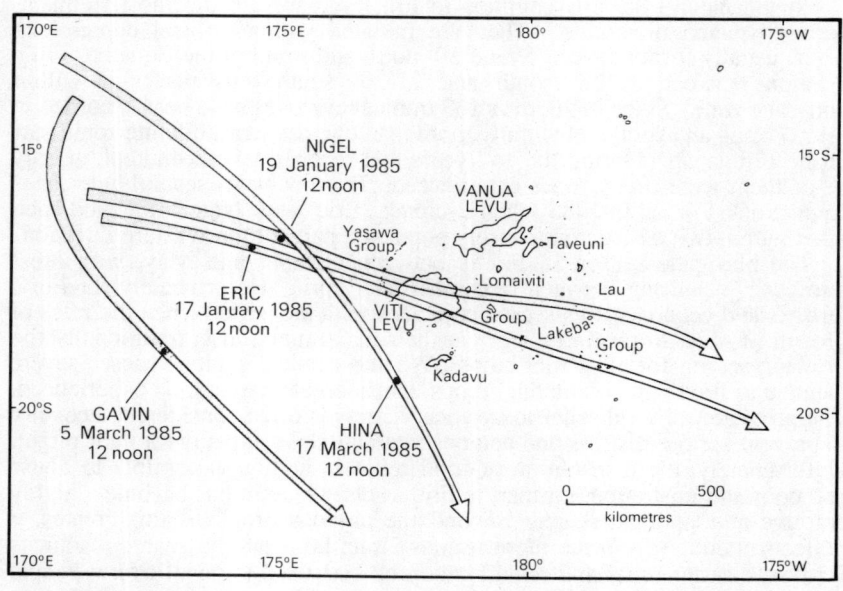

Cyclone Nigel approached Fiji on a similar trajectory. On January 19, it struck Fiji slightly north of the path that had been followed by Eric (Figure 1). The centre of the cyclone passed over the town of Ba at 1800 hours and moved rapidly towards the Lau islands. At about 0400 hours on the 20th of January at Lakeba, close to the centre of the cyclone, winds of about 120 km/h, with gusts to 170 km/h, were recorded.

Both cyclones brought widespread damage to the densely populated districts of the Western Division of Viti Levu. The worst hit areas were between Nadi and Ba in the west, the Keyasi area in Nadroga and the islands of Viwa, Waya and Naviti in the Yasawas. The damage to houses was staggering in its visual effect, its extensiveness and cost to people. Thatched *bures*, squatter shacks, low-cost houses and costly substantial dwellings all suffered. Of the twenty-seven people killed during the cyclones, fifteen deaths were from falling walls and roofs and flying debris. As well, there was extensive damage to schools, electrical installations, the telephone system, Nadi airport facilities and equipment, hospitals and health centres, and Fiji Sugar Corporation plant and equipment. Fortunately, there was a surprisingly low level of damage to the large pine plantations in the district, and the major part of the annual sugar crop had already been harvested and crushed[1].

Other agricultural losses were reported to be severe. According to Ministry of Primary Industries reports, the damage to livestock industries in the Western and Central Divisions was extreme (Table 1). The commercial poultry and piggery industries apparently suffered most, and poultry production came to a temporary halt. At the time, the future looked bleak for the many smallholder farmers who were already burdened with heavy debts.

Post-disaster appraisal of crop damage is an extensive task and needs to be undertaken systematically. Immediately following the cyclones, the Ministry of Primary Industries gave priority to the assessment of food crop damage. The Ministry's initial survey showed that coastal areas, river banks and flood plains had suffered greatly, and even interior areas of Viti Levu had experienced crop losses (Table 2). Although department heads recognised that this information required verification, past experience (because of the demand by government decision makers for quick figures) had been that the original survey figures were the ones most often used, despite likely inaccuracies.

Discussions with agricultural field officers following cyclones Eric and Nigel revealed that because of the haste with which they were to estimate crop damage, it was not possible to visit every farm and village. Since most figures, therefore, were obtained from interviews, and not actual site investigations, the tendency was towards exaggeration; both on the part of the

---

1   A large proportion of the approximately 100,000 tonnes of cane still unharvested, was badly damaged. Because of the general disruption of services, the Government decided the sugar mills would not reopen that season, and standing cane would not be harvested. Farmers with unharvested cane were paid the full season's price for their crop.

Table 1
Summary of Stock Losses Caused By Cyclones
Eric and Nigel, Western and Central Divisions, 1985

	No. of farms affected	Stock losses no.	value ($)	Other losses[a] ($)	Total losses ($)
Beef cattle	108	100	15,550	54,446	69,996
Dairy cattle	65	217	23,205	92,574	115,779
Pigs	13	340	10,910	132,951	143,861
Poultry	20	na	93,102	1,321,044	1,414,146
Goats	93	1,309	42,340	185,785	228,125
Total	**299**		185,107	1,786,800	1,971,907

[a] 'Other losses' refer to buildings, fences, dwellings, stock feed etc.
na Data not available

Source: Compiled from Ministry of Primary Industries files (unpublished).

farmer or villager in the hope of receiving some sympathy and free rations, and on the part of government workers impressed with the 'urgency' of their task and encouraged to err on the side of generosity. In any case, the common practice in Fiji during the past decade has been to begin the distribution of food rations even though the initial agricultural surveys were still in progress.

Relief rations were issued soon after cyclone Nigel struck, that is, on the 20th January. At first, food was cooked and eaten at evacuation centres. Those wanting free food had to go to the nearest centre and be fed there. After a few days, rations were apportioned and distributed at these centres. Neither arrangement was popular, and people wanted food to be delivered to them because of the inconvenience of attending the centres and the fear that their damaged, and therefore unsecured, houses might be looted during their absence. Rations were also delivered directly to villages and settlements. This distribution of food, and also tents for temporary shelters, proved to be very controversial as some people believed that certain recipients of assistance were undeserving and distribution was unfair.

Figure 2 shows the period over which provisions were distributed following cyclones Eric and Nigel. Within nine days of the cyclones,

Table 2
Summary of Crop Damage Caused by Cyclones Eric and Nigel in the Western and Central Divisions, 1985

	Area Damaged (ha)	Estimated Value ($)
Cassava	1,349	1,653,512
Other root crops[a]	1,477	2,877,150
Tree crops[b]	13,370	1,464,301
Vegetables	505	1,226,472
Maize	223	64,650
Peanuts	4	3,242
Pulses	178	177,930
Rice	256	244,230
Pineapples	20	17,000
Cocoa	5	3,800
Yaqona	66	677,800
Total	17,453	8,410,087

[a] yams, taro and sweet potatoes
[b] coconuts, bananas, pawpaw, mangoes, breadfruit etc.

Source: Compiled from Ministry of Primary Industries files (unpublished).

$1,862,473 worth of food (or 58 per cent of the total) was allocated to people who had directly experienced the cyclones and others who had been marginally affected. Table 3 describes the types and quantities distributed. These foods were almost all imported, and the millions of dollars spent did not benefit the farmers with produce to sell or the small businessmen. The highest expenditure was on rice and flour, both of which were readily available in shops.

Figure 2
Rate of Expenditure on Food Relief After the 1985 Cyclones[2]

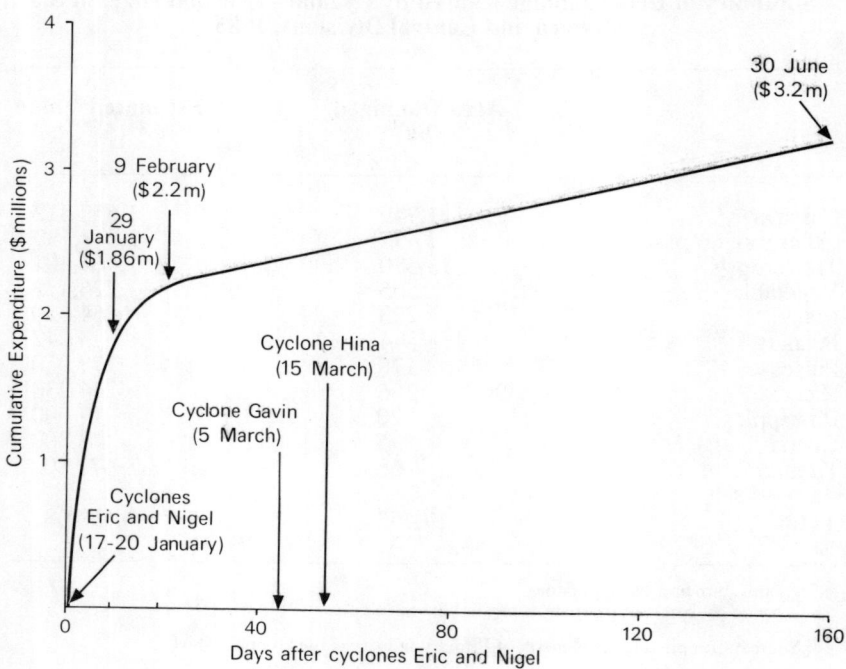

THE DISTRIBUTION OF FOOD RELIEF

In describing the types of abuse that the food relief system was subject to and fostered, it is not denied that many needy people received aid. Nor is it in any way intended to denigrate the difficult work undertaken by usually conscientious civil servants and others during stressful times. The civil

---

2   Figure 2 refers to all four cyclones which affected Fiji during 1985. Cyclones Gavin and Hina did not come on land but caused heavy rain and strong winds over parts of the Fiji group. Expenditure on food relief after March includes food rations given for these cyclones, but this was negligible by comparison to expenditures on Eric and Nigel.

Table 3
Summary of Rations Issued for Cyclones, 1985

	Central	Division Eastern	Western	Northern	Grand Total
Population fed	86,514	32,156	157,037	40	275,747
Net cost ($)	859,534	468,776	1,901,444	296	3,230,050
Rations issued					
Rice (kg)	294,744	282,657	715,760	161	1,293,322
Sugar (kg)	67,740	61,506	149,257	50	278,553
Tea (kg)	7,500	5,994	47,439	-	60,933
Skim milk (kg)	440	-	127,145	-	127,585
Jam (tins)	13	-	-	-	13
Salt (kg)	7,212	2,651	21,828	3	31,694
Flour (kg)	199,697	213,353	598,192	50	1,011,292
Sharps (kg)	-	-	69,600	-	69,600
Biscuits (kg)	7,777	36	74,916	-	82,729
Margarine (kg)	172	-	60	-	232
Corned mutton (tins)	103,185	3,168	43,080	-	149,433
Corned beef (tins)	135,341	41,476	24,897	48	201,762
Tinned fish (tins)	123,795	108,281	47,634	63	279,773
Curry powder (kg)	28		53,700	-	53,728
Cooking oil (litres)	60,455	14,235	131,580	20	206,290

Source: Compiled from Ministry of Rural Development, Rehabilitation and Rural Housing files (unpublished). Covers period 20 January to 30 June 1985.

servants, upon whom much of the post-cyclone work falls, are drawn from a small manpower base.   In the days and nights immediately following a cyclone they often work very long hours under pressure, not least because they are often victims of the cyclone themselves and must leave their own family to go to the assistance of others.   The abuses which occur cannot consistently be blamed upon the government, its civil servants nor the general community, but rather on a relief system which has worked itself into a state where dependency and misuse are factored into the whole process[3].

The immediate distribution of rations following a cyclone ignores the fact that although near-maturing food crops may be damaged, unless they have somehow been completely dislodged and blown away, deeply silted over, or inundated by sea-water, they are usually not beyond harvesting. Because of the need to harvest crops promptly that would otherwise spoil, there is usually an abundance of food in the days straight after a cyclone. The critical period for shortages is more likely to be two to three weeks later, when current crops have been consumed and the new ones are not yet ready for harvest. Recognition of this fact would reduce the apparent urgency with which crop damage needed to be assessed. As Figure 2 shows, large quantities of food were distributed in the days immediately following cyclones Eric and Nigel. Much of this was unnecessary distribution and a wastage of resources.

During the two weeks after the cyclones interviews were conducted by the author with farmers, villagers and civil servants involved in the relief programme. Also inspections were made in areas of reported agricultural damage as well as in the municipal markets at Sigatoka, Lautoka, Nadi, Ba and Rakiraki. All of these markets were selling a good range and quantity of foodstuffs, including root crop staples. On one of several similar occasions, a woman at Lautoka market who had just arrived from Wainibuka with a large carrier-load of *dalo* and cassava was interviewed. She said that she and people in her village were receiving full relief rations[4].

Instances were found of food having been distributed to farmers who had suffered little damage, and where harvestable crops had been left to rot. One such case was in Sigatoka Valley, where a mature crop of maize had become lodged but was harvestable. The farmer, however, had decided to leave it to rot, and when asked why, he explained that he needed it as evidence of crop damage so he would be granted rations and other assistance by the agricultural survey teams. Unfortunately, this type of thinking was widespread.

Parts of Tailevu Province were affected by cyclones Eric and Nigel as they passed overhead. The intensity of cyclones usually decreases as they pass over the land mass of Viti Levu, and in Tailevu there was not the extent of damage apparent on the western coast. At a village meeting in Tailevu in February, the supply of rations was discussed with villagers. They had received free food, although they had made no request for it, and then believed they had not been supplied enough. However, they admitted openly

---

3   Indeed, this was recognised by the government following the cyclones of 1985, and a review of the Emergency Services Procedures was undertaken later that year by Air Vice-Marshall Nicholas Carter and the author. It is not clear, however, whether the guidelines suggested in that review have been followed closely during public emergencies since late 1985.

4   Similarly in Ovalau, following flooding later in 1985, food rations were supplied to villagers. Some villagers were known to have brought carrier-loads of produce into the Levuka market, and loaded the same carrier with free food rations to take back to their village.

that they were in no distress regarding food and had a lot of crops they could use. In describing what they considered to be 'enough' the central issue was their perceptions of equity with other people. Another common idea was that it was not pragmatic to 'look a gift-horse in the mouth', for if they were to turn down freely-offered aid they believed they might be overlooked on future occasions. Also, it could be considered impolite to refuse assistance from the government.

The generosity of relief officials in some areas exacerbated problems in others. With a senior officer of the Ministry of Primary Industries, the author toured areas where particularly high levels of agricultural damage had been reported. One of these was in Ra Province. On inspection, the damage was found to be slight: even breadfruit remained on the trees. When asked how misreporting had occurred, a government officer explained that this was a deliberate effort to obtain for local people the amount of rations that those in a neighbouring district with comparably light damage were receiving. The extraordinary statement was then made by the officer that his district would 'forego' claims for food relief and agricultural rehabilitation this time, conditional on their receiving relief after the next cyclone. It was apparent that the 'potlatch' mentality was affecting some government officials as much as anyone else.

There have also been allegations by survey personnel that their recommendations not to supply food relief have, at times, been overruled by more senior civil servants. The only apparent motivation for this is political pressure placed on, or exerted by, these senior officers.

There was, of course, another side to this problem. One incident observed was where a villager had reported to his local agricultural officer a loss of 12 hectares of cassava. When the officer replied that this could not be so because on a recent visit to that village he had noted less than three acres of cassava planted, he was bluntly told to hold his tongue, or else. Later in 1985, there were reports from Lomaiviti of a visiting politician who was pressed for virtual automatic granting of food rations following local bad weather. He was warned, only partly in jest: "*qarauna na tiki*" (beware of the way we will tick the ballot papers).

Clearly, there was distribution of free food rations to virtually anybody in the affected areas of the western districts immediately following the cyclones. Workers at Nadi airport told how they had been encouraged to put their names down for relief although they were on full pay and their jobs were not disrupted. Similarly, many school-teachers, civil servants and other salaried people were supplied with food, or had their names added to the ration list. Sugarcane farmers, who had received their annual cane payments and, therefore, arguably did not lose their means of livelihood, received free provisions. There was at this time abundant food in the shops and the markets. Criteria regarding the recipients of rations were set but, in the event, these were hard to verify and sometimes apparently ignored. The criteria were simply stated as "affected people with (a) no regular source of income and (b) dependent entirely on farming for food and income"[5]. It was easy for almost anyone to claim eligibility for either category, and not be checked upon.

Police investigated some reported cases of ration abuse, following allegations such as that some local government officials had supplied rations and tents only to those with whom they were acquainted. It was also widely asserted that some people collected more than their share by visiting more than one distribution point, or by declaring a false number of dependents. There were also reports of the hoarding of rations and that whole truckloads of provisions were not delivered to the correct places but illegally diverted. There were political issues involved also such as the decision not to supply rations to squatter settlements.

For the first time in the history of the country a food riot was reported. This took place at one of the relief centres at Lautoka where bus loads of people staged a demonstration which developed into a fight over food[6]. Although it was a small one, it was significant in displaying the expectations of the people for handouts regardless of whether they deserved rations or not.

THE EVOLUTION OF DEPENDENCY

Tropical cyclones have always been a hazard of life in Fiji. Traditional mechanisms of coping with natural disasters no longer operate, for they evolved within a much simpler and smaller society than exists in Fiji today. Unfortunately, in disaster-prone Fiji, the cultivation of low-risk disaster resistant crops, or 'famine food' is considered by most people as no longer necessary for survival. Also, there has been a gradual decrease in the diversity of food crops grown by villagers and other rural dwellers and food storage and preservation, either by traditional or introduced methods, is no longer considered necessary. In a few decades there has been a shift from self-reliance to dependency[7], and from consumption only of local produce to mass distribution of imported food.

A benevolent government will supply plenty of free food whenever a natural disaster occurs, and dependency on the government increasingly is taken for granted. In this way the ability of the people to cope, using proven methods and local resources, has weakened further. The general attitude has become to accept all you are given, and demand all you expect, or, foolishly, you will miss out. The system allows no rewards to the selfless or the self-

---

[5]   These criteria were given at the Divisional Commissioners' Meeting, Lautoka, February 1985 (author's notes).

[6]   There were suggestions at the time that the riot was orchestrated by political opponents of the government.

[7]   Food dependency is a phenomenon noted elsewhere by Thaman (1979, 1982b, 1984) and others (for example, McGee 1975, Sharma 1985).

reliant, much as the government might extol these virtues. Problems in the disaster relief process were clearly exposed by cyclones Eric and Nigel which, by severely damaging a highly-populated region, stretched the system to reveal its flaws.

To prevent the perpetuation and escalation of dependency it is necessary to review the current system of post-disaster assessment and decision-making procedures. Many of the problems described above stem from inappropriate operational practices, the politicisation of relief activities, and the general propensity to over-react initially when a cyclone occurs.

There is a tendency for those in authority to treat all cyclones similarly and hence the criteria for deciding upon relief activities has become, basically — do what was done previously. This seems inappropriate and may foster the idea in the minds of recipients and aid officials that everyone is entitled to specific goods regardless of their real needs. More relevant information or messages coming in from the field may be ignored.

While there are advantages to a central relief coordination system, this tends to assume complete authority with a top-down mode of operation. This becomes a problem when officers at lower levels (departments and district levels), who may have better local knowledge and information, become isolated from decision-making. It has been the experience of some officers that they have conducted considerable field surveys only to find that their reports are not used and decisions about relief activities have rolled on regardless of them. One example of this occurred after an agricultural officer had completed surveying a village which had suffered some damage. The villagers had themselves decided that they did not want immediate food relief. The next day, while he was conducting the survey at a neighbouring village, the officer learned that food was already on the way from Suva to be delivered to all villages in the district, regardless of the agricultural survey or the peoples' decision to be self-reliant.

A major problem in the coordination of relief activities is the exaggerated sense of urgency that usually accompanies the distribution of free rations and other aid. As already mentioned, there are usually quantities of storm-damaged food that need to be used before spoilage occurs. Relief that is too hasty often preempts the results of even the preliminary agricultural surveys. It also reduces the ability of surveyors to assess real levels of damage and real needs. Furthermore, the rush to distribute rations is wasteful for, in this manner, large amounts of money may be spent where they are least needed. Longer-term community and agricultural rehabilitation that may help reduce vulnerability to some forms of damage is relatively neglected.

One simple remedy for some of the problems in the relief system is to seek accurate information on damage from the field and to use this information as a basis for decisions regarding the types and extent of assistance to be given. The surveys must be timely, yet accurate, and work towards identifying the real needs of those who have suffered hardship. Survey officers must be instructed in ways of accurately assessing damage for, in the emotion and confusion that follows a cyclone, it is easy to misjudge the extent of losses[8]. Often things are not as bad as they might first appear. Furthermore, crops are affected differently in any one event or depending on the type of natural disaster which has occurred. When it is widely known by people that relief will be given only to those who really need it, and following well-defined guidelines, then some of the abuse in the system will be reduced.

Consideration needs to be given to delaying food distribution to allow the proper assessment of needs and to encourage the use of alternative foods. This would assist in a move away from virtually automatic and universal relief to carefully defined 'needs-based' relief. It would also increase public recognition of the value of damaged but salvageable crops and the food supply in the markets and shops. Further, it might encourage rural people to readopt some of the traditional methods of famine relief and traditional foods that previous generations relied upon.

In the longer term it is necessary to question how appropriate an emphasis on food relief is. With better post-disaster assessment may come an improved capacity of the government to communicate to international aid donors the types of post-disaster assistance Fiji most requires. The money usually spent in the days immediately following a cyclone could be better used in longer-term rehabilitation or development projects. Thought needs to be given to ways in which self-help can be fostered and the recipients of relief given some valid choices in the process of post-disaster rehabilitation. The long-term goal should be self-sustaining development of the people and enhancement of their self reliance.

---

8   Two handbooks providing practical guidelines for field surveyors were prepared by the Pacific Island Development Program (Campbell and Chung 1986).

8

THE IMPACT OF A ROAD

Margaret Chung

ROADS AND RURAL DEVELOPMENT

In the literature on rural development, roads are described as a critical element in the expansion of modernisation. In particular, their role is to link rural areas with regional towns and settlements higher up the urban hierarchy, providing access for rural people to public services, sources of change-inducing information, and markets. This increased interaction, it is generally assumed, will promote structural and contextual changes in the rural economy, such as changes in modes of production and organisation, and increased commercialisation and capitalist penetration. These changes will be reflected in the increased distance and volume of the movement of people, increased cash cropping and local entrepreneurial activity, increased household incomes, and improvements in the quality of rural life, all of which may work to reduce migration from the rural areas.

Such assumptions are central to the spatial strategies for regional development that were adopted in principle in the Fiji Government's Seventh (1976/80) and Eighth (1981/85) Development Plans (Fiji Central Planning Office 1975, 1980; Atkins 1983; McLennan Magasanik 1984). This set of policies to promote regional development in Fiji was by 1986 only in its very early stages of implementation. It was however, not too early to examine some questions as to the extent to which people were likely to respond in the manner that policy-makers anticipated, for some of the important elements were already in place as part of earlier developments. An obvious example of this was roads and improved transport facilities. Had existing roads had the effects on rural economies and population mobility that were assumed in these present policies?

Blaikie *et al.* (1977:4) comment on the striking contrast between the optimistic estimations expressed in feasibility reports and the consensus found in many studies as to the very limited nature of effects attributable to road provision. Within this consensus there is further divergence regarding the types of effects.

Why is the literature on the impacts of roads so equivocal as to their benefits? Of course, one consideration is the specific conditions that relate to each unique location. In general, however, McCall (1977:56) argues that claims about the benefits brought by roads are suspect because the so-called 'development effects' are usually assessed through the most superficial, easily measurable and quantifiable transport effects. They are, therefore, usually confined to agricultural production increases while longer-term structural impacts are neglected. This chapter suggests two further problems in assessing the impacts of roads. The first is that, depending on the length of time which has elapsed between completion of the road and initiation of the study, survey results may capture either short-term (more favourable) or longer-term (often less favourable) effects. Secondly, it is often difficult to disengage the effects directly attributable to roading projects from changes occurring more generally in the national economy. These arguments will be illustrated by reference to the Monasavu road which was built between 1977 and 1979 through central Viti Levu, Fiji. They are based on a review of road impact studies and fieldwork conducted in 1986 in Wainimala *tikina*, which is located in the northwest section of Naitasiri Province (Figure 1). The methodology on which the fieldwork was based is detailed elsewhere (Chung 1987).

The Monasavu road, which links Serea with Monasavu in the northern section of Wainimala *tikina*, was built primarily to provide access from Suva to the construction site for a hydro-electric power scheme at Monasavu. That the road required for the power scheme also provided road access to the people of Wainimala was their good fortune, for they had long wanted a more reliable form of transport than the river and a less arduous one than travelling by foot or horseback. The completion of the road provided Wainimala people for the first time with easy access to all the urban centres of Viti Levu. Previously, when people rafted down the river or walked out of the district, movements to markets were predominantly downstream to Serea and then to Nausori or Suva. Now, the road provides an easy route over the mountains to markets at Tavua and Ba on the north coast. It is likely, however, that despite the power scheme, the road would have been built eventually. Its construction was given third priority in the national roading programme in the late 1960s, and the upper Naitasiri Province was an area targetted in DP8 for development investment, focussed on the growth of a regional centre at Vunidawa, extension of welfare services, and regional expansion of transport infrastructure (McLennan Magasanik 1984).

Figure 1
Viti Levu and Study Area

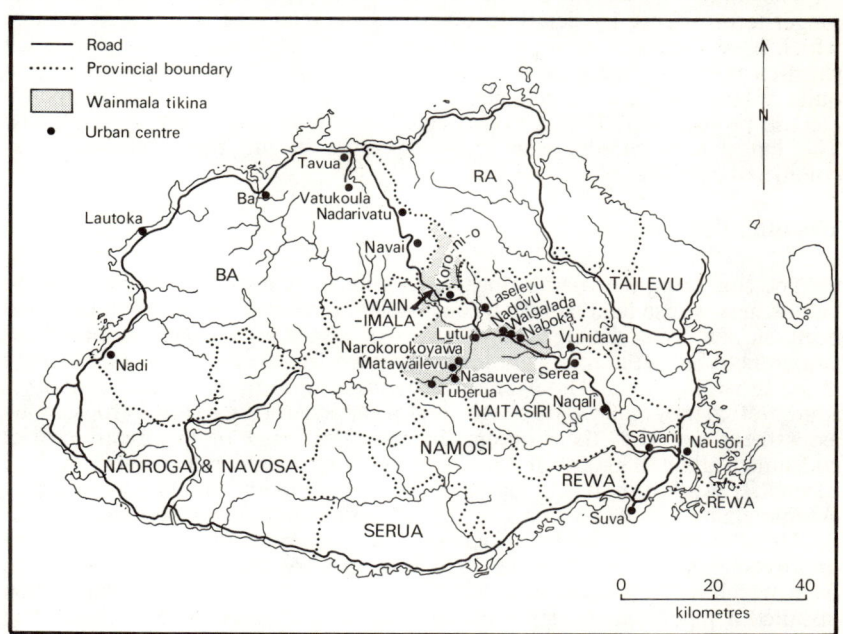

EFFECTS OF THE ROAD

A pattern commonly noticed by rural development workers in Fiji, but rarely acknowledged in the literature, is of an initial period of local activity and the promise of change which, in the longer term, slowly regresses to a slightly modified version of the old life. It is interesting to note that of a number of studies of specific road developments, those which found the most positive effects (Ward 1970, 1975; Hugo 1981) were often had been conducted less than two years after road construction; those which found least substantial benefits usually had been conducted after longer periods (e.g. Airey 1984; Leinbach 1983; Blaikie *et al.* 1977). Of course, not all such studies can be thus categorised (e.g. Southern 1973; Bouchard 1972). This pattern of change ties in with the increasing awareness that many road projects, in the absence of complementary investments and in the longer term, fail to generate the developments expected of them (Airey 1984:192).

The following section of this chaper illustrates this pattern of short and longer-term effects by detailing the types of economic and social change which have occurred in Wainimala since road construction. Generally the short-term effects had played themselves out within five years — which is quite a long period — but some work continued at the Monasavu hydro-electric project until 1984 and this acted to extend some short-term effects. The longer-term effects were those apparent at the time fieldwork was conducted in 1986.

The initial effects

The first thing the road brought was money: compensation payments to landowners whose land had been converted into roadway or whose timber had been cut and crops damaged in the process, wages for villagers employed as labourers to build the road, and income gained from selling food and *yaqona* at the urban markets. The Monasavu hydro-electric project site was another source of money, providing wages and a market for local food crops. One assessment was that the workers for the third stage of the hydro project consumed about $50,000 of locally-grown root crops and vegetables (Fiji Electricity Authority, n.d.). However, this figure included a large number of Wainimala households over a long period of time and may be too high.

Then came a sudden increase in Government aid for village improvements. At Nadovu, in 1978 road construction polluted the stream from which village water was drawn. The Public Works Department then installed a piped water supply to the village. Similarly, other villages had piped water supplies installed around this time. As Government officers could move easily along the road, other innovations were introduced to the district such as water-seal toilets and concreted drains.

This initial period of prosperity was also one of optimism, for people had long blamed their lack of 'development' on the absence of a road and now, it appeared, all their hopes were capable of fulfilment. One immediate response from the roadside villages when the road first opened was to market available food crops and wild foods. It is very difficult to assess the extent to which this occurred for no market records exist, but several community leaders from the district reported that some roadside villagers sold much of their *dalo* and *yaqona* crops although these had been planted mainly for household consumption. These sales were often to middlemen from beyond the district who bought directly from villagers at 'farm-gate' prices. Those who had sold most of their *yaqona* then had to wait for three to four years before another crop matured.

This sudden surge of interest and activity in producing crops for the market only lasted as long as the local surplus of produce and until people became aware of the costs and benefits of marketing their crops. Prices for agricultural crops fluctuate widely in Fiji's local market, and unless one has a steady, guaranteed market outlet, the profitability of a crop can change drastically in the time between planting and harvesting. This is particularly true with slower-maturing crops. When the crop also has a low value to bulk ratio, such as *dalo*, transport costs for areas remote from the market further reduce profitability and it is difficult for traditional farmers to compete with more commercially organised producers who are located closer to the markets. The market for seasonal wild food crops, such as *duruka*, is often good for there is a high demand during the short season. But there also is a lot of work involved in collecting the limited amounts that can be transported to the road or along it and competition from other sellers can be strong. Although it may at first appear an easy matter to market agricultural produce, there are many factors farmers have to consider: who will do the work, how to obtain or control other resources necessary for market production, the material and social costs of harvesting, transport and marketing, and whether, in the whole scheme of things, the extra effort is worthwhile.

The early optimism about the opportunities a road would bring was apparent in discussions with people in the upper reaches of the Wainimala River who must still walk several hours to reach the Monasavu road at Balea (Figure 2). It is the general opinion that the absence of a road to their villages is their single greatest disadvantage. Such a view may be considered indicative of others in the district before they gained road access. Typically their plans for when the road might finally reach them are ambitious:

When the road comes, do you think you people will sell more crops?
>Plenty, because of the road.

What will you plant?
>Yaqona, *dalo*, bananas, *vudi*, breadfruit, pawpaw.

Do you think you will sell these?
>Yes, because of the road. Oranges, *duruka*, everything.
>>*(Upper Wainimala villager)*

>The road will change our lives. A lot of crops will be sold — cassava, bananas, *dalo*, *duruka*.

Do you think a lot will be sold?
>Yes — all this food we've planted, but it's difficult to get it to Balea. We don't have a horse. When the road comes, all these things will earn money for us. We'll eat less and more we'll sell.
>>*(Upper Wainimala villager)*

Interviews with roadside farmers revealed changed attitudes and expectations seven or eight years after the completion of the road. For the most part, they still rarely sold crops other than *yaqona*. When asked why, their explanation generally was that transport costs, the limited quantities which could be carried on the bus and the problems of selling in the market made most crops 'uneconomic' unless prices were especially good. At the

Figure 2
Location of Public Services in Wainimala

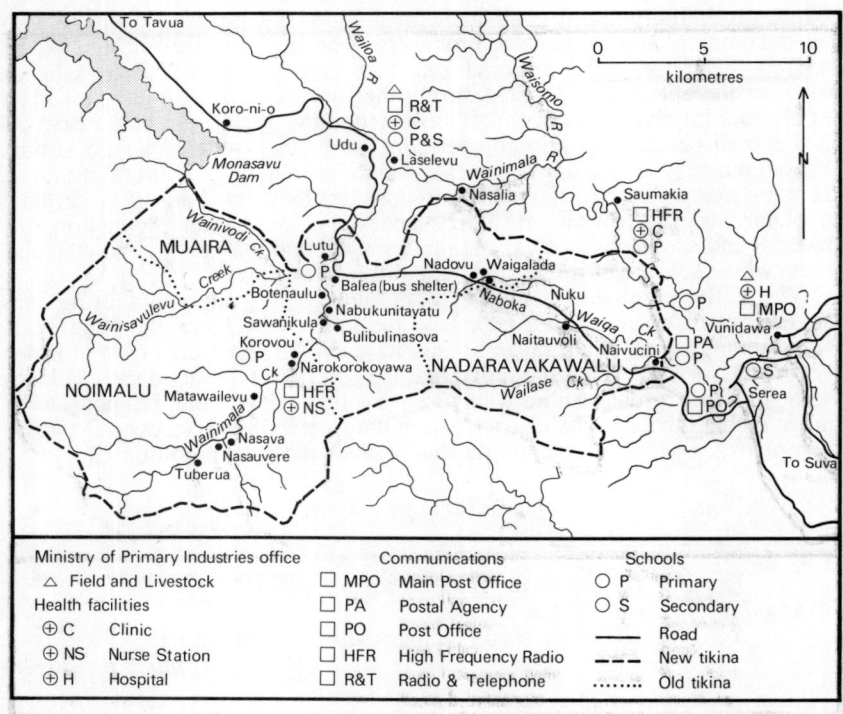

time of field-work, for example, the market price for *dalo* was around $2 a bundle. Farmers in Wainimala believed this price would need to almost double before selling *dalo* would be worth their while. Wild foods, such as *ota* (edible fern), and uncultivated tree crops, such as oranges, provided further examples of market problems. Although it grew wild in abundance, *ota* was rarely offered for sale because it was considered difficult to harvest and sometimes did not sell well, thus wasting the work, a return bus-fare, and a frustrating day in the market.

During construction of the Monasavu dam, between 1978 and 1984, the road had much more traffic, and roadside sales of oranges earned villagers easy money. After that, with lighter traffic, most of the crop needed to be taken to markets elsewhere. The early season price of around $10 a bag was considered 'worth it', but this price usually halved during the peak of the season. Agricultural economists might dispute such values, but it is the farmers who calculate the price as it reflects their economic and non-economic costs and their perceptions of value. *Yaqona*, which has a high value to weight ratio, remained the main crop marketed from Wainimala[1].

Some of the money the road brought was spent on conspicuous consumption, as Rutz (1977) and Griffin (1978) reported in the Waidina Valley and Namosi after road construction in 1965 and 1976-7 respectively. One type was social trips to and from the towns, as people acquainted themselves with the new dimensions of personal mobility. The bus service, which expanded close behind the road construction teams, also provided a new social scene: as well as meeting friends and relatives on the bus, one could greet them as it passed along the road. Also it helped to import new things into the district such as beer sold to villagers at high prices by the bus drivers.

> In this village, they were paid more than $30,000 by the Government as compensation for the damage done to their crops by road construction. They got that money and since no good advice was given to them, they started to drink. That is a lot of money, but most of it went to Carlton Brewery and only some to their houses.
>
> *(Village leader)*

While this leader probably exaggerates the sum spent on beer, drunkenness amongst village men became a problem of considerable concern to local leaders. Eventually, with the help of the churches, it was curbed and in some villages community leaders placed restrictions on drinking alcohol.

Money was spent on houses and village facilities, which mostly took the form of large concrete community halls and churches. Large amounts of money available in the district also were channelled to district projects. For example, $10,000 was raised by villagers of Waibasaga, Matainasau, Lutu, Nadovu, Botenaulu and Nabukenivatu for improvements to the Muaira District School (*Fiji Times*, December 4, 1980) and the people of Noimalu raised a large sum of money to rebuild the Noimalu District School in concrete blocks. Villagers throughout Fiji are also required to raise money to support the Fijian provincial administration. In 1978, for example, each

---

1   Sofer (1985:430-1) explains that *yaqona* is currently the most profitable crop in several of the economically disadvantaged areas of Fiji — in particular Kadavu, parts of Cakaudrove and Lomaiviti, and Bua. "All these areas may be classified as peripheral areas in Fiji — that is where farming, the principal activity, is marked by non-capitalist relations of production, low capital-labour ratios, and the continual presence of a significant amount of subsistence production. In addition, the most common type of settlement in these areas is the traditional Fijian village."

tikina within Naitasiri was required to raise $6000 for the province (*Fiji Times*, October 11, 1978).

The main change in housing was the increased substitution of corrugated iron for bamboo and thatch. Villagers of the upper Wainimala valley, still without direct road access, stated that they would first improve housing and village facilities when they did get road access. The relative improvement in accessibility provided by the Monasavu road had greatly increased the use of corrugated iron in this area already. It was, however, more common in villages with road access than those at a distance from the road, because of the difficulty of transporting it by horse or on foot.

New businesses sprang up along the road: new village shops, a tea and coffee shop at the bus stop at Balea, and villager-owned carriers. Few lasted long, due to poor management and because the local entrepreneur's hopes of success were based on the affluence that immediately followed the road. Before this local wealth dissipated or dried up at the source, as road-work and later the Monasavu hydro-electric project came to an end (in 1979 and 1984 respectively), these businesses could survive but as money became scarcer most collapsed. Their demise was helped by the intrusion into the district of outside enterprises: bread vans which came every day, and mobile foodstores and second-hand clothes sellers which came once a week or so. Several shops closed because of considerable credit extended to relatives and neighbours. The tea and coffee shop was closed by the Government Health Department because of poor hygiene. Carriers, with their business viability strongly challenged by bus operators from outside the district, were recalled by the Fiji Development Bank due to arrears in loan repayments. One pickup truck purchased with land compensation payments, and used in a carrier business, lasted only three weeks before being written off in a collision.

The road produced some immediate residential changes. Several men who had been working in town returned to their roadside villages after the road was completed for it now appeared that the district was really developing. There was also a small on-going movement out of the villages to land along the road. This was in response to several factors, one of which was access to land-holdings which previously had not been used because of their location and distance from the village[2]. Another factor, common throughout rural Fiji, is a move away from the sometimes burdensome communal demands of the village to become *galala* (independent farmers) on a leased portion of *tokatoka* or *mataqali* land. This trend has been encouraged by Government lending agencies which will only advance loans on land held under specific lease agreement.

This first wave of change brought many new things but it was soon apparent that the benefiits had been quite superficial, at least in the short term. Very little of the money that came with the road was invested in improving the productive capacity of village agriculture. Investments in local transport

---

2   Rutz (1977) similarly reported that following the construction of a road through the Waidina Valley (1965) people actively asserted their rights to land near the roadside.

and other businesses were often unsuccessful. It was not only the local people who had innocently expected that all their problems would be over. Civil servants questioned were equally naive. They took the peoples' failures to convert these apparent opportunities into real benefits as evidence of their inadequacy and the inflexibility of traditional society and agriculture. Clearly, such an explanation is too simple.

Longer-term changes

Field-work for this study was undertaken in early 1986, some seven years after the completion of the road. Undoubtedly, the road had altered the lives of the people in the district (and even those still distant from the road) but a traveller along the Monasavu road would see little sign of the dramatic changes that improved transport facilities have reputedly brought in other parts of the world (Hugo 1981; Leinbach 1983).

The changes in Wainimala have been subtle, for a number of reasons. The land tenure system has so far mitigated against a restructuring of society and the expansion of rural landless and poor (cf. Hugo 1981). There has been little change in the mode of production, although the cash cropping element of the semi-subsistence farming system has become important. Peoples' incomes are insufficient to support a local transport industry in competition with the bus and this limits traffic along the road. Other local entrepreneurial activity is inhibited by the intrusion of outside businesses. Despite improvements in household incomes, Wainimala people do not have (or do not consider themselves to have) the disposable income to significantly increase their personal mobility. Before the advent of the road, transport as far as Serea could be free (although it was not necessarily so) if arduous; now a trip to Suva and back requires an immediate cash outlay of at least $5 to $6 for bus fare. The road has brought some improvements in rural life, in particular, better access to public services — although not completely so in the case of medical facilities. In most respects, however, Wainimala remains where it has been in the political economy of Fiji since colonial times: a region of semi-traditional semi-subsistence agriculture, peripheral to Fiji's economy and society.

Commercialisation with access to markets. A common observation in the South Pacific region and elsewhere is that the expansion of commercial agriculture tends to follow road construction (Ward and Proctor 1980; Ward 1982; Doulman 1976; Leinbach 1983; Airey 1984). In Wainimala the road has encouraged the expansion of *yaqona* cultivation within the framework of semi-subsistence village agriculture.

Yaqona has long provided part of the cash requirements of Wainimala households. In the last decade there has been, to some degree, increased planting, harvesting and marketing of *yaqona*, both because of the improved accessibility of the market and higher market prices. It is impossible to precisely measure this increase because of the paucity of pre-road and post-road information (cf. Griffin 1978). Generally, production figures are difficult to obtain where there is a large subsistence or semi-subsistence sector and local market transactions are unrecorded. The few figures available from official agricultural records were clearly unreliable. Estimating production increase is further complicated by the long period that it takes *yaqona* to mature — from three to five years; its ability to stay in the ground indefinitely as a form of bank account until the farmer needs cash; and the manner in which it is planted — in scattered patches of favourable soil on the hill slopes and interplanted with subsistence crops.

Villagers were generally of the opinion that production had increased and was still increasing in response to the current good prices for *yaqona* and the road access for marketing it. Others, however, suggested that production had not increased very much and it was rather the rapid increase in *yaqona* price that made earnings much greater.

That the increase in production cannot have been very great is suggested by the quantity marketed. Most farmers interviewed estimated their annual sales to be between three to five sacks full, generally valued at between $500 and $1000. If one takes an average yield of 4kg per plant at an average price of $6 kg, these returns approximately represent twenty to forty plants harvested. The maximum reported values for the previous years' harvest were $2500 and $3000.

Interest in *yaqona* production was not confined to the villages along the road, but had spread throughout the region to others less accessible. Thus, in this regard there was little discernible difference between the road's impact on villages near and away from the road.

Little change in production methods. The increased commercialisation of *yaqona* reveals the flexibility of subsistence village production and its ability to respond to changing opportunities for participation in the market (Ellis 1983b:34). Nevertheless, district farmers had not otherwise changed their mode of production. Farming retained its semi-subsistence, shifting character and its close links with traditional culture and lifestyle. Villagers worked on their smallholdings and, depending on the occasion, might cooperate on the basis of their *tokatoka*, *mataqali*, church or village. Production remained centred around traditional products with no market-led diversification into other crops or products. There had been little investment in productive capacity and few farmers invested in new inputs.

It is not that district farmers did not wish to change; most hoped that their agriculture would develop to support a more comfortable life style. Rather, it appears that they did not know what to do; hardly surprising given the complexities of their situation and the absence of agricultural extension work by the Ministry of Primary Industries (MPI).

Why have the improved accessibility and transport facilities provided by the Monasavu road been insufficent forces to induce much expansion and reallocation of resources within local farming systems? This complicated issue can be dealt with here only briefly, but the general constraints on smallholder agriculture are summarised by Hardaker *et al.* (1984:202).

As Blaikie *et al.* (1977: Appendix iii) explain, the extent to which such development takes place is dependent on the capacity of agricultural systems to expand and reallocate resources. The physical restrictions of land and suitable soils, the agrotechnical requirements of *yaqona* cultivation and the long maturation period of the crop are limiting factors. It could be risky to invest resources too heavily in this crop and disregard subsistence requirements, for farmers have no quarantee that *yaqona* planted today will realise the same returns when harvested three or four years later. Other factors include social and cultural values about productivity and accumulation which are reinforced by the land tenure system. Farmers were hampered by a lack of investment in their means of production and, with rising aspirations and costs of living, it is difficult to see from where such investment could come. Large projects, such as one organised by a Christian youth group at Nadovu, may be one approach but despite the supposedly communal nature of Fijian society, there is no record of success in such projects beyond a few years. Farmers were also handicapped by distance from markets and competition from commercially-oriented farmers closer to markets.

In particular, the road had provided little new access to change-inducing information. One service which had not come along it was agricultural extension. There was one agricultural field officer at Laselevu but his impact was slight because the policy of the MPI is to concentrate on commercial farmers and encourage them to produce commercial crops, such as cocoa, or go into cattle production. There is little official interest in traditional semi-subsistence farmers and their crops, particularly *yaqona*. This is despite the fact that *yaqona* is demonstrably an important crop for Wainimala people and those of other economically marginal areas of Fiji, and overall is possibly the second most important cash crop in Fiji after sugar (Ellis 1983b:17).

The semi-subsistence orientation of agricultural activities may change as people develop other aspirations. There was some evidence that this change was underway:

> Now that I'm earning more money I have to use it on more things too. Church fund-raising, weddings, school fees, things we need for our household, things we need for our village. You see, the more money we earn from our farming the more money also we have to use on our lives and on things to do with the village because we are living in the village. I also bank some of my money. This is for the times when there is a *leqa* [problem or event] or for going to see the doctor or some other emergency I am faced with.'
>
> *(Farmer, Nadovu)*

It was also true, however, that although Wainimala farmers were doing well for the moment, their situation was vulnerable. Beyond *yaqona*, they produced little that could provide them sufficent cash flows. Almost anything they produced could be produced more efficiently by commercial farmers elsewhere. In Fiji, as market demand and prices have increased, the production of traditional crops has been taken over by commercial farmers who have greater financial resources, more efficient production systems and better access to the market than semi-subsistence farmers.

Changes in market destinations and arrangements. One positive effect of the road was that it had eased the transportation of *yaqona* and given farmers more control over their choice of market and marketing arrangements. The bus can carry more *yaqona* over a longer distance than a horse, and it provides a pleasanter journey to market than walking for two days over steep and muddy terrain. Before the road was constructed, most *yaqona* was sold in Suva where competition is greater because it is also the market for *yaqona* coming in from the main producing areas: the eastern islands and Taveuni. Suva was the most accessible market in pre-road days as the road-head at Serea was about two-days walk away or downstream if one travelled by river. From Serea there was about a two-hour bus ride to Suva. Much less often, farmers would walk across the mountains to the northern Viti Levu markets at Tavua, Lautoka and Ba.

> Before, when we planted and harvested our crops, we used
> to wonder where to take them to sell. Today we can argue
> about going to Ba, Lautoka, Tavua or Suva to sell.
>
> *(Farmer, Nadovu)*

Specific market prices are conveyed by word of mouth. But most farmers expected prices to be higher in Tavua, Ba and Lautoka during the sugarcane harvest season (approximately April to November) as *yaqona* consumption rises with the presence of the sugar harvesting gangs. During the other months of the year, or when there are high prices, farmers looked more towards the Suva market. There is a choice of two buses in either direction every day — unless the bus breaks down or bad weather closes the road.

With better accessibility, farmers can choose to sell at the village to other villagers who serve as local middlemen, to middlemen who occasionally come to the district looking for a supply of *yaqona*, to middlemen at the market, or they can retail it themselves. Local middlemen were used when only a small amount of *yaqona* had been harvested and when the farmer did not think it worthwhile travelling to market. Middlemen from outside the district were not sold to as often as previously for people were aware that the 'farm-gate' prices they offered were not very good. Most farmers sold their *yaqona* to a middleman in the market as they could complete the transaction quickly. Increasingly, however, people were realising the best value for their *yaqona* by selling it themselves in the market and getting the full retail price.

In early 1986 there were seven market stalls at the Ba market and two in the Tavua market rented on a long-term basis by Wainimala people.

This flexibility in marketing arrangements had the important effect of increasing the returns from *yaqona*. The average producer prices for *yaqona* estimated by Ellis (1983b) in Table 1, column 1, are based on the assumption that the producer received 65 per cent of the market price. This shift in marketing strategy suggests both that these figures are too conservative and that the prices received by producers had increased even more dramatically since the early 1970s than Table 1 might suggest.

Local entrepreneurial activity. It has already been explained that an immediate effect of the road was the setting up of local businesses, but few lasted long. By early 1986 two small village shops existed in Nadovu and Lutu. Of the study villages off the road, Matawailevu had a shop and near Nasauvere a *galala* was establishing another. A shop at Korovou also served the people of Narokorokoyawa. The range of goods sold was limited to such basic items as kerosine for lights, tinned fish, flour, sugar and batteries. The light local trade had been captured mostly by businesses from outside the district. Two vans from out of the district sold vegetables and used clothing once a month. Other needs were supplied by travellers returning from town. The bread van finally stopped its trips in 1985 due to poor patronage.

It was difficult for a local transport business to develop to compete with the bus for despite the restricted carrying capacity, the need to conform to bus schedules, and the relatively high freight rates ($1 to $2 per bag of produce), it was still cheaper to travel by bus that to hire a carrier. When people bought corrugated iron or large amounts of other materials they sometimes hired a carrier from town to return to the village and, if all went well and was planned in advance, another group of men might wait with their produce to take advantage of the discounted return trip.

One more promising type of business activity was building village houses. Two men who had gained building experience working away from the district, earned money occasionally in this way. One of them as well had a chainsaw and ripped logs into timber for sale to villagers.

The quantity of goods transported. Improved transport facilities had resulted in an increased amount of goods taken in and out of the district, but this increase had not been dramatic for several reasons. First, *yaqona* has a very high value for its bulk. Secondly, farming activity in the district otherwise is directed more at subsistence requirements than at production for the market. Thirdly, because of the low incomes earned by Wainimala farmers, the lack of investment sources from which to buy vehicles, and the effective monopoly of transport business by bus operators from outside the district, people are largely dependent on the bus for transportation. This reinforced the need to take small amounts on each trip to the market.

Table 1
Estimated Producer and Market Prices for Yaqona, 1970-1985
($ per kg)

	(1) Estimated producer price	(2) Mkt price A	(3) Mkt price B	(4) Mkt price C
1970	1.198	1.99	nc	na
1971	1.196	1.96	nc	na
1972	1.200	1.93	nc	na
1973	1.258	1.99	nc	na
1974	2.109	3.29	nc	2.50
1975	2.744	4.22	nc	3.95
1976	3.070	4.72	4.66	4.30
1977	3.397	5.23	4.93	na
1978	3.398	5.23	4.41	na
1979	3.406	5.24	4.57	5.00
1980	3.361	5.12	4.96	na
1981	3.425	5.27	4.88	na
1982	3.744	5.76	6.47	na
1983	na	na	7.04	na
1984	na	na	8.77	6.00
1985	na	na	9.07	7.00

nc Available before 1976, but not collected.
na Data not available.

Sources:
(1) Ellis (1983b: Table 5).
(2) Calculated from *ibid,* following Ellis' assumption that producer price was 60 per cent
    of the retail price in 1970, moving up to 65 per cent of the retail price by 1975 and
    remaining so.
(3) Compiled from weekly market reports, *Fiji Times*, 1976-85.
(4) Unpublished figures, Fiji Development Bank, 1986.

Another reason why people carried small amounts of produce is the
manner in which produce is marketed. Men usually took the *yaqona* to
market and most often sold to market middlemen. Such trips generated the
largest amounts of cash and the transactions were completed quickly.

Produce which required the seller to remain in the market (such as oranges, *duruka* or *dalo*) was often taken by women who would remain in the market — even sleeping there at night — until it was sold. As a rule, they planned to remain no more than two or three days and so limited the produce taken to what probably would sell in this time.

The demand for consumer goods. One often observed effect of roading is an increased demand for consumer goods. This is most apparent where improved transport encourages agricultural specialisation and thereby the purchasing of a greater proportion of food, and stimulates a demand for other goods which had a high transport component in their prices prior to road construction (Blaikie *et al.* 1977:38). This is barely the case in Wainimala, for although farmers produced, marketed or earned more from *yaqona* than previously, this had not been substantially at the expense of subsistence food production. Incomes in the district had risen but there was still not much money available to spend on imported food or other consumer items.

From discussions with women and observations of household activities, it was apparent that households in roadside villages bought more food than households away from the road, and this may be indicative of the change that has occurred in roadside villages over time. Food purchases were generally basic items such as tinned fish, cooking oil, sugar, flour, breakfast crackers and tea. Because they usually made more trips away from the district, people in roadside villages were also more likely to buy fresh meat or fish from town. The main dietary change appeared to be in breakfast food; where before they ate *kakana dina* (traditional root crops) at every meal, roadside people now often ate pancakes or *roti* (Indian unleavened bread) with tea for their morning meal. However, such imported food was still considered a luxury and constituted only a small part of the household's food. Away from the road the more traditional diet persisted. Root crops and vegetables such as *rourou*, *bele* and *ota* were eaten for every meal.

In roadside villages some houses had western-style furniture such as beds, settees and chairs. Apart from the beds, this furniture was not regularly used for it is Fijian custom to sit on the floor and generally it is considered rude to sit higher than other people. Most such furniture was a relic of the initial period of prosperity.

Impact upon population mobility. Another expected effect of improved transportation is an increase in personal mobility. There had been an increased volume of people moving but again, the increase had been quite small. Indeed, some people even believed that people now travelled less than previously because improved transportation enabled more produce to be carried per trip. There may be some truth in this, for a major effect of the road had been that it saved time and effort. Data on trip frequencies suggest that people in roadside villages make more non-market trips than those without direct road access. Observation of bus passengers also suggested that more old and very young people now travelled than would be likely by foot.

Figure 3 shows the reported trip frequencies of adult members of forty households, twenty from roadside villages and twenty from the villages in the upper Wainimala valley which lack direct road access. These household members comprised eighty-two individuals: forty-four males and thirty-eight females. Two provisos must be made with regard to the interpretation of these figures. First, it is apparent that there was under-reporting of the annual trips, but it is particularly difficult to collect data when accuracy relies on recall and a defined time division in a society which is not overly concerned with time. Despite this under-reporting, the responses were sufficiently similar to suggest that the overall pattern is accurate. Secondly, the on-road and off-road distinction provides only a very crude measure of change, for even the villages without road access had relatively-improved accessibility.

Nevertheless, a comparison of movement behaviour between road-side villages and villages without direct road access suggests a greater volume of travel. Interesting features are that the biggest increase has apparently been in womens' travel and that trips are made to a wider number of destinations (Figure 3).

Even so, it is equally noteworthy that people did not appear to journey out of the district very often. Table 2 shows the average number of reported trips per individual for the previous month and the previous year. People did not have the money to spend on unnecessary bus fares or to enjoy the amenities of the towns. Despite the much quoted attraction of the 'bright lights' of the urban areas, commonly little effort had been made to experience the brightest of these: very few women admitted to ever watching movies in town or visiting bars or night clubs. Although the men more often said they had been to these places, usually it was once or less a year, with younger men going more often than older men.

The majority of shopping trips to Suva for both road-side and non-road villagers involved a same-day return, and this was commonly expressed as one of the major benefits of improved accessibility. People left from Lutu or Balea around 8.00 a.m. and Nadovu about 8.30, and arrived in Suva between 11.30 and 12 midday, quickly completed their errands and shopping, boarded the homeward bus before it left Suva at 2.00 in the afternoon, and reached home around 5.30 or 6 p.m.

The often expressed opinion of town life was that it was difficult if one had little money: the town 'ate up' money and one could not eat without paying cash for the food. This negative — or pragmatic — view possibly stemmed from the fact that few people from the district had succeeded in establishing themselves in secure jobs in town. The majority had only experienced urban life as low-paid labourers or semi-skilled workers, often living in difficult conditions in the peri-urban Fijian settlements. Such attitudes which contributed to the short duration of trips to town were reinforced by the absence of many relatives or contacts with whom to stay there. Trips to Tavua where there was nearby a settlement of district people (Lomalagi) were, however, generally of several days duration.

Figure 3
Frequency of Reported Move by Destination,
Wainimala Villagers, 1986

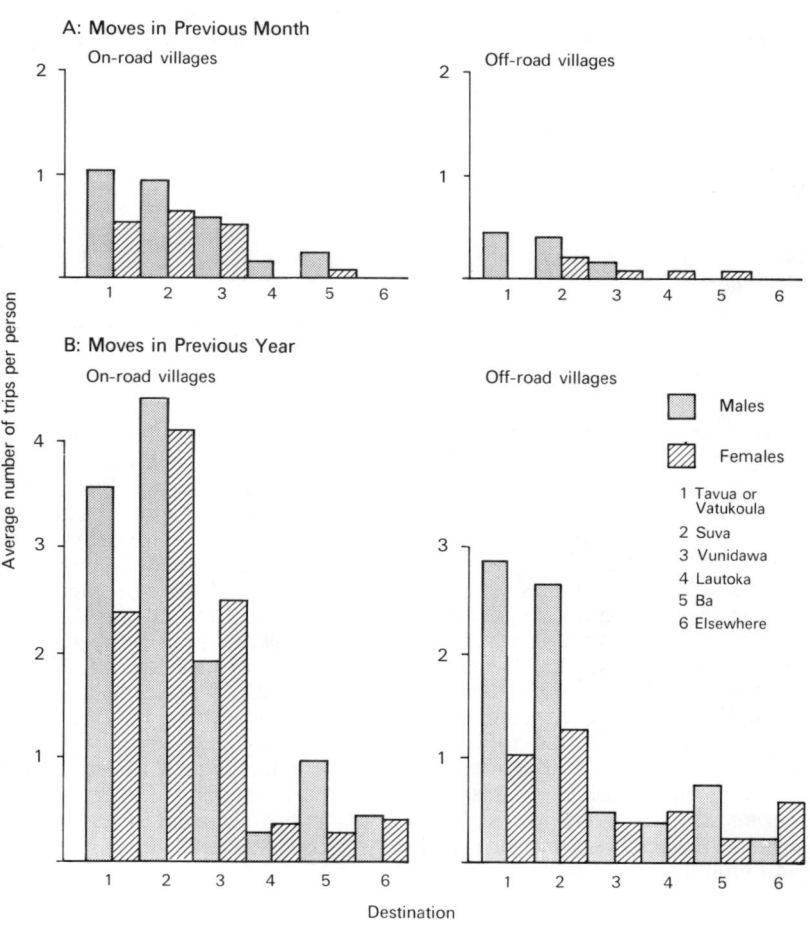

A: Moves in Previous Month

B: Moves in Previous Year

Average number of trips per person

Destination

Males

Females

1 Tavua or Vatukoula
2 Suva
3 Vunidawa
4 Lautoka
5 Ba
6 Elsewhere

Source: Table 2.

113

Table 2
Average Frequency of Trips for Wainimala Adults, 1986

Destination	Previous Month On-road villagers	Previous Month Off-road villagers	Previous Year On-road villagers	Previous Year Off-road villagers
Tavua	.7	.3	2.6	1.9
Suva	.6	.3	3.8	2.1
Vunidawa	.5	<.1	1.8	.5
Lautoka	<.1	<.1	.3	.3
Ba	<.1	<.1	.5	.5
Elsewhere	0	0	.4	.6

Source: Interviews, Wainimala, January-April, 1986.

Another dimension of population mobility is migration from the district. An examination of the residential histories of around 1100 Wainimala people of four generations revealed that throughout the colonial and post-colonial periods the dominant pattern of mobility had been for them — usually the men — to periodically engage in wage labour elsewhere — mostly in urban areas — to help support the rural lifestyles of their families and communities (Chung 1987). Interviews with a broad spectrum of district people strongly suggested that in the past decade people had less often left the district for work elsewhere, a finding which was supported by the small number of the *de jure* population absent and working elsewhere in early 1986. Partly this was because of improved opportunities for earning cash in Wainimala, and thus might be considered a positive effect of the road. In a broader context, however, there appeared to be three interrelated factors affecting present mobility decisions of Wainimala people: the retrenchment of the unskilled and semi-skilled urban job market in Fiji, the improvement in the prices of *yaqona*, and the extent to which family elders had accepted the conventional wisdom of the rural-urban drift and its supposedly attendant evils for young rural migrants.

Local recreational traffic. There was an active social life in the district, centred around church functions and group visits to neighbouring villages. For road-side villages, such trips had been made easier, and possibly more frequent, by the presence of the road and bus service. Some people claimed, however, that the road had served to decrease intra-district personal interaction, for before construction of the road when people had to walk out of the district, it was always necessary to sleep or rest at villages along the way. In this way strong and cohesive relationships developed between people of the district. Now that people rushed past on the bus there might be fewer opportunities to develop such relationships.

Access to rural public services. Better access to local public services and improvement in the quality of these services is a further expectation of road development. The present location of rural public services in Wainimala is shown in Figure 2. This discussion centres on the two most used: the schools and medical facilities.

The quality of education facilities had improved in the district since the advent of the road. In 1978 a junior secondary school providing education up to fourth form level was established at Laselevu. Existing primary schools at Laselevu, Lutu and Korovou reputedly benefitted from the new road in that their staffing levels and quality improved dramatically. Previously, few teachers wished to be posted to these schools, resulting in serious staff shortages and, in some cases where disgruntled staff were appointed, poor work performance. Several of the longer-serving and dedicated teachers were people of the district. The principals of both Noimalu and Muaira District Schools in 1986 reported that staffing shortages were no longer a problem. The management committees of the schools were quick to improve school facilities with the initial prosperity that came with the road. People of the district also noted that the performance of many students had improved markedly. The road had also made it easier for students from distant villages to travel home for the weekends.

The improvement of facilities was even more marked for district medical services. Since the establishment of the road the medical centre at Laselevu had been upgraded and a doctor stationed there. The health station at Narokorokoyawa had also been improved although it was still only staffed by a district nurse. In early 1986 a nursing station was under construction by villagers at Nadovu but the posting of a nurse there was still dependent on the further upgrading of the facilities provided by the villagers.

The situation with regard to the accessibility of medical facilities was more complicated than for schools, for the need for these services is often more urgent and cannot be planned in advance. The provision of a road resulted in more and higher qualified medical staff being posted to the district but despite their commitment to work they cannot be at their posts permanently. They must attend meetings, visit villages, relieve staff in other districts, and attend to personal matters away from the district. Even where there was both a doctor and a nurse, they were sometimes both absent. There was no way of communicating this information to the local people who then had the frustrating experience, having made their way to the clinic, of finding nobody there. Problems were aggravated by a tendency to delay seeking medical attention until a person's condition was quite serious. Nevertheless, the improved accessibility to medical facilities was commonly mentioned in interviews as one of the greatest benefits of the road.

The main medical centre for Wainimala is at Laselevu. This site was chosen long before the existence of the road, for in the time of river transport it was about the highest point on the river which could be safely navigated by outboard motor driven punts and therefore commonly visited by government officers[3]. However, even villagers in the immediate vicinity must either wade across the river to use the facilities or travel further down river to the nursing station at Saumakia.

The road had improved accessibility to services at Laselevu, Vunidawa and Suva — but in good weather only and when the bus timetable can be adhered to. In bad weather the improvement is less evident, as is illustrated by the hypothetical example of a sick villager at Lutu (Figure 2). She is virtually dependent on the bus to reach the medical facilities at Laselevu, Vunidawa or Suva, for little other traffic uses the road. She is unlikely to use the river: villagers on the upper reaches believe the hydro-electric dam at Monasavu has lowered the level of the river, making travel more hazardous. If the bus is running that day there is no particular problem. She might ride to the bus stop near Laselevu, get off the bus, walk about one mile to the river bank, wade across the river which is moderately swift and in places thigh-deep on an adult, and visit the doctor should he be there. If she manages to be back on the road within an hour and a half, she would be able to return to Lutu by bus the same day. Otherwise she must sleep in the village at Laselevu.

But should the weather be bad, problems begin to arise. In wet weather, crossing the river at Laselevu suddenly becomes impossible and it is necessary to travel by bus to Vunidawa. In 1986, a bridge was under construction to Vunidawa but it was still necessary for road users to take a punt across the river to the medical station[4]. When the river is high, the punt is unable to cross. Should river conditions become worse (as they do approximately five times a year) the Naqali bridge on the road between Vunidawa and Suva becomes impassible. This stops the bus service and all other traffic on the road, and although she is standing on the road, the Lutu villager is denied access to medical facilties as much as if that road did not exist. She cannot even reach the nursing station at Narokorokoyawa because the river there also cannot be crossed when the water is high.

This discussion of the location of medical facilities demonstrates that provision of a road does not of itself always improve access to rural public services. It also demonstrates another problem of rural public service provision: as Funnell (1976:91) reports, where population distributions within a region are uneven or low, differential accessibility can become very great.

---

3   It was possible to travel by boat further upstream to Lutu, but increasingly hazardous.

4   The partly completed bridge was swept away by flood waters in April 1986, and by early 1988 was still not rebuilt.

He noted that the very sharp distance-decay functions often reported around rural public services point to the fact that the centres in which facilities are located effectively provide for only a limited proportion of the surrounding population.

This examination of the effects of the Monasavu road suggests that, in the longer term, there had been little real change in the rural economy of Wainimala. There had, however, been some improvements in the quality of life in the district. By improving accessibility to markets and providing the opportunity to 'play' market conditions, the road had helped district farmers to exploit current good prices for their *yaqona*. However, improved accessibility had not been a suffcient force to change methods of production within the district. As Blaikie (1980:69) explains, an essential characteristic of semi-subsistence agriculture is limited choices and, therefore, vulnerability: this vulnerability remained, for their present prosperity depended on their *yaqona* crop and the market for this could come under attack from more efficent commercial farmers elsewhere. While local incomes had risen with better returns from *yaqona*, they were still quite low. There had been little expansion of local business or few new opprtunities for non-agricultural employment in the district, other than village house building. In the case of the local transport business, the success of the bus companies and the failure of local carrier operators acted to reduce local peoples' ability to capitalise on the opportunities theoretically provided by road access.

This conclusion as to the economic benefits of the road runs counter to, for example, those of the studies conducted in Papua New Guinea by Marion Ward. Her study of the Rigo road concluded that there had been considerable benefits 'even' in the comparatively short period of two years, (Ward 1970:77). Perhaps had the present study been conducted as soon after completion of the Monasavu road our conclusions may have been more similar. To the extent that patterns of short-term and longer-term impacts similar to those demonstrated by the Monasavu road can be observed elsewhere, the variation in the timing of impact studies may explain some variation in their conclusions.

THE IMPACT OF CHANGES IN THE NATIONAL ECONOMY

In assessing the impact of any project, it is necessary to consider the effects of events occurring outside the project area. In the case of the Monasavu road we have seen rising incomes, increased commercialisation of the *yaqona* crop, and a reduction in the number of people working away from the area. It would be tempting, perhaps, to claim these as benefits of the road. However, these 'effects' are more closely related to two broader trends in the national economy: the rapid increase in *yaqona* prices and the reduction in opportunities for short-term unskilled or semi-skilled urban employment.

The increase in *yaqona* prices

In 1986, the economy of Wainimala rested almost solely on *yaqona* production — as it has to varying degrees throughout the colonial and post-colonial periods. As already noted, it is difficult to assess accurately the extent to which *yaqona* production has increased since construction of the Monasavu road. What is clear, however, is that this has been a period of phenomenal increase in the *yaqona* price, of the order of 180 per cent in current terms since 1974 (Table 1, column 4). This increase only fortuitously coincided with the existence of the Monasavu road. The larger market forces controlling *yaqona* prices have nothing to do with the provision of the road and are beyond the control of the Wainimala people. The road has, however, facilitated Wainimala farmers' ability to gain the most advantageous prices on this market by providing them access to all Viti Levu markets and enabling them to adopt better marketing strategies.

Ellis' estimated producer prices for *yaqona*, the full market prices his estimations were based on, together with *yaqona* market prices complied from weekly reports in the *Fiji Times* and from Fiji Development Bank figures, have been assembled in Table 1. Values in columns 2, 3 and 4 do not coincide very closely; this reflects the use of different sources of information and the general difficulty of accurately calculating market prices. Ellis' figures end at 1982 and, therefore, do not show the quite spectacular increase in price since then. If the change in marketing arrangements is taken into account, it is clear that returns to farmers have effectively risen even faster than these figures suggest.

Of course, real incomes in the district have not risen to the extent that the *yaqona* prices have, for price increases have been closely followed by inflation, as shown by the Consumer Price Index (Figure 4). The CPI is only partially relevant to the lives of Wainimala people, for it is calculated on the basis of goods and services that people in the district do not consume; nevertheless they are affected by the general rise in the cost of living by way of items that are consumed and by greater transport costs. Their cost of living is also driven higher by new patterns of increased consumption (such as of imported foods) and perceptions of need that have been influenced by improved accessibility.

Subsistence agriculture is almost universally characterised by limited options (Blaikie 1980:69). Beyond *yaqona*, Wainimala people produce little that could provide them sufficent cash inflows. Although the road has allowed them to exploit current good market conditions, they remain very vulnerable for almost anything they grow can be produced more efficently by commercial farmers elsewhere. There is clear evidence that the present high prices for *yaqona* are attracting the attention of commercial growers, as has happened in previous periods of good returns. Several commercial ventures in other parts of Fiji propose to, or have begun to, produce *yaqona* on a large scale. One venture alone is scheduled to soon release *yaqona* onto the market in quantity, representing in 1988 7.2 per cent, in 1989 7.0 per cent, and in

Figure 4
Relationship Between Increase in *Yaqona* Prices and Consumer Price
Index, 1968-72

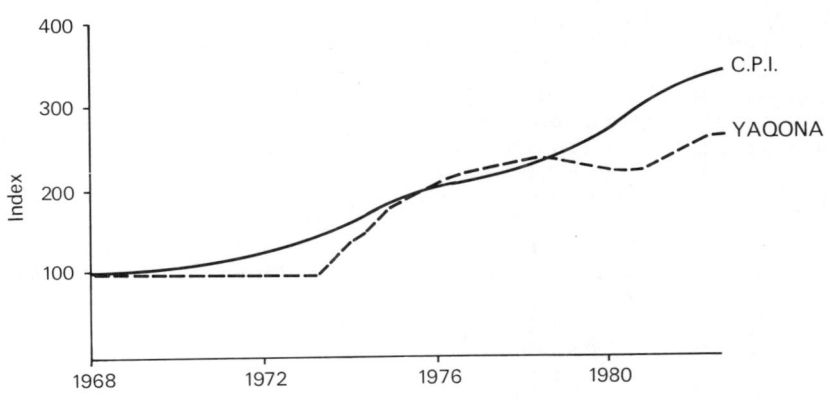

Source: Sofer 1985:421

1990 3.5 per cent (at 1989 levels) of total estimated production in these three years respectively (Fiji Development Bank, unpublished data). As no firm data exist as to the price elasticities of *yaqona* nor its substitution effects, it is impossible to predict the effect of this quantity on price. Previous boom and bust cycles in *yaqona* production resulted in semi-subsistence farmers being forced from the market. Again, such events are beyond the control of Wainimala people and beyond the sphere of influence of the Monasavu road.

The retrenchment of the national labour market

Increased cash returns from *yaqona* have reduced the need for Wainimala people to find work beyond the region and this is fortuitous, for in the period since the mid-1970s the national labour market has contracted sharply.

Throughout the colonial and post-colonial periods, Wainimala people who have left the district in search of employment have gone mostly to unskilled or semi-skilled labouring jobs in urban areas and of short duration (Chung 1987). For men, this involved labouring in mines, factories, quarries, building sites, etc; and for women, domestic service or cafeteria kitchen work. The general entrenchment of the national labour market, and of this employment category in particular, was detailed by the Fiji Employment and Development Mission (Bienefeld 1984:201-2). Although the early 1970s was a period when the labour market was absorbent, after 1975, Bienefeld reported, there was a marked decline in the rate of growth in formal wage and salary jobs. This decline in the growth of the job market coincided with a bulge in the national population structure, and a sudden increase in the number of people joining the job market. He noted that the rise in unemployment levels was substantially less than would have been expected from the number of jobs available in the formal wage salary sector. He therefore concluded that many people must have been absorbed into self-employment, unpaid family work, and village employment. By Employment Mission calculations, this type of employment must have grown by about 3.3 per cent per year between 1975 and 1980. This conclusion was corroborated by the 1982 Employment Survey, which suggested that between 1976 and 1982 the increase was more than 35 per cent, enough to make the figures after 1980 plausible. The increase in the number of villagers probably represented more the ability of the semi-subsistence sector to absorb excess labour than to employ this excess labour.

Again, this trend in Fiji labour force absorption has coincided with the construction of the road but is determined by forces beyond the bounds of Wainimala and even Fiji. Its effect, in combination with improved opportunities for earning cash in the district, has been to reduce the number of people looking for short-term employment elsewhere and to encourage the return of some people to Wainimala who were working outside the district.

CONCLUSION: ROADS IN RETROSPECT

This paper has examined two problems in assessing the impact of roads. The first is that the timing of impact studies should take into consideration time-differentiated effects. The second is that impact studies need to look beyond the project boundaries to consider broader structural changes in the national economy. Developments in Wainimala following construction of the Monasavu road further demonstrate that roads may be a necessary but clearly not sufficent condition for agricultural development (cf. Blaikie *et al*. 1977; Airey 1984). The contrast between the optimism regarding the effects of roads that is often apparent in planning documents and the limited positive effects that subsequent studies reveal, should be a matter for concern. It is apparent that development, however defined, requires more than a road and a regional development policy for which transport improvements are a critical item in initiating socioeconomic change may be a prescription for disillusionment. McCall (1977:64) suggests that roading projects are politically popular because 'rural roads are a symbol of state beneficience in health, water supplies, education, etc.' As we have seen in the case of Wainimala, provision of a road cannot alone induce sufficent economic change to remove the structural bases of the regional, sectoral and social inequalities which exist between the traditional and modern sectors of Fiji's economy. Policies which directly dealt with such inequalities would probably be much more difficult to design and politically less expedient.

Fording a river, Wainimala

The Monasavu Road

9

LAND SETTLEMENT AS A RURAL DEVELOPMENT STRATEGY

Tim Bayliss-Smith and Patrick Haynes

LAND SETTLEMENT AND AGRARIAN CHANGE

Regional imbalance has become one of the most pervasive features of the human geography of less developed countries, as a result of regional or urban bias in the patterns of population growth, expansion in economic opportunity, and innovation in technology. At a certain stage of rural transformation, 'land settlement' or 'agricultural colonisation' is often seen as part of the answer to this problem. Modern resettlement schemes are occurring in the context of steady and rapid growth in both population and, in the broad sense, technology and are an integral part of the whole process of state planning that has come to be called development.

Phase I: Local resettlement

Belshaw (1984) has recently proposed a three-phase model which provides a useful basis for classifying land settlement schemes. Phase I (local resettlement) occurs when an expanding rural population can be accommodated by short-distance migration to vacant land of similar potential to that which it already occupies. This process is spontaneous and usually involves minimal dislocation of existing social networks.

Traditional land tenure practices are adopted by the settlers, although there is a tendency for communal tenure systems to be modified through time into *de facto* freehold, particularly if perennial cash crops are planted and other land-saving capital formation occurs, such as drainage and terracing. Belshaw (1984: 272) comments that it may well be futile for the state to attempt to play a prominent role in this phase, but "both efficiency and equity gains can often be secured from low-cost, pump-priming public investment in physical infrastructure, e.g. roads, domestic water supply and basic health facilities".

In Fiji, in the early part of this century the expansion of Indian smallholder settlements outside the perimeter of cane farming can be seen as a spontaneous phase I colonisation process, constrained only by legal restrictions on land acquisition from the indigenous Fijian population.

During this phase, and alongside spontaneous resettlement, there may occur (as in New Guinea) the growth of large-scale production units and the allocation of unused areas to forest reserve. At this stage this sector poses no major efficiency or equity problems, even though it has limited multiplier effects. It is typically land-extensive, management intensive, and often involves high-risk monoculture buffered by state or multi-national institutions. Its advantage to the state is that production occurs from otherwise little-used resources, while locally some employment is provided, an opportunity usually exploited by individuals on a short-term basis. Circular mobility between villages and plantations has been the typical response of Pacific islanders to this opportunity (Bedford 1981; Ward 1980a).

Phase II: Inter-regional resettlement

The second phase begins when settlement opportunities within the jurisdiction of local ethnic groups are closed off as a result of the end of local resettlement and allocation of vacant land to extensive forms of land use. At this stage "the transcending and unifying power of the nation-state is required to create an inter-regional planning framework for the transfer and absorption of newcomers into what is often perceived as a socially as well as physically hostile environment" (Belshaw 1984: 273). These formal 'land settlement' projects, termed 'agricultural colonisation' in South Asia (Farmer 1957, 1974; Samarasinghe and Samarasinghe 1984), may well lead to a later period of spontaneous, phase I-type settlement. It is at this stage that extensive forms of land use come under increasing attack, both politically and physically. In Africa, forest areas and game reserves have proved particularly vulnerable, while in the Pacific the coconut plantation sector has come under pressure — for example, in the Solomon Islands — to either develop unused land or else return it to local communities. Where the state itself has a vested interest in retaining exclusive control, through public institutions involved in cattle ranching or forestry, conflicts can be particularly difficult to resolve. Growth of rural populations and the monetisation of an increasing proportion of rural production means that a *de facto* land market generally emerges in this phase, but it need not lead to the creation of a rural landless class except in urban areas. Circular migration continues to enable individuals to retain some residual rights to rural land.

Phase III: Intensification

The onset of phase III (intensification) is marked by the closing off of a frontier of fertile land anywhere in the rural sector. If there is still spontaneous resettlement then it is into low-potential areas liable to drought, soil erosion or flooding, and it "becomes more a part of the problem than its solution" (Belshaw 1984: 274). This is the phase of intensification of existing activities, but land settlement can still play a limited role when a radical change in land use occurs. Such an opportunity is presented by land reform, for example, through the redistribution of *hacienda* land in Latin America (Smith 1984), and by irrigation or land reclamation schemes (Chambers 1969; Harriss 1984). The large scale of state investment in such schemes means that the planners desire to retain management control over land and water use, so that short-term tenancy arrangements may be adopted. These arrangements may act as a disincentive for investment and discourage continued commitment to scheme participation, but, on the other hand, freehold title may lead to undesirable levels of land accumulation (Belshaw 1984:277). In other ways, too, difficult trade-offs between efficiency and equity objectives will become more frequent for planners in this phase, with the desire to reduce rural unemployment, through small holdings, often conflicting with the simultaneous desire to maximise marketed surplus, through larger farms where Green Revolution or mechanised technology becomes feasible (Brookfield 1979; Ward and Proctor 1980).

Although the forms of state intervention that are needed vary in these different phases of rural transformation, at all stages land settlement has proved to be popular with planners. One reason is that schemes of this kind seem bound to satisfy both efficiency and equity objectives. Land settlement combines under-utilised land and labour resources so as to raise production for, it would appear, rather low unit costs. Regional 'efficiency' is thereby enhanced. But, at the same time, such schemes provide new self-employment opportunities to underemployed families or to new entrants to the labour force, in both cases assisting directly the poorest sections of the rural community.

In practice, however, the results of state intervention have been mixed, as a number of studies in South Asia, tropical Africa and Latin America have shown (e.g. Farmer 1957, 1974; Chambers 1969; Lehmann 1974; Ward and Proctor 1980; Jones *et al.* 1982; Belshaw 1984). This chapter discusses land settlement in Fiji, and the extent to which its history has conformed to the sequence of phases outlined above. Reference is made, in particular, to data collected on Taveuni and elsewhere by a UNESCO/UNFPA study in 1974-1976, and to a study of the Seaqaqa scheme in western Vanua Levu by Atkins Land and Water Management Ltd., during the period 1982-1983. The underlying objective is to determine to what extent land settlement itself is an appropriate solution to the problems of efficiency and equity that countries such as Fiji are beginning to face.

LAND SETTLEMENT IN FIJI: THE INDIAN FRONTIER

The Fiji group contains islands differing widely in size and ecological problems, yet these potential sources of inequality are less important in practice than those which derive from the land tenure system. The unequal distribution of land relative to demand means that today in some areas and on some islands the people's land requirements are still easily satisfied by means of phase I-type processes of local resettlement; whereas elsewhere there are phase II schemes for long distance resettlement or even phase III intensification.

By the time of Cession to the British Crown in 1874, between 23 and 28 per cent of the best land on the main islands had already been sold by the Fijian chiefs to Europeans for plantations, though many of these were never developed (Ward 1965: 121). For the native (Fijian) land remaining under communal tenure, colonial land policy in effect fossilised the pattern of allocation of circa 1874, transforming a flexible system of traditional land annexation and redistribution into an artificially rigid one of strict inheritance within the clan (*mataqali*) group (France 1969). The result has been that those *mataqali* favoured by accidents of history in the period immediately prior to Cession found themselves with abundant land, whereas other *mataqali* were, and remain, disadvantaged.

Phase I: The haphazard frontier

The Indian immigrant population, or rather the 40 to 60 per cent who elected to remain in Fiji after their period of indenture was complete, found themselves from the late 19th century onwards in a situation where freehold land was virtually unobtainable, but where leases to small plots of native, Crown or freehold land could still be acquired, particularly in the period prior to the 1940s when the Fijian population was still village-based, subsistence-oriented, and recovering slowly from earlier depopulation. Most Indian settlers established themselves as close as possible to the sugar estates, which provided a market for surplus produce and a continuing source of casual employment. Thus there emerged a frontier of Indian land settlement spreading out from the cane areas. By 1917 there were 12,000 Indian farmers independently established, nearly 60 per cent of them as tenants on native land, and another 25 per cent using European freehold land on annual tenancies. Only 166 Indians had obtained freehold title to land, forming a small group of larger-scale proprietors with holdings averaging between 70 and 100 acres (28 and 40 ha). At the other extreme there were 1,500 tenants of Crown land with average holdings of three acres (one ha) representing a class of smallholders dependent on wage employment to supplement subsistence production. Anderson (1974: 55) comments:

There is no doubt that a process of economic differentiation was occurring in rural areas. ... the appearance of landlord-tenant relationships among Indians, for example, and of the *jemindar* (sharecropper) systems of sugar-cane production. Had tenure systems favoured (or at least not impeded) its manifestation in land proprietorship, a more sharply-polarized agrarian structure would probably have emerged.

As well as being relatively egalitarian, these settlements were also haphazard in form and distribution and fluctuating in composition (Mayer 1961). The patches of land that were available were scattered, and until 1940, native land was only available on ten-year leases. A high turnover in population occurred either because leases were not renewed or because settlers decided to move on or return to India (Chandra 1980).

Phase II: Sugar company settlements

During the early period of Indian resettlement (phase I) the land tenure system acted as a constraint on the emergence of inequities amongst the settlers. The organised settlement schemes of the Colonial Sugar Refining (CSR) company in the 1920s and 1930s achieved the same result, but in this case efficiency rather than equity was the primary intention. Inasmuch as the subdivision of estates was the rationale for these schemes, they can be said to represent a jump to phase III intensification of rural settlement and production. However, in Fiji, this stage occurred long before the frontier of land available for extensive resettlement was closed. Rather than representing intensification, these settlement schemes reflect the demands of sugar cane production, where inter-regional resettlement (i.e. phase II) is not technically feasible unless rail or road transport to local crushing mills is also available. It is this dependence upon capital-intensive infrastructure that has lead to the intensification of Indian settlement around Lautoka, Labasa, Penang and the other milling centres.

Organised land settlement first became necessary for CSR in 1920 when indenture was abolished, and it became clear that maintaining a plantation labour force would soon be an acute problem for the estates (Ward 1980b: 6). With labour problems and low prices most of the European growers withdrew from the industry, and most of the leased estates reverted to CSR. The initial CSR response to this problem depended on the location of land. Estates close to the mills either were subdivided into smallholdings leased to tenants under company supervision or, alternatively, were run as company estates. Land further away was subdivided into 50 to 60 acre (20 to 24 ha) blocks which were leased to Indian planters, who themselves subleased or employed plantation labour. After 1925, however, the independent tenant smallholding was increasingly adopted by CSR as a better means of ensuring a reliable cane supply with fewer of the overhead costs incurred in supervision or estate management.

In 1925, only 10 per cent of cane output came from tenants leasing CSR land, whereas 52 per cent derived from CSR estates. Ten years later the situation was reversed, with 52 per cent of cane produced by CSR tenants on holdings predominantly 10 to 20 acres (4 to 8 ha) in size, depending on land quality, and only 5 per cent grown on CSR estates. The remainder came from the almost extinct European estates (7 per cent) or from farmers contracted to CSR but leasing native or freehold land (Anderson 1974: 73). Cane growing became overwhelmingly an Indian occupation, with only 553 Fijian growers and two Europeans enumerated in 1943 out of a total of 8589 growers (Shephard 1945). By 1952, the number of Fijian growers had shrunk to 101 out of a total of 9842 (Twyford and Wright 1965: 181).

Between 1935 and 1945 the cane perimeter within which CSR settlement schemes operated was virtually static, but beyond, in the dry zones of Viti Levu and Vanua Levu, the frontier of Indian settlement not based on cane continued to advance. The Indian population grew at the rate of 2.3 per cent per annum from 1921 to 1936, and then at 3.4 to 3.6 per cent per annum throughout the next thirty years, in the context of a national economy with very limited expansion in non-agricultural employment. Many of the new Indian farms were located beyond the reach of the cane railways, and concentrated instead on maize, rice and other crops, and on pastoralism. New markets for sugar after 1950 enabled CSR to issue new contracts to some of these mixed farmers, who were drawn into mill catchments by rail extension plus the use of lorry transport for the cane. On Vanua Levu the cane perimeter was extended by rail construction westwards from Labasa as far as the Wailevu Valley, but the scattered Indian settlements that lay beyond remained isolated from Labasa — for example, the settlements in the Tabia Valley, in the Seaqaqa region, and along the Dreketi River.

Origins of state involvement

The effect, if not the intention, of CSR land settlement policies was thus gradually to exclude the Fijian population from the most lucrative and dynamic sector of the rural economy. The Fijians were left with subsistence agriculture and copra, both increasingly unsatisfactory as a basis for rural welfare. As Fisk (1970) pointed out, the subsistence sector, however affluent, is essentially stagnant, so that economic advancement for Fijians in the post-war period began to depend heavily on copra, an industry that has been described as having "the almost medieval structure of ... low capitalisation, high labour coefficient, ancient technology, minimal R & D input, and archaic systems of marketing and transportation" (Brookfield 1977; 136).

By 1960 the process of local resettlement was virtually complete. Population growth among the Fijian community was beginning to match the continued expansion of the Indian population, and land was becoming an increasingly sensitive political issue. Overgrazing, frequent burning and soil erosion were all too evident on some marginal land, particularly in western Viti Levu, and there were signs also of rural under-employment. Yet population movement away from the cane districts to other parts of the country where Fijian land was not fully utilised was surprisingly limited. One constraint was uncertainties in land tenure: "the area which may eventually be leased is unknown until the native reserves have been declared. The N.L.T.B. is unwilling to approve leases in advance of declaration and the slow rate of reserve demarcation and proclamation has seriously hindered land settlement" (Ward 1965: 130).

The year 1960 did not represent in Fiji the end of phase I of land settlement, since for Fijians in particular the process accelerated in the 1960s and continues to this day in places with good cash cropping potential such as Taveuni, Koro and interior Viti Levu. It does, however, mark the beginning of a second phase, that of formalised inter-regional resettlement schemes. These have been very different in character from the pragmatic CSR schemes for estate subdivision in the inter-war period. For the Indian community the cane settlements simultaneously achieved efficiency and equity to a remarkable degree, with CSR providing overall control in a way which the British colonial government was not willing to consider. The attitude of government changed after 1960, with the onset of comprehensive development planning in which land settlement occupied an important place.

LAND SETTLEMENT FOR FIJIANS: BRITISH COLONIAL EXPERIMENTS

During 1960 a development plan for the coming decade was prepared, with a heavy emphasis on expenditure for improving communications and agriculture. The underlying intention was clearly to boost economic growth in the Fijian sector of the economy, as a means of reducing racial tensions and as a necessary precondition for ultimate political independence. Land settlement was an important component of this plan, since it seemed to provide the most efficient means whereby Fijian farmers could escape from all of the constraints which Spate, Burns and other reports of the time had identified. Watters (1969a: 261) summarised these constraints as follows:

Cultural. Some traditional motivations and attitudes persist, so that Fijians fail to respond fully to economic stimuli.

Structural. Preconditions for economic growth in rural areas, particularly capital, transport and markets, are absent and obstacles in the form of common land tenure systems and communal labour obligations are present.

Physical. There are perceived deficiencies in soil resources, in the available agricultural technology, or in security from climatic hazards, compounded in some cases by rates of population growth which reduce the net returns from growth.

By resettling independent farmers (*galala*) on new land remote from existing villages it was hoped that a new society of Fijian peasants would emerge, market oriented, innovative, and free from communal restrictions. The settlers were to be selected from the ranks of effectively landless *mataqali*, so that equity as well as efficiency would be promoted. To initiate and finance the proposed land development and settlement schemes a Land Development Authority (LDA) was established in 1961. Watters (1969a: 274) echoed the consensus view of development planners:

> Here, clearly, is the type of institution needed to promote the settlement of interior pockets of land by Fijians and others as independent farmers on secure tenancies. If such institutions can avoid the twin dangers of excessive paternalism and bureaucracy and their planning is technically sound, they could play a crucial role in rural development and accelerate the rate of social change in Fijian society.

On paper, progress of land settlement appeared to be rapid. In 1965, over 1000 new farmers were established by the LDA, mainly on Viti Levu, double the number of the previous year. In 1967, 5140 new farms were created along new feeder roads, occupying a total area of 40,000 hectares (Watters 1969a: 274). Yet before the end of the 1960s, "this ambitious programme quickly failed and collapsed altogether" (Brookfield 1979: 36). After the spectacular failure of a 'showpiece' scheme at Lomaivuna in 1968 the LDA was run down and, just before Independence (1970), was abolished, its remaining functions being distributed among the established government departments.

Why was this land settlement programme regarded as so unsuccessful, and indeed by what criteria should we evaluate 'success' or 'failure'? A brief glance at two such schemes indicates that despite apparent failure, land settlement schemes might well loosen the grip of cultural and structural constraints on economic growth, but in ways unforeseen by the schemes' initial architects.

Sawani-Serea road

The origins of the settlements along the Sawani-Serea road in south-west Viti Levu have been traced by Ward (1965: 182) to 1954/55, when the road link to Suva was first constructed. Lau islanders visited Sawani village and negotiated informal land leases at Waibau through traditional means. These spontaneous settlements were then formalised by the NLTB, who organised a subdivision into blocks averaging 6 hectares, which were occupied mainly by migrants from resource-poor islands in southern Lau. Initially, the settlers planted taro and *yaqona* for the Suva market, as did local villagers many of whom took advantage of the new road link to establish new farms outside their former villages. In the 1960s, however, the settlers were encouraged to shift the focus of their activities to banana production, in order to benefit from the agricultural extension effort that accompanied the LDA's much larger Lomaivuna settlement scheme which was carved out of forest in this same area. By the end of 1963, 200 settlers were established at Lomaivuna on 10 acre (four ha) holdings. In the first year over 100,000 cases of bananas were produced, but success was short-lived: falling yields, disease and hurricane damage brought the banana farms to the point of collapse within five years, at which time the government withdrew all supervision. Government establishment costs per farm were high, averaging F£1,200, which included the cost of land clearance and planting, feeder roads and electricity supply. In addition, there were personal loans to settlers, most of which were never repaid (Ward 1965: 182-186, Watters 1969a: 274; UNESCO/UNFPA 1977: 160-161).

To what extent the settlers shared the gloom and despondency of the development planners is, however, unclear. After the collapse of bananas some settlers did leave Lomaivuna, a few permanently, but those farmers that remained changed to taro, *yaqona* and subsistence cropping, supplying the expanding Suva market with great success (UNESCO/UNFPA 1977: 161). At the 1976 census, Lomaivuna settlement had a population of 1515 in 235 households, of which 193 were Fijian, 18 Indian and 25 other. Although detailed studies have not been done, it would appear that the original 200 blocks have more than maintained their initial population. Despite the disruptions that resulted from inappropriate land use planning in the 1960s, the Sawani-Serea road settlements seem to support Ward's (1965: 186) verdict on the initial Waibau subdivision of 1956, that it represents an important stage of change from shifting, semi-subsistence cultivation to stable commercial small-holding farming by Fijians.

Taveuni

In the early 1960s three subdivision schemes of the LDA were established on the island of Taveuni (Brookfield 1979). The object was to establish coconut-cocoa farms of about eight hectares, with marketing channels to be developed aided by the Cooperatives Department. By 1967, three initial schemes were in operation, although with varying degrees of completeness and success. Meanwhile, the enthusiasm for subdivision of villagers elsewhere in Taveuni had, in Brookfield's view (1979: 39-40). "got out of hand":

> Almost every village set up its subdivision scheme, but the plans did not meet approval .... Only a minority of the settlers moved onto the blocks to live; most found their blocks too remote from the villages, and only a few elements in the programmed network of access roads were ever constructed. By 1970 most blocks lying any distance from the roads lay untouched, or had less than a hectare cleared, planted and then neglected.

As in the Sawani-Serea road settlements, the failure of the main cash crop (on Taveuni, cocoa) appeared to mark the end. Three schemes on Taveuni were actually implemented through the various stages of survey, establishment, supervision, and issue of leases. Even on these schemes not all leases were issued, but at first this land was treated by occupants as though they had been (Brookfield 1979: 37). In 1969, there were 132 listed cocoa growers, 93 on settlement schemes, but remoteness from fermentaries, disease and low prices meant that by 1973 cocoa production had virtually ceased. However in the mid-1970s, there was a revival of the settlement movement, based not on export crops but on *yaqona* and taro, again serving the Suva market. In 1976, Brookfield found (1976: 9) that:

> Men who had lost interest have returned to their blocks to resume clearing and planting, perhaps establishing houses on their blocks for the first time ... new settlement clusters have begun to arise under local leadership, creating in effect new semi-independent foci of rural settlement, separate from the parent villages.

Unfortunately, by 1983, pressure from *mataqali* owners had forced out those settlers whose leases had never been formalised in the 1960s (Bayliss-Smith *et al*. 1988). The failure of Government to follow up the spontaneous local resettlement process of the mid-1960s, despite its mid-1970s revival, meant that an opportunity for a more effective land reform in Taveuni appears to have been lost. The measure of success which was achieved occurred "in spite of the failure of the grandiose plans of which it formed a part, and in spite of the collapse and extinction of the organisation created to serve it" (Brookfield 1979: 51).

THE SEAQAQA SCHEME: LEARNING FROM MISTAKES?

After Independence, in 1970, central government's planning for rural development became dominated by two urgent priorities. The first was the need to reorganise and strengthen the sugar industry, which despite the growth of tourism still accounted for about one-fifth of GDP and two-thirds of domestic exports. In 1970, the industry was in a state of turmoil, as the cane contract between the millers (South Pacific Sugar Mills Ltd., established by CSR in 1962) and the growers became the subject of acrimonious dispute. The settlement that was eventually achieved was unacceptable to CSR, who decided to abandon altogether their interests in Fiji. All their assets were acquired by the Fiji Government who set up, in 1973, the Fiji Sugar Corporation (FSC). Meanwhile sugar production was in decline, falling to a level that in both 1974 and 1975 was only 82 per cent of the average annual production between 1966 and 1970.

The second urgent need was to involve the indigenous Fijian population more fully in commercial agriculture. The five-year Development Plan published in 1975 stated that "Government is committed to achieve a more equitable distribution of the fruits of development in this plan period", which implied an emphasis on "the rural population generally and the Fijian population in particular" (Fiji Central Planning Office 1975: 5).

The Seaqaqa settlement scheme was attractive in that it promised to help fulfil both these objectives of sugar expansion and Fijian involvement. In retrospect, it has also been justified by its contribution towards the objectives of a more regionally balanced pattern of development. This regional objective was only implicit in Development Plan 7 (1975), but became more explicit in DP8 (1980).

Resources and hazards

Seaqaqa is located within western Vanua Levu (Figure 1), which is today still one of the least-developed lowland regions of the country. Prior to the initiation of the settlement scheme in 1974 the area that has become known as Seaqaqa was sparsely settled, with about 150 Indian and 50 Fijian families whose production was limited to subsistence crops and a small marketed surplus of cattle, rice, root crops and *yaqona*.

It is an area of rolling to hilly land crossed by small streams draining into the Dreketi River. Until the 1950s access was possible only by river or along footpaths, but by 1960 there was a road link from Labasa to Dreketi which passed through Natua, the village later chosen as the site of Seaqaqa township. The World Bank estimated in 1976 that only about half of the area was of moderate slope suitable for cultivation, but with soil conservation measures another 25 per cent could be developed for citrus or other tree crops. Most of the soils where sugar cane was proposed are red latosolic clays and clay loams, strongly leached, acid and deficient in nutrients. The World Bank report commented that the soils are "erodible and of poor water retention capacity. They will need careful management and heavy fertilizer applications to yield satisfactorily" (World Bank 1976: 7).

Rainfall averages 2.5 to 2.9m with, on average, only four dry months each year (i.e. months with less than 100mm rainfall). This climate would appear to be ideal for sugar cane but, unfortunately, year-to-year variations are substantial. Analysis of the rainfall data for three stations shows that drought conditions (i.e. months with less than 60mm rainfall) can occur for several consecutive months. For example, there have been four occasions in thirty-one years of records when four consecutive drought months have been experienced. Droughts of this duration represent a severe hazard for small cane farmers. Hurricane-force winds and associated torrential rainfall also occur, with major damage experienced on three occasions in the last hundred years of records (Atkins 1983).

Figure 1
Western Vanua Levu
Average Household Incomes, 1982-1983

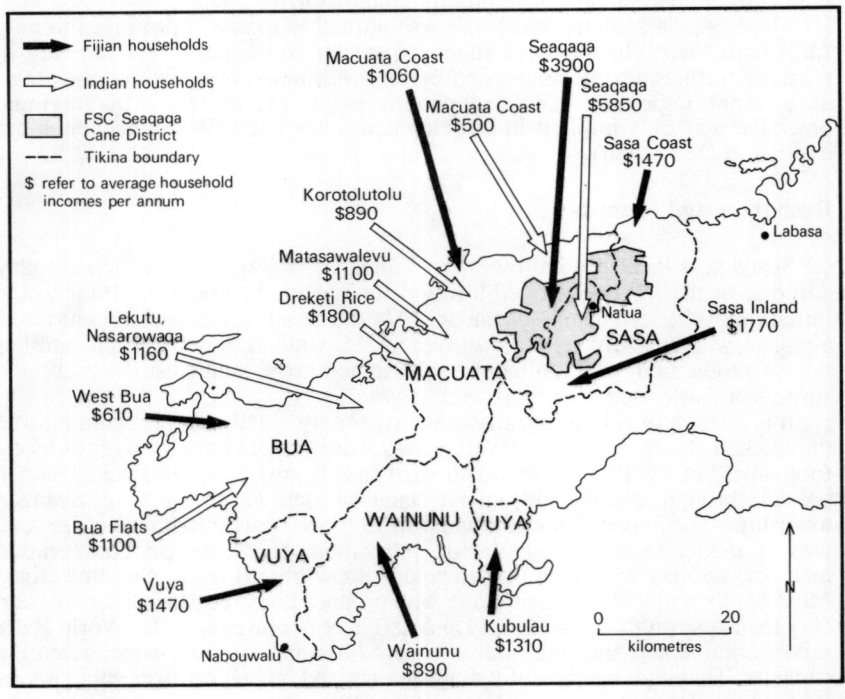

The scheme in outline

Land settlement at Seaqaqa was started in 1974 by the Fiji Government as part of a larger plan which also included improved drainage of existing sugar cane land near Labasa and elsewhere, and the enhancement of cane milling capacity. As a consequence of World Bank funding Seaqaqa was established as a special project in 1976. The expanded scheme was planned to settle some 800 farmers on six-hectare cane plots, occupying some 5,000 hectares of land. However, because of the uneven topography and variable soils, more than three times the area required for sugar cane was occupied. In total the project area covers some 18,000 hectares of native land, which was subdivided by NLTB and made available on thirty-year leases. In 1981, the scheme ceased to have special project status and it is now administered as a normal cane district by the FSC.

The cost of the settlement scheme itself was estimated at $18.4 million, including land clearance, construction of roads, acquisition of tractors and implements, cane transport facilities, and the development of a new township at Natua (renamed Seaqaqa). Additional costs were incurred in land drainage and seawall construction elsewhere on Vanua Levu, to bring the total cost of the project to $22.25[1] million, of which 46 per cent was estimated to be in foreign exchange (World Bank 1976)[2]. According to the original plan for Seaqaqa, a mixed cropping pattern was anticipated by the World Bank (1976: 8):

> In addition to sugar cane, each farm is being planted with about 1 ac of mixed citrus and 0.1 ac of pineapples for the local market. Subsistence rice, root crops and vegetables would be grown on small plots ....

This intended pattern of supplementary cropping has not so far received financial or extension support from FSC, whose exclusive concern for sugar

---

[1] The original cost estimates in the 1976 World Bank report were in U.S. dollars. The first estimate was $US21.5 million (then $F18.4 million), rising later to $US26 million ($F22.25 million).

[2] To achieve some perspective on these figures, it is worth recalling that in 1965 the Bua Flats rice scheme on Vanua Levu only cost in total F£5000, of which F£3200 was contributed by the settlers themselves, in order to establish 67 new farms (Watters 1969a: 274). This cost represents only about $210 per farm at 1982 prices. The Lomaivuna banana settlements on Viti Levu involved 200 farms on the Sawani-Serea road, at an average cost (in 1982 prices) of $8800 per farm. When Lomaivuna was officially abandoned as a banana scheme just before Independence it was regarded as an expensive fiasco. Five years later Seaqaqa, costing $18.4 million to establish 800 farmers and about 100 service personnel in Seaqaqa township, represents (at 1982 prices) an expenditure of $33,800 per household (farm and town). This astonishing escalation in real costs is a measure of the Government's determination to maintain the sugar industry, and of its continuing commitment to land settlement as a strategy for rural development.

cane production is reminiscent of the exclusive focus on bananas in the Sawani-Serea scheme and on cocoa in the settlement schemes on Taveuni.

The extent of under-utilisation of land resources in the Seaqaqa scheme was shown in a sample survey in 1983 by Atkins Land and Water Management (Gunasekera *et al*. 1983). The total land area within the scheme is 18,038 hectares — 53 per cent of which is rated as class II or class III land — 5008 hectares are planted with sugar and a further 380 hectares are recorded as growing citrus, rice or coconuts. It appeared that, on average, 1 hectare was allocated for food crop production on each farmstead, implying that altogether some 850 hectares are devoted to various non-cane crops. Of the land on which cane was cultivated, 610 hectares was land classed as more suitable for tree crops or grazing. Some 12,646 hectares are classified as unused, of which 4200 hectares or 44 per cent was potentially suitable for arable farming.

Evaluation of the scheme: Efficiency

The Seaqaqa scheme represents a very large financial commitment for a small country like Fiji. Throughout the late 1970s expenditure on the scheme amounted to at least 10 per cent of all government expenditure on economic services. Loans to Seaqaqa settlers accounted for 30 per cent of all agricultural loans made by the Fiji Development Bank during this period (Fiji Bureau of Statistics 1983a: 32, 48). To what extent have the scheme's production objectives been fulfilled?

The World Bank estimated that 800 cane farmers at Seaqaqa should produce by 1980 about 200,000 tonnes of cane each year, representing raw sugar exports of 25,000 tonnes (World Bank 1976: ii). When measured against these projections the project is undoubtedly successful. In 1979 cane production was 241,000 tonnes, and by 1983 Seaqaqa's output had reached 316,000 tonnes from 837 farm holdings (35 operated as an estate by NLTB, the remainder individual farms).

This resounding success in terms of total production unfortunately has not been matched by foreign exchange earnings on the scale envisaged by World Bank, because their calculations were based on the exceptionally high sugar prices of 1975. The World Bank calculated in 1976 that the 200,000 tonnes of cane projected for Seaqaqa would earn $6.85 million in foreign exchange. This target has been met, but only because output has been much higher than was anticipated. With the exception of 1980, prices received by farmers for sugar exports have been declining steadily in real terms since 1975. Although the EEC-subsidised price of $25 per tonne that farmers now receive is two and a half times the 1973 price, the consumer price index in Fiji has risen by almost exactly the same amount, and cane production costs have risen in real terms even more. At Seaqaqa, fertiliser and harvesting costs alone now amount to $15 per tonne, and lorry transport to the mill cost a further $6 per tonne. With Fiji's sugar production exceeding its EEC quota, and with the world price that is received by FSC for the remainder falling in 1983 to the equivalent of $12 per tonne of cane, there seems to be little immediate prospect for improvement. The resulting erosion in real incomes has been counteracted by increased productivity, but only for the efficient farmers. The overall success of the settlement scheme in production terms in fact obscures some important variations between farmers in performance.

Evaluation of the scheme: Equity

In any group of new settlement farmers, differences in economic performance are to be expected, but at Seaqaqa there is evidence that by 1983 at least 20 per cent of settlers were in grave financial difficulties. On one level it can be argued that the poor performers at Seaqaqa suffered from a combination of unexpectedly low cane prices, inadequate technical knowledge, poor financial management, and/or lack of motivation. At another level it can be suggested that the nature of the scheme itself is at fault, and that settlement schemes smaller in scale, less dependent on imported technology, and organised more flexibly might have a better prospect for long-term success than the present project.

Evidence of varying performance comes from a farm survey carried out by Atkins Land and Water Management consultants, together with records provided by the Fiji Development Bank (FDB) and the FSC (Atkins 1983; Gunasekera *et al.* 1983). These data showed that three groups of Seaqaqa settlers can be identified. The first group (about 200 farmers) appears to be financially sound, a middle group (about 500) is solvent but vulnerable financially, while the bottom 150 farmers are in considerable financial difficulty. Those farmers in the top group have net farm incomes in the range $5000 to $10,000 per year. At the other end of the scale are those with net incomes of $2000 or below, of whom a substantial number were accumulating increasing debts. The Fiji Development Bank estimated in 1983 that at least ninety farmers were unable or unlikely to meet their loan commitments, and in 1984 an even larger number were said to be in this category.

Table 1 identifies some of the characteristics of a random sample of thirty-one farmers who allowed examination of the FSC records of their gross cane income and expenses, and the details of their loan repayments to FDB. The poor performers (ten farmers with net cane incomes of minus $3169 to plus $1472) plant less cane, obtain a much lower yield, yet have higher fertiliser costs per tonne harvested than the remainder. The results suggest that they are under-utilising their total land holdings, and are using expensive fertiliser inefficiently. They are also burning a higher proportion of the crop, a procedure which facilitates harvesting but reduces cane quality, and may reflect the difficulties of these farmers in obtaining enough labour for cane cutting.

Indian farmers do slightly better than Fijian farmers on all of the above performance indicators, but not much of the statistical variation in the sample can be accounted for in this way (Table 2). Nevertheless, on the whole, a

Table 1
Data for 31 Seaqaqa Farmers, 1983
By Income Group

	Size of net cane income		
	-$3,169 to +$1,472	$1,957 to $5,040	$6,217 to $10,341
Sample (number of farmers)	10	12	9
Characteristics of farmer			
Average age	33	47	41
Number of years on farm	6.2	6.6	7.0
Size of household	6.3	6.8	7.3
Average costs and returns ($)			
Fertiliser	881	1,205	1,653
Harvesting	1,538	3,008	5,235
Net cane income	414	3,728	8,265
Farm data			
Area in cane (ha)	4.4	6.1	7.4
Area of farm (ha)	22	22	25
Amount of cane cut (t)	148	284	509
Efficiency			
Proportion of farm planted with cane (%)	20	24	30
Cane yield (t/ha)	34	42	69
Fertiliser costs per tonne cut ($)	5.95	4.24	3.25
Harvesting costs per tonne cut ($)	10.39	10.59	10.28
Cane burnt (%)	24	29	12

Source: Field Interviews, FSC Records and FDB Data (for details, see Atkins 1983 and Gunasekera *et al.* 1983)

Table 2
Data for 31 Seaqaqa Farmers, 1983
By Racial Group

	Fijians	Indians	Total
Sample (number of farmers)	17	14	31
Average costs and returns ($)			
Fertiliser	1,222	1,241	1,230
Harvesting	3,025	3,370	3,180
Net cane income	3,230	4,614	3,855
Farm data			
Area of cane (ha)	5.7	6.1	5.9
Area of farm (ha)	24	21	23
Amount of cane cut (t)	294	319	305
Efficiency			
Proportion of farm planted with cane (%)	24	29	26
Cane yields (t/ha)	52	52	52
Fertiliser costs per tonne cut ($)	4.16	3.89	4.03
Harvesting costs per tonne cut	10.29	0.56	10.42
Cane burnt (%)	26	14	20
Non-cane income[a] ($)			
Average per farm	472	981	700

[a] Non-cane income data are available for 22 Fijian and 18 Indian farmers, but figures shown here exclude one exceptional Fijian farmer (supplementary income of $5000) and one exceptional Indian ($50,000)

Source: Field interviews, FSC Records and FDB Data (for details, see Atkins 1983 and Gunasekera *et al.* 1983)

higher proportion of Fijians are experiencing financial difficulties, as shown by the numbers who in 1981 did not succeed in producing enough cane to cover the credit allowance made by FSC at the start of the season to cover input costs. This credit, known as the Farm Basic Allowance (FBA), is estimated by FSC field staff according to the amount of land the farmer has prepared and made ready for planting and is expressed in terms of the anticipated production of cane to be delivered to the sugar mill in Labasa. In 1981, only 53 per cent of farmers at Seaqaqa succeeded in meeting their FBA repayments. Of these successful farmers 32 per cent were ethnic Fijians while 78 per cent were ethnic Indian.

Despite the growing number of near-bankrupt settlers, the majority of all Seaqaqa farmers have managed to achieve incomes that are substantially in excess of rural incomes elsewhere in western Vanua Levu. A number of surveys of Fijian villages and Indian settlers in other parts of the region (Atkins 1983; Bayliss-Smith 1983; Gunasekera *et al*. 1983) have shown that average household incomes on the settlement scheme are not matched by those of any other section of the agricultural population (Figure 1). It is true that many people elsewhere in the region have access to a subsistence income which, to a surprising degree, the Seaqaqa settlers have not yet achieved, but even taking this fact into account there is no doubt that the Seaqaqa scheme has sharpened the differences between various sections of the rural population in Vanua Levu.

Unfortunately, the example of the Seaqaqa settlers is not one that can be imitated by other farmers in the region, since without FSC infrastructure, transport and cane contracts they are totally excluded from cane production. The participation of outsiders is limited to wage labour in the cane cutting season, and the Seaqaqa scheme is heavily dependent on migrant workers for this task. In 1982, 1600 cane cutters out of a total labour force of almost 2000 came into the Seaqaqa region from outside. These migrants were mainly Fijians, and included over 500 from the islands of Lau and Lomaiviti in Eastern Division (Table 3). The workers received around $5 per day gross, but living costs and, for village groups, communal savings schemes absorbed a high proportion of this wage.

Illustrative of the unrewarding nature of cane cutting are the 236 Lau islanders recruited by the Lau Provincial Council for the 1982 season (Table 4). The Council provided free transport for the men, who came from seven small islands. Gross pay averaged $1.46 per person/day during the five month season, of which living expenses and contributions to communal schemes accounted for almost half, leaving only $0.83 per day for the cutters themselves. The fourteen villages from which they came each gained on average $727 in communal savings, but the average of $127 net which each person earned (much of it spent locally in shops, bars and buses) amounts to a trivial individual reward whatever the compensations in communal prestige. The work itself is regarded as exceptionally hard, and living conditions (including diet) leave much to be desired.

Table 3
Number and Origin of Cane Cutters at Seaqaqa,
Harvesting Season, 1982

Place of origin	Number of cane cutters	Percentage of total
Northern Division	1,391	70.0
Seaqaqa and local[a]	387	19.5
Other Macuata[b]	270	13.6
Bua	392	19.7
Cakaudrove excluding Taveuni	171	8.6
Taveuni and Qamea islands	171	8.6
Eastern Division	532	26.8
Lomaiviti group	178	9.0
Moala group	57	2.9
Northern Lau	134	6.7
Central and southern Lau	93	4.7
Kadavu group	18	0.9
Not specified	52	2.6
Central Division	65	3.3
Tailevu	65	3.3
Total	1,988	100.0
Fijian	1,723	86.7
Indian[c]	265	13.3

a Refers mainly to cutters from Seaqaqa itself, and also to a few from immediately adjacent villages.
b Refers mainly to villages inland from Seaqaqa and to Korotolutolu, Batiri, Dreketi, etc.
c Of the Indians 234 were from Seaqaqa itself, 20 were from nearby locations, and 11 were from Bua.

Source: Data in Ellis (1983a: 34) and Atkins (1983: 42).

Table 4
Gross and Net Pay of Lau Islanders Recruited by
Lau Provincial Council to Cut Cane at Seaqaqa,
1982 Season ($)

Month (number of cutters)	Gross pay	Accom. costs	Savings for village schemes	Net Pay Total	Net Pay Per person
June (236)	7,940	2,260	2,260	3,420	14.50
July (236)	9,019	260	2,260	4,499	19.06
August (192)	9,139	1,510	1,870	5,759	30.00
September (193)	11,753	2,240	1,880	7,633	39.55
October (193)	9,102	1,910	1,910	5,282	27.37
Season's Total	46,953	10,180	10,180	26,593	25.33
Average (per person-day)	1.46	0.32	727	0.83	127 (per season)

Recruits came from Moala (3 villages), Vanua Balavu (3), Kabara (1), Nayau (2), Cicia (3), Ono (1) and Matuku (1).

Source: 'Lau 21/45 Cane Cutting', file in District Office, Lakeba (unpublished).

The organisation of labour supply to Seaqaqa, with its elements of communal coercion and local government subsidy, seems very like an archaic form of articulation of pre-capitalist village production to an intrusive plantation sector, rather than an integrated process of development that provides mutual gains to farmers and their work force. It should, therefore, be seen as part of a process whereby peasants in peripheral regions become conscious of their marginalised status, thus increasing the political pressures for more integrated development or alternatively promoting a more permanent migration of wage labour.

IMPLICATIONS FOR DEVELOPMENT PLANNING

Rural development strategies that depend heavily on capital-intensive schemes, such as Seaqaqa, can lead to substantial macro-economic problems of foreign exchange indebtedness, as the experiences of a number of Third World countries have recently shown. For land settlement schemes establishment costs (roads, land clearance and social infrastructure) are inevitably high, but if these costs are all concentrated into a three- or four-year period (as at Seaqaqa), then a dependence on expensive imported machinery and expertise becomes inevitable. The establishment of 800 farms in such a brief period places an intolerable burden on local resources and, all too often, the bottlenecks are avoided by means of foreign, not local, resources.

Also it can be argued that in planning land settlement schemes greater consideration should be given to the particular requirements of each farmer and each holding. In most schemes emphasis is on a particular crop or enterprise, with a massive investment in extension staff and specialised infrastructure which has the effect of reducing flexibility of response by farmers and planners to changing ecological or market conditions. A shift of emphasis by planners to individual holdings would encourage a fuller use of the particular production opportunities of each farm, in order to maximise farm income. The wider range of farm enterprises which is likely to follow from this approach has several additional advantages. It provides farmers with greater security against adversity, it encourages them to develop an independent decision-making capacity, and it forms a framework in which market forces can influence the type and quantity of produce without traumatic change. For such an approach to be successful planning teams must include farm management specialists. This is imperative since the choice of enterprises requires a knowledge not only of land use potential, but also of marketing opportunities and the provision of an adequate cash flow.

Farmer selection in settlement schemes is also crucial to their success. In some cases selection may not, for a variety of reasons, be appropriate, but it is still important that consideration be given to the training of farmers and their continued support. The Seaqaqa project shows what can happen when the selection of settlers is dictated by over-riding political imperatives, and where preparation and support are inadequate. In the case of Fiji the concept of equal participation by ethnic Fijians and Indians is understandable. At Seaqaqa the government's desire for a much greater Fijian participation in sugar has lead to 448 Fijian settlers being selected compared to 339 Indians and 13 others (Sovasova 1980). However, within the accelerated timetable that World Bank support required, difficulties were experienced in finding enough Fijians who were not only keen to participate in commercial agriculture, but who were also prepared to abandon those traditional social obligations that proved to be incompatible with commercial farming. In practice, this commitment has proved easier for Fijians who migrated to

Seaqaqa from other islands than for those whose origins were local, and whose loyalties were therefore split between cane farming and continued participation in Fijian village life.

The problem of farmer preparation is put into perspective when we contrast the situation in Fiji with that elsewhere. In countries with a tradition of commercial farming, it is usual for agricultural land to be made available only to individuals with professional qualifications and farming experience. In Seaqaqa, several holdings are occupied by individuals whose previous experience is almost entirely restricted to subsistence farming of root crops, and who have little or no experience of commercial production. The Fijian situation is further complicated by the superimposition of commercial responsibilities upon traditional obligations. An assumption of planners in the 1960s was that subdivision and settlement of native land would create a new class of independent (*galala*) farmers, free from traditional obligation. This has not proved to be the case, so that ethnic Fijian farmers become subject to dual responsibilities which can only detract from their performance in the commercial sector.

While some training for potential settlers should be provided, it is unrealistic to propose the two to three years of schooling followed by a similar period of practical experience that is normally assumed to be necessary in western countries. Two realistic options are available which would overcome this impasse. Settlers could either be supported by a farm management service, or holdings could be developed as independent commercial units with all operators becoming participatory stake-holders. This latter approach has been suggested for Trinidad, in a situation where much agricultural land is owned by the State and can therefore be managed in this way without individual or communal land rights being threatened.

CONCLUSION

As in many Third World countries, planners in Fiji are aiming for a type of rural development which contributes to national growth yet diminishes regional disparities, and which rewards entrepreneurs but does not exacerbate social inequalities. It would be surprising if any one project were to be simultaneously successful in all these different ways, in particular, perhaps, land settlement projects which involve inexperienced farmers adopting an unfamiliar technology in a new environment.

This paper has tried to place the Seaqaqa scheme in its historical context, as a bold attempt to implement an interregional resettlement scheme in a country where spontaneous resettlement (phase I) is no longer politically feasible, and where previous (phase II) efforts had been generally unsuccessful. An exception was the sugar cane smallholdings organised under strict company supervision during colonial times, and it is by sticking closely to this model that Seaqaqa has been successful in production terms. At the same time the dangers of dependence on a single export crop have again become apparent, particularly as the area is remote from the Labasa mill making transport expensive, and has a cropping system that makes large labour costs almost inevitable. The success rate for Seaqaqa settlers is at present much better than for other recent settlement schemes in Fiji, but the problems of integrating indigenous Fijians into commercial farming have not been fully solved. For reasons of cost alone this is not a strategy for rural development that can be widely adopted, and in a country where land rights are jealously guarded and where rural populations continue to grow, subdivision and settlement are at best temporary solutions to development problems. These problems might better be tackled by means of phase III initiatives, to achieve an intensification of production on existing holdings.

Seaqaqa landscape

10

THE ADOPTION OF RICE BY VILLAGE FIJIANS[1]

John Overton

RICE AND THE GREEN REVOLUTION IN FIJI

State efforts to increase substantially rice production in Fiji and thereby achieve self-sufficiency may be likened to a Pacific Islands 'Green Revolution'. Certainly the strategies employed — be they the introduction of new high yielding varieties, irrigation schemes, land development, extension services, price support and improved marketing infrastructures — bear many similarities to programmes in South and Southeast Asia. Yet here the similarities end. Rice is the staple food for only about half of Fiji's population and rice has only been established in Fiji for a relatively short time. Indigenous Fijians still rely on root crops (cassava, taro and yams) as their staple foods and rice is little consumed or produced. This chapter argues that if the Green Revolution is to be promoted in Fiji, it must involve Fijians a great deal more than at present but, in doing so, major constraints (land, labour and technology) will become apparent.

Rice has been grown in Fiji for a little over a century, being introduced with indentured Indian labourers on sugar plantations. For most of the ensuing years, rice cultivation was restricted to small household subsistence plots in the sugar areas (a smaller area than the present sugar areas of Figure 1) and its expansion was restricted by the Colonial Sugar Refining Company

---

1   This paper appeared first in a workshop on 'The Green Revolution in South and Southeast Asia in perspective', held at the Research School of Pacific Studies, Australian National University, Canberra, 10-12 April 1987. The author acknowledges the assistance of Josefa Raibosa and Mesake Tukai in gathering data, Paula Taukei for his helpful insights into the Agricultural Development Programme, and Barbara Banks and Michael Bourke for their comments on earlier drafts.

(CSR) which was concerned to maximise sugar production. Rice was allowed only on wetland unsuitable for sugar and there was no sugar-rice rotation. The colonial government in the 1930s and 1940s began Fiji's first official rice development programmes in response to low sugar prices and high imports of rice. More land in the sugar country went under rice, there was an extension into new areas, such as Dreketi and Taganikula in Vanua Levu (see Figure 1), and a few Fijians even began to cultivate rice on a small scale. A 75 per cent increase in area under rice resulted, which was all but reversed in the 1950s when sugar prices rose steadily (Fiji Ministry of Primary Industries 1985:1). However, as late as 1958, rice output was still dominated by sugar cane farm production (Ward 1965:168). The sugar constraint on rice was removed in part with the closure of sugar operations on the wet (southeastern) side of Viti Levu, first at Navua in 1922 and, more importantly, at Nausori in 1959. This freed up areas of Indian-farmed land for rice and laid the basis of the industry.

Figure 1
Rice Producing Regions of Fiji

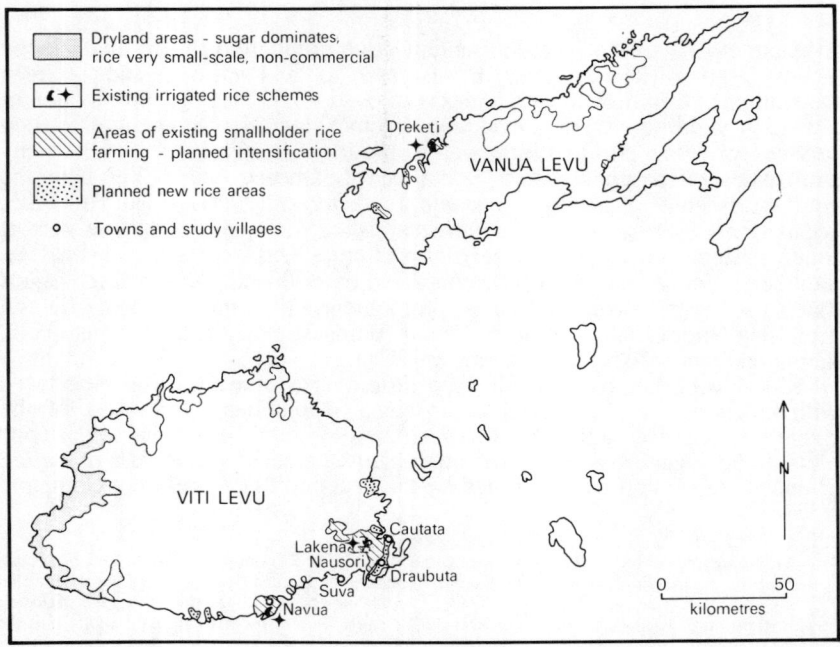

Since 1960, the disengagement of rice and sugar has continued. The sugar areas expanded considerably, especially in the 1970s, and household rice production has continued there, but the real growth has occurred with regional specialisation of rice on non-sugar land. After Independence in 1970 there was another drive for self-sufficiency and this led to the establishment of large-scale (by Fijian standards) irrigation schemes for rice first at Lakena and later at Dreketi and Navua. Despite the virtual economic failure of these schemes[2], there has been recent strong re-affirmation of the self-sufficiency policy. Fiji, throughout the 1970s, imported 50 to 60 per cent of its rice requirements but has set an ambitious target of 90 per cent self-sufficiency by 1990 (Fiji Central Planning Office 1985: 63, see Table 1 and Figure 2). It is also hoped that the programme will generate more rural employment and raise incomes, especially as rice farmers are amongst the poorest in rural Fiji.

In brief, the strategies being adopted to achieve this goal include)[3]:

Price support. In 1986, rice producers were able to obtain in excess of $300 per tonne guaranteed on delivery at the government rice mills[4]. The cost is passed on to consumers and imports are restricted through quotas and duties to match the high price of local rice.

Improved marketing. Traditional marketing channels, involving small-scale mills and local markets have been recognised as efficient, especially for traditional varieties. There is no direct price support, though the high prices offered at the government mills and dietary preferences for traditional varieties mean that prices offered to growers are as high, sometimes higher, through these smaller-scale mills. The government mills do give the official price and handle most of the production of the new varieties.

Extension services. There has been a major expansion in specialist extension advice for rice, increased local research, more farmers' credit available through institutions, such as the Fiji Development Bank, and there are plans to establish pools of government machinery for hire to farmers.

---

2   These schemes involved very high costs for land development and operation. They were capital intensive schemes with heavy machinery being used for clearing and harvesting, and pump irrigation, and there was a programme of land re-apportionment. See UNFAO/Fiji Ministry of Agriculture and Fisheries (1982:32), Fiji Ministry of Primary Industries (1985:1,49), Australian Agricultural Consulting and Management Co. (1982, n.d.).

3   Interestingly, most of the finance for these projects will come from aid sources: hurricane relief aid for much of the road and reclamation work in Central Division (Australian Agricultural Consulting and Management Co., n.d.); Australian aid in Western Vanua Levu (Australian Agricultural Consulting and Management Co., 1982); loans from the Asian Development Bank; and Japanese and Chinese aid for separate rice projects.

4   This was over three times the price received by Australian rice growers in 1986.

Figure 2
Rice Production and Consumption, 1971-1990

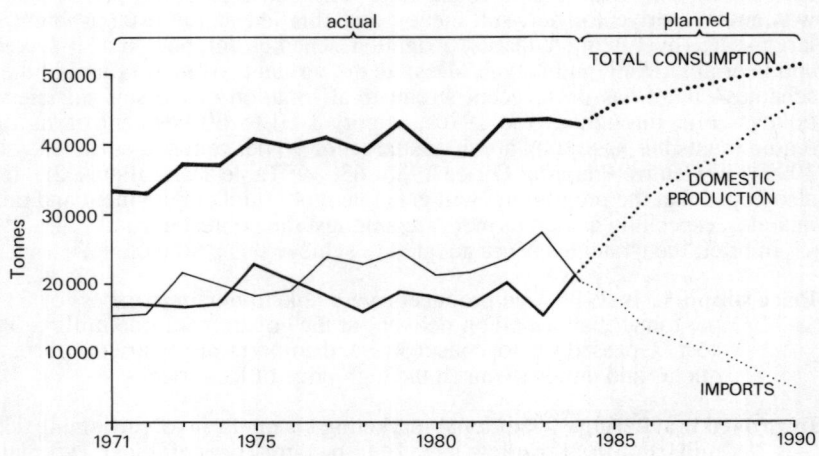

Land development. As well as the above measures to increase output in existing rice areas, new areas are targeted for expansion. Drainage, levelling, clearing, gravity-fed irrigation, and improved transport infrastructure are being carried out by government agencies. It is planned to bring an additional 1670 hectares in Vanua Levu and 2500 hectares in Southern Viti Levu under cultivation in this way. Also, gravity-fed irrigation schemes are targeted for about 1800 hectares of mostly existing rain-fed rice areas (Fiji Ministry of Primary Industries 1985: 60-66).

The magnitude of this recent rice intensification programme in Fiji can be gauged from some of the targets set (Figure 2 and Table 1).

There is to be a 105 per cent increase in rice output from 1984 to 1990, a 67 per cent increase in annual area harvested and a 46 per cent increase in area under rice, all impressive targets for a six-year period. Much of the growth will come from a conversion of single-crop rainfed systems to double-cropped gravity-fed irrigated systems, but the increase in area is significant. When the regional dimension is considered, it must be noted that the Northern Division (Vanua Levu) will experience the greatest extension in irrigated area (mostly on the Indian smallholding Dreketi, Korokande and Bua

Table 1
Rice Production Targets, 1984-1990
(tonnes)

	1984[a]	1986	1987	1988	1989	1990
Production	22,246	33,552	36,193	38,396	42,530	45,576
Imports	20,665	13,169	11,500	10,269	7,172	5,162
% self-suff.	52	72	76	79	86	90
Employment	25,000	25,550	25,950	26,150	27,50	27,700
Ha irrigated[b]	588	1,221	1,674	1,774	1,974	2,444
Ha rainfed	8,468	10,562	10,391	10,681	10,821	10,761
Tot.ha/year[c]	10,436	14,178	14,964	15,824	16,574	17,444
Yield/ha/year	2.13	2.37	2.42	2.43	2.57	2.61

[a] actual production
[b] increase is also gravity-fed schemes including conversion of areas from rainfed — hence rainfed areas may decline. Main season crop only, annual production from irrigated areas will be double the area, allowing for off-season crop.
[c] includes area of off-season crop.

Sources: Fiji Ministry of Primary Industries (1985); Fiji Central Planning Office (1985:63).

schemes)[5]. But also the Central Division (Southeastern Viti Levu), it is planned, will experience an 85 per cent increase in rainfed rice area as well as larger percentage increases in irrigated land. There will be some planned expansion of rice within the western sugar areas but the Central Division is to be the major focus for the development of new rice lands.

In such a programme, there are obvious problems to be faced. A doubling of rice output in six years will require substantial financial, technical and infrastructural changes. However, one of the major problems will be land. At present, probably in excess of 95 per cent of rice in Fiji is grown by Indo-Fijians but ethnic Fijians have title to 83 per cent of the country's land area, though, in reality, the land situation is not as simple as these figures suggest, for much of the Fijian land is hilly and unsuitable for any agriculture and also there is a very large area of Fijian land leased by Indo-Fijians (Ward 1985, 1987, Overton 1987). Most of the planned increase in output of rice — perhaps 80 per cent — will still be dependent upon Indian smallholder

---

[5]   There is a planned decline in rainfed acreage of 13 per cent but a planned increase of 621 per cent in irrigated area in Vanua Levu.

production. Nonetheless, rice land is in very short supply. The importance of sugar in Fiji's economy precludes major expansion in the western areas and most of the existing land elsewhere that is suitable for rice is already heavily cropped with rice, vegetables or root crops. Attention is being turned to Fijian land that has not been leased and which lies in the flat and fertile delta or valley regions of Southeast Viti Levu.

Thus, if the targets for expanding rice area are to be met, they must involve Fijian land and Fijian farmers. It happens that such a policy fits with present objectives of increasing the participation of ethnic Fijians in cash-cropping and raising their incomes. For the Green Revolution to succeed in Fiji, therefore, there must be not just the introduction of new technologies on an existing rice-farming base, but the comprehensive grafting of a whole new type of agriculture (intensive rice cultivation) and a new cash crop onto a complex of predominantly root crop cultivation situated on largely communally-owned land and mixed commercial/subsistence production.

Certainly there are possibilities. Many Fijians in the targeted areas are already engaged in commercial agriculture (vegetable and root crop market gardening); a number have proved successful with rice; there does appear to be land available; there is some surplus labour in the villages; and because it is not widely consumed by Fijians, increases in output should all be marketed. But the task is immense. Of the planned 4150 hectare total increase in rice area in 1984 to 1990, over two-thirds will be in the Central Division and of this, an estimated 73 per cent will have to occur on Fijian-owned and farmed land[6]. For the whole country then, perhaps 50 to 60 per cent of the planned increase in area (though not output) will be in the hands of Fijians. It will be a 'Green Revolution' not just because of the colour of the fields, but also because of the inexperience of many farmers.

This chapter examines the possible progress and consequences of this revolution with reference only to Fijian farmers and draws upon fieldwork in two villages in Viti Levu, and upon a wider survey of Fijian rice farmers in Central Division, the Agricultural Development Programme (ADP) Benchmark Survey, in 1985[7]. It examines the two models for Fijian rice farming (group and individual) and some of the developments and problems encountered in the implementation of the programme to date.

---

6   Of the 2818 hectare increase, 1320 hectares will be on Fijian group farms and about half of the rest (a very conservative estimate) will be on individually-operated Fijian farms, making a total of a 2069 hectare increase in Fijian rice area.

7   The study of Cautata and Draubuta is part of the author's research on changing patterns of Fijian agriculture, carried out in 1985-6 in the two villages and two settlement schemes. Household interviews and field surveys have been conducted as well as archival and air photo research. The larger study (in terms of the number of interviews) was conducted by the Ministry of Primary Industries, Fiji (with the author's participation) as part of a benchmark survey of about 40 per cent of all rice farmers (39 per cent of 1587 Indian rice farmers and 45 per cent of 248 Fijians) in the Central Division in 1985. The results of this survey appear courtesy of the Ministry of Primary Industries.

FIJIAN RICE ADOPTERS

Individual Non-Village Farmers

Although Fijians are new to rice farming and many will adopt the crop in the next few years, it must be recognised that many are growing it now and some remain who first grew rice in the 1930s. For the whole of the Central Division in 1985, Ministry of Primary Industries records revealed that there were 248 Fijians planting rice, 205 of these being full-time farmers. Extrapolations from the ADP Benchmark Survey lead to the conclusion that about 20 per cent of the area in smallholder rice in Central Division was in the hands of these Fijians[8]. Whilst around half of the sample interviewed have begun to grow rice since 1980 (many since 1984), 40 per cent had adopted in the '60s and '70s and 11 per cent before 1960. Therefore, there is a large body of Fijian experience in rice growing, even if previously on a small scale and using basic techniques and traditional (Indian) varieties.

Around three-quarters of these present Fijian rice farmers are located outside the villages on secure freehold or leased land.' They have individual farms which are run on a largely commercial basis and are mostly free from everyday village or communal obligations. Many have good land, are relatively highly capitalised, and are successful capitalist farmers. Comparison of survey data on present (mostly non-village) Fijian rice growers and Indo-Fijians (Table 2) reveals that there is no *a priori* reason for distinguishing between the two ethnic groups. Indeed, if anything, the Fijians, with more land, have higher incomes, grow more rice and have taken out more agricultural loans. In general, too, they are much better off than Fijian villagers who often have less secure or high quality land, little access to credit and lower incomes.

Clearly, Fijians can make, and have made, successful rice farmers. Away from the villages, their rice areas, yields and farm incomes (more than doubled by off-farm incomes) compare favourably with their Indian neighbours and, from the official point of view, this group of Fijian capitalist rice farmers will be treated under the rice schemes in much the same ways as Indo-Fijians, with the emphasis on intensification, price support and extension services.

Individual Village Farmers

When attention is turned to the villages and village land, this image of progressive, prosperous and, sometimes, experienced Fijian rice farmers

---

8   Nearly all the rice grown in Central Division is smallholder rice. The major exception is a large-scale farm, Consolidated Agriculture Ltd. (Conag) at Navua, which cultivates 500 ha.

Table 2
ADP Benchmark Survey — Basic Data on Rice Farmers
Central Division, 1985

	Fijians	Indians
Sample size	111	583
Av. size holding (ha)	16.68	3.85
Av. area under rice 1984 (ha)	2.66	1.76
Av. yield 1984 (t/ha)	1.11	0.99
% with freehold land	30.2	19.8
% with agricultural loans	65.3	54.4
Av. rice income ($/year)	617	478
Av. farm income ($/year)	1,142	774

Source: ADP Benchmark Survey, 1985, Ministry of Primary Industries, Suva (unpublished results).

comes into question. Draubuta and Cautata are two Fijian villages close to the Suva-Nausori urban area; they lie on the Nausori 'rice perimeter' and are within the target area for rice expansion. Many of the village households rely on non-farm cash income, though household food production is important for some and cash cropping for many. Land is scarce in both villages. Cautata has over 100 households and about 220 hectares of village land; Draubuta some 60 households and 161 hectares. In Draubuta, 28 hectares have been leased, mainly to Indians (see Figure 3). In both village areas, there is land that is very suitable for rice. Draubuta lies on the floodplain of the Rewa River and alongside one of its distributaries, whilst Cautata contains some good flat land (when drained) behind the mangrove margin. However, there are considerable areas of heavy bush in Draubuta (important for tree crops and ritual use) and in Cautata, hillocks and swamp land restrict the cultivatable area considerably. When these physical factors are overlain across *mataqali* (clan) land boundaries, it is apparent that only some of the villagers (those in *mataqali* with good land) have access to rice land. Thus, the five 'bush' *mataqali* in Draubuta (of the fourteen 'live' *mataqali* units) cannot engage in rice farming unless they can get leases (whether formal registered or informal *vakavanua* leases) to another *mataqali*'s land. This has proved almost impossible in recent years, such is the pressure on land, though

Figure 3
Draubuta — Rice and Land Tenure, 1985-1986

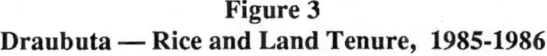

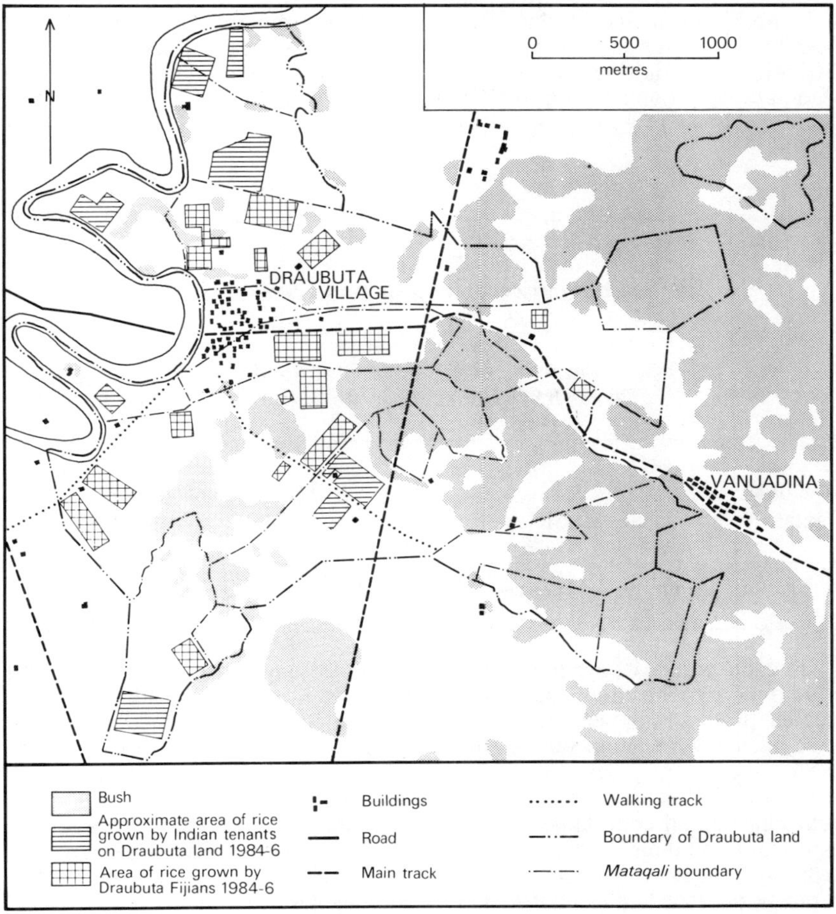

one Draubuta farmer from a 'bush' *mataqali* has managed to get a registered lease to a patch of good rice land owned by another clan (Overton 1987).

The shortage of *mataqali* land is seen as the main obstacle to future expansion. Nearly half of the respondents in both villages stated that land shortage and the reluctance of the rest of their *mataqali*, let alone another clan, to grant them more land, restricts them considerably.

There were seventeen Fijian households growing rice in Draubuta in 1985 and fifteen in Cautata. As with the non-village growers, a small number of them have grown rice for many years, but most are recent starters. Because of difficulties in acquiring land and because most were trying rice for the first or second time, the areas were smaller on average than the ADP samples (Tables 2 and 3) but there was considerable variation in areas within, if not between the villages.

Table 3
Area Under Rice, Draubuta and Cautata, 1986

	Total area (ha)	Mean ha/ household	Standard deviation	Range
Draubuta	19.20	1.20	1.14	0.08 - 4.05
Cautata	22.66	1.51	0.96	0.40 - 4.05

Source: Field surveys and interviews, May-June 1986.

In each village, there have emerged some leading growers (five in each) with over two hectares under rice. The rest, mainly new adopters have smaller plots and appear to be experiencing a little more difficulty. There have been few absolute failures, despite major flood damage in Draubuta in 1986 (they were given government assistance to replant) and inexperience there and in Cautata. Indeed, the only two who later abandoned rice were both elderly and complained that they were now too old themselves for the hard work and their sons had left home. There were, however, some growers in both villages who were clearly struggling with low yields, crop damage (from birds, weeds and leafroller) and shortages of equipment (ploughs and sprayers). Their future is uncertain.

Capital is a major constraint. Bullock teams, ploughs and, occasionally, the cost of land clearing are major costs for villagers who have few savings and often restricted access to other sources of income[9]. The shortage of implements ranked on a similar level to land shortage as a barrier to future expansion. For farmers outside the villages on freehold or registered lease land, access to credit through the Fiji Development Bank is relatively easy. But where land cannot be used as security for a loan (the FDB will only accept a formal lease, not communal land), credit is very difficult to obtain. In Cautata, however, four have been able to get loans in excess of $1000 as part of a government experiment lending to village farmers. It has not been continued. In Draubuta, only two have managed to secure loans from the FDB and one was lucky enough to get a large loan from American aid. The majority are dependent upon usually meagre savings or informal credit to finance rice development. It is likely that the credit/capital constraint will remain a considerable obstacle to these individual village farmers.

Labour requirements are less of an obstacle to development. For rice, most pre-harvest tasks can be carried out by the farming household, though for harvesting, larger numbers are required for up to a week. The differences observed between Cautata and Draubuta are illuminating and have implications for the future of Fijian rice schemes. In Draubuta, all labour for rice farming came from within the village and mostly from the household or relatives. No payments in cash were made. Workers were 'paid' in kind: cigarettes, meals, *yaqona* and, rarely, some of the output. In other words, there was no monetised labour absorption and no real extra employment generation within the village as a result of rice development. In Cautata, however, perhaps because more people are engaged in off-farm employment (creating a greater awareness of the opportunity cost of labour), nine of the fifteen farmers employed extra village labour for cash payments. Though the periods of employment were short, for harvesting only, there were flows of money from the rice growers to labourers who were often very short of land and dependent on casual work. Thus, whilst the Draubuta model of payment in kind might assist capital-scarce growers to become established, the Cautata cash payment model will have to be adopted in the future if the benefits of the rice schemes are to be spread more widely amongst Fijians.

Another difficulty facing individual village rice growers is the shortage of technical advice. Whilst the Ministry of Primary Industries has helped establish new areas by draining wetlands and clearing and levelling fields, extension services seem to be lacking, especially in Cautata. A number have complained that the difficulties encountered with pests, diseases, and spraying have not been met by extension workers who 'only appear at harvest time'. It is apparent that some of the growers just do not have the knowledge to successfully adopt rice. Others, however, are thriving without advice.

But despite these problems, rice remains very popular with growers; its main attraction, according to farmers, may be summarised as 'good, quick and easy money'. Rice matures much faster than root crops (a return can be

---

9   Most land clearing, levelling and drainage has been carried out by Ministry of Primary Industries bulldozers. Some complain that the area prepared has been too small for them.

had 120 to 150 days after planting), the price is good and secure, and farmers do not have to sit all day at the Suva market trying to sell their crop. Payment is in a lump sum upon delivery at the Rewa Rice Mill at Nausori. It is apparent that, at $300 per tonne, the rewards to labour are much higher for rice than for *dalo* and cassava. This pecuniary advantage of rice is likely to sustain interest and output in the crop.

There was an interesting secondary advantage given by over half the respondents. Rice was being used more and more for home consumption. It could be stored for long periods, was a popular food for breakfast, though some were using it as a staple food for two to three months of the year, and one household used it also as poultry feed. There is evidence, then, of a partial dietary substitution of rice for root crops amongst Fijian rice farmers, if not other villagers. At the least, rice is becoming an important complement to root crops in some household diets.

Given this dietary substitution, it could be expected that there may be some land and labour reallocation from root crops to rice and a decline in the output of the former. Farmers were asked if rice farming had affected their cultivation of other crop[10]. The results were varied (Table 4).

Table 4
Change in Area of Root Crop Cultivation as a Result of Rice Adoption (number of responses)

	No Change	Less root crops	More root crops
Draubuta	12	5	0
Cautata	10	3	2

Source: Field interviews, 1986

For most farmers, then, there has not been any major decline in staple food production since adopting rice. All grow only one rice crop per year and many stated that they could deal satisfactorily with their other crops at other times of the year. Two in Cautata even said that growing rice motivated them to give more attention to farming and their root crops. For these farmers with

---

10 Because of the lack of time-series data on village cropping, it has not been possible to quantify the substitution of rice for root crops on village land and reliance must be made on farmers' estimates and comments.

no negative impacts on root crop production, it is probable that rice has utilised surplus labour time. Traditional food production and its labour inputs have been readjusted to accommodate the new crop. It is too soon to tell whether such a reorganisation will lead to the concentration of root crop output at certain times of the year and shortages at others, though the increase in household consumption of rice suggests that this might occur.

The 25 per cent of respondents whose root crop production had declined are significant. Their main reason for a decline was the increased labour input into rice, leaving less time for other crops. There is little or no surplus labour available for this group. Most stated that they had reduced root crop production to the level of household needs, having previously sold considerable surpluses at the urban markets. This substitution of one cash crop for another may have important consequences for future supply of marketed root crops to meet the needs of urban Fijians, as this region is one of the main *dalo* and cassava producing areas for the Suva market. A dual marketing structure is emerging, whereby one staple (rice) is on a protected, price supported market and the other (root crops) operates through a free market. Whilst this is satisfactory for rice producers, it may not be so beneficial from long-term and national perspectives. Root crop staples are often better suited to the flood-prone Rewa delta areas, they have very low input costs, their technology is widely known, and there is a stable (if unprotected and highly competitive) market demand in the towns.

Whilst farmers whose output of root crops had declined believed this was the result of a labour/time effect, it is clear from field surveys that there has been considerable encroachment of rice onto root crop land. Figure 3 shows the distribution of rice areas in Draubuta village. As well as the 19 hectares of Fijian-grown rice, there are a further 28 hectares of land leased to Indian smallholders who are growing rice on most of their land. Rice has occupied a significant portion of the best cleared land close to the village and the Wainibokasi River. Root crops have seemingly 'retreated' back to the bush margins and into bush clearings. There seems to have been, then, a division of village land, (and by implication, of *mataqali* specialisation in land use) into rice-dominant and non-rice areas. Similarly at Cautata, the flat lands that have been drained for rice are coming to be dominated by this crop and household root crop gardens are found on the hill slopes.

Thus, the adoption of rice by individual Fijian village cultivators has been generally recent and responsive. There are some failures, or near failures, but many find it a profitable and successful crop. Because it has been a recent innovation in the villages studied, some of the longer-term consequences are not yet apparent. However, preliminary results have shown that there will be important effects on village land (exacerbating shortages), village labour (limited generation of wage employment), crops and diets (rice partly replacing root crops), and socio-economic inequalities (rice farmers with land will prosper alongside those with little or unsuitable land).

Village Group Farms

In response to some of the land, labour and capital constraints facing individual village Fijians wanting to adopt rice, the Fijian government has encouraged the development of group farms, usually made up of the members of a single *mataqali* and part of its land. Members of the group provide the labour and, eventually, the full management. The land constraint is thus eased because the group decides to devote a piece of land to rice, rather than allocating land and rice incomes to an individual. Similarly, the capital constraint is overcome as groups can register as cooperative societies, which are eligible to apply for loans (regardless of land security), and members contribute some of their savings to the group to help establish the schemes. There is also a political dimension, as the present Fijian state can deal with the apparent contradiction between modernizing and commercializing village agriculture on the one hand, and preserving traditional authority and society on the other by promoting communal ventures.

The Agricultural Development Project for Central Division, plans forty-four *mataqali* group farms covering a total of 1320 hectares. Given that this accounts for 47 per cent of the planned increase in rice area in the Division, the importance of this strategy can be recognised. In contrast to individual farmers (especially those within villages) government assistance to and direction of the group farms is substantial and direct. As well as land development (clearing, levelling, and drainage), the Ministry of Primary Industries has assigned workers to oversee credit applications and all stages of work. For most group farms, there will be a full-time, government paid extension officer assigned to a single group farm (or 'cluster' of two or three). This person will act as a manager, organising labour, overseeing planting, maintenance, harvesting and accounts, and being responsible for training a local replacement. Loans taken out for machinery and the manager's house will be repaid under the supervision of the manager (who will stay until the loan is repaid), thus reducing the possibility of default. Loans will average $39,000 per group farm. The majority of the farms will be rainfed-only schemes with one crop of rice (sometimes two) and off-season crops such as maize and vegetables.

Whilst the rationale for the group farms and their planning has been impressive, the results to date on the first of the farms in operation have been poor. Two farms were studied, Veitauni and Drauvutu.

Veitauni group farm was one of the first to be started and is located inland on the flats of the Waidina River. It began in 1984 with Canadian aid money, unlike others planned which will not involve external aid. The scheme is headed by a retired senior civil servant in Naqali. It is a large scheme, covering two villages (Naqali and Viria), five *mataqali* and 130 members. It began enthusiastically, with 18 hectares developed, a good response to the call for labour and the full area planted. Since then, it has regressed. The first yield was poor with only 11 tonnes marketed, loan approval and cooperative registration have not been completed, (thus) machinery has had to be hired, labour has been difficult to obtain in subsequent seasons, morale has sunk, and there have been disputes between the *mataqali*. In 1985, only 4 hectares were planted.

The main benefit of the Veitauni scheme may not be rice output but lessons for agricultural planners. It is now recognised that the scheme was too large and future group farms should be restricted to single *mataqali* or smaller *tokatoka*. It has also been suggested that the initial input of aid may have had negative effects by creating an aid-dependence mentality among the members and the view that if things went wrong, the government or the donors could salvage them. Finally, the need to have credit available from an early stage is vital.

Drauvutu is a smaller, single *mataqali* operation. It is situated roughly half way between Draubuta and Cautata, again on the Nausori rice perimeter. Much of the land adjoining this project has been made suitable for rice due to the construction (using hurricane relief aid funds) of a sea wall behind the mangrove swamps to prevent salt water intrusion. The *mataqali* involved is socially cohesive, having moved away from their village some ten years ago to form their own settlement near their land. They have thirty-two members, a total of 123 hectares of land and 2.8 hectares developed for rice. The scheme began in 1986. Again there have been bottlenecks with loan and cooperative registration and initial operations have used members' savings. The first crop yielded 1.3 tonnes/hectare, below the target of 3 tonnes/hectare but respectable for a first crop and favourable compared to Veitauni and even some established individual producers.

Observation of an important meeting between Ministry of Primary Industries extension workers and the group members in June 1985, reviewing the first year's operation, was illuminating. There was an impressive approach of consultation and information, not direction on the part of the officials. Mistakes were identified and discussed and the group reached a decision on two major points: to reinvest its $400 profit from the first crop into the second; and to try a combination of rice and maize as off-season crops. There was an evident consensus and commitment in the group. Labour for the scheme is drawn from the members, it is casual, and unpaid, so that there is a large outlay of energy on the part of the group with, as yet, little monetary reward. In short, Drauvutu is a cohesive, energetic and promising group farm.

Thus there are distinct prospects for group farming in Fiji. In many areas, where land is short, it may be the only way for *mataqali* to release productive land; it also allows for economies of scale in production, use of machinery and extension advice; and it may be a way of utilising surplus rural labour equitably. If group rice farming is to succeed on the scale envisaged though, (and be extended into other types of farming), the lessons of Veitauni and Drauvutu must be learned. The preconditions for survival, let alone success, should include: a sound communal base for the group, small and committed and with good leadership; managerial assistance for the loan repayment period, training of local replacements and constant consultation and advice;

and rewards for the participants — if labour remains unpaid and the trained replacements receive little remuneration, wage alternatives elsewhere may create labour shortages, especially of those more skilled.

But there remain reservations. There is a fundamental problem of trying to mobilise a communal mode of production for capitalist agriculture. Also, it must be recognised that, no matter how strong the group, they are surrounded by alternatives, and group rice farming must compete for land and labour with off-farm employment, individual farming and social obligations. Fiji has a complex but competitive and capitalist rural economy.

PROBLEMS AND PROSPECTS

Fiji is unlike many countries which have adopted a 'Green Revolution' approach in rural development in that rice is not an indigenous crop and that it is a staple for only half its population. Yet for most rice producers in Fiji — Indo-Fijians — the strategies adopted (new varieties, irrigation, infrastructure and more inputs) and, one suspects, the consequences (increased yields, costs and limited employment generation) have been similar. In Fiji, however, there has been a major difference in that a significant proportion of planned increases depends upon the incorporation of indigenous Fijians (hitherto not rice producers) into the rice economy. Despite some failures, there are signs that this is occurring and Fijians have made successful rice farmers. They have adopted not only a new crop but whole new production technologies.

The reasons for these early and tentative signs of success may include:

Availability of resources. There is some surplus labour (after reorganisation of labour time) and some surplus land (after drainage and clearing and despite the tenurial obstacles).

Compatibility with existing systems. There has been relatively little disturbance of traditional staple root crop production, although there are signs that substitution is taking place in diets, labour time and land for some farmers and in some areas. Therefore, rice can develop alongside root crop production, the latter providing a safety net if rice fails. Commitment to the new crop is not absolute.

Price. The price received for rice has been kept artificially high. If government policy changes to lower the minimum price or if falling marketed supply of root crops leads to an increase in the price of these staples, there may well be a threat to the competitive advantage of rice.

Agronomic skills. Many Fijians are good farmers and can grow rice well.

As yet, possible disturbances to rural Fiji resulting from the efforts to encourage Fijians to engage in rice farming are not apparent. Failures may be explained by poor planning and design (as of the Veitauni group farm), bureaucratic obstacles (for credit), or inexperience of farmers. However, there are wider processes operating that are profoundly transforming the Fijian rural economy and, in this sense, the effects of the rice schemes need to be monitored closely.

Dietary and food supply effects may appear soon. If the substitution of rice for root crops in rural diets and rural land continues, it will spread to the towns as root crops rise relatively in price and rice gains more acceptance in the Fijian diet. In this case, the most economically efficient allocation of agricultural land, labour and capital between root crops and rice will not be made if the market price of the latter is subsidised artificially at a high level, and the former suffers by comparison with the vagaries of the open market. Traditional root crops are still probably the best suited staple foods for Fiji and should not be neglected alongside rice.

One of the likely major impacts in the rice areas will be on land and labour. With an already felt shortage of land, the larger area under rice, whether farmed on an individual or group basis, will increase that pressure. It will become extremely difficult for outsiders and even *mataqali* members to get land, let alone extend cultivation; the value of land (expressed through transfer of leases or informal rents) will continue to escalate; pressure will be placed upon land or bush that is unused or set aside for non-commercial crops and ritual use; and land disputes will intensify. For labour, there is probably some degree of surplus (either in farmers' time or with the increasing number in villages with little land) that can be absorbed. But with more individual commercial farming, awareness of off-farm alternatives and the widespread appearance of monetised economic relations within the villages, it is improbable that the very low or zero cash value of agricultural labour (as evidenced in Draubuta) can be assumed in the future. Rice farming, even if on a group basis, will have to compete for village labour.

With such demand on land and labour, differentiation within village Fiji will continue to occur. Groups farms may act as a brake on this process if they prove successful and if they distribute the rewards to all participants. Given relatively even material standards of living, if not traditional status or land endowments, the Green Revolution in village Fiji does not seem to be exacerbating any existing inequalities. In fact, it favours farmers rather than chiefs or off-farm wage earners, those previously better off. However, there will be a clear advantage to those with secure access to land and those who are profitable farmers. Rice incomes are high, relative to other cash crops and despite the higher costs of production. For those with unsuitable land or little land, rice can only offer them limited and low-paid casual wage employment. That may accelerate   differentiation between semi-proletarians and 'big peasants' in village Fiji.

One constraint on this process may be the high cost of production and overcapitalisation of rice farming. If the early years of price support, extension advice, credit (for some) and good yields give way to market competition, rising input costs, buying of inappropriate machinery (such as tractors), and indebtedness, rice farmers could suffer major reversals. There are more macro considerations as well. Rice consumers, the Fiji Government and aid agencies are funding the protection and development of the rice industry. With falling marginal returns, especially as the country approaches self-sufficiency, these costs may be perceived as politically and economically untenable. The cost of the Green Revolution in Fiji is the maintenance of an industry that is producing rice at over double the world price[11].

---

11 Many of these conclusions have been overshadowed by recent political events. On a brief visit to Draubuta in 1988, the author noted some major changes. Nearly all the Indian tenants living close to the village had moved away and, in an least two cases, relinquished their leases; several men from the village (including two rice farmers) had left to join the army; and no rice was being grown. Fijian rice farming, it seemed, had become another casualty of the coups. Paradoxically, however, government efforts to promote rice farming had brought benefits to the village: a new road linking Draubuta to Nausori (paid for out of 'rice development funds') was nearly finished as was the electrification of the village (from Chinese aid).

11

THE DISSOCIATION OF CROP AND LIVESTOCK PRODUCTION ON SUGARCANE FARMS

Imam Ali

INTEGRATED CROP-LIVESTOCK SYSTEMS

A major strength of smallholder agricultural systems is the ability of farmers to obtain relatively high yields per unit area of both subsistence and commercial crops through intensive diversified crop and animal husbandry. Evidence indicates that this strength has been eroding because of increased emphasis on commercial, primarily export, production of single crops, at the expense of diversified production (Hardaker *et al*. 1984; Ali 1986a,b). This chapter attempts to examine some of the effects that an emphasis on sugarcane production, at the expense of a diversified crop-livestock system, has had on smallholder farms in the sugarcane belts of Fiji. More specifically, it examines the changing role of livestock production on smallholder sugarcane farms in the Yaladro area of northern Viti Levu from 1971 to 1983.

Until this century, in many developing countries, livestock and crops formed a complex rather than being separate entities (Borgstrom 1980). They were part and parcel of single agricultural systems, in which animals provided meat, dairy products and wool or hides, and did not require a food supply from beyond the farm. As well as yielding small surpluses for sale, animals also served as 'waste-disposal units' and 'lawn mowers': they were often fed on kitchen and other domestic wastes (in the case of poultry and pigs) or allowed to graze weeds and crop residues. They also provided traction and transport (non-fossil-fuel-dependent), organic fertiliser, and, in some cases, even fuel. In many societies, they also had important spiritual or religious value and were used in ritual exchange. However, despite the positive attributes of an integrated crop-livestock complex, modern agricultural development plans continue to dissociate the two, thus making the long-term future of the small farmer more precarious.

From the onset of smallholder systems of sugarcane farming in Fiji, it had been common practice to keep animals such as bullocks, horses, cows, goats, chickens, and ducks. Bullocks and horses were reared as draught animals, cows to provide milk (either consumed fresh or processed into yoghurt and ghee) and as breeding stock for replacement bullocks, and goats and poultry to supply fresh meat or eggs. Surplus animals and animal products were occasionally sold to neighbouring townspeople or used to discharge ceremonial obligations on occasions such as weddings.

In spite of the important role played by livestock in cane areas, they have received relatively little attention from geographers, economists and agriculturalists. In fact, there have been few studies conducted on the cane farming areas of Fiji that have focused on the role of livestock.

Some consideration has been given to the subject by Derrick (1965), Kerr and Donnelly (1969: 181-185), Anderson (1974), Mayer (1961), and Chandra (1980). Most of these studies either looked at livestock in terms of dairying in the wet zone of Fiji (Navua and Tailevu), on coconut plantations and in Yaqara (the dry zone), or tried to show the importance of cattle as draught animals on smallholder rice and sugarcane farms. None of them really detailed the wider importance of the crop-livestock complex in the provision of meat, eggs and dairy products[1].

Furthermore, although policy-makers and Fiji's development plans (Fiji Central Planning Office 1975, 1980, 1985) have advocated diversification of agricultural production, it has been directed at the national rather than farm-level. Fiji's Development Plans Seven and Eight, for example, outline strategies for increasing production of crops and livestock on a virtually monocultural basis. Neither mentions the crop-livestock complex in sugarcane areas, let alone stresses its importances as a possible way to increase productivity. Development Plan Nine suggests horizontal diversification in terms of growing more food for self-consumption but there is no mention of expanding the crop-livestock complex in the cane areas as a means of increasing productivity and enhancing national and on-the-farm self-sufficiency. This chapter argues that more encouragement should be given to the expansion, or at least maintenance, of balanced crop-livestock complexes on smallholder Indian and Fijian sugarcane farms in Fiji.

---

[1]   Others who have examined livestock production in the Pacific are Patridge (1979), Camoens (1985), Quartermain (1980), and Wilson (1984). Among these, Patridge and Wilson again focus on livestock rearing in isolation from crop production. Camoens and Quartermain do discuss the incorporation of livestock into mixed farming systems, with Quartermain (1980), briefly referring to livestock production on small-scale sugarcane farms in Fiji.

THE CROP-LIVESTOCK SYSTEM IN YALADRO

This chapter draws upon a study of land use changes in Yaladro cane farming area near Tavua, Ba Province, Viti Levu, over a twelve-year period from 1971 to 1982. Most of the data were collected between September 1982 and April 1984, by means of a questionnaire and empirical observations. A survey was made on a sample of twenty-six smallholder cane farms comprising 306 hectares — out of a total of fifty-four holdings. The sample included six of the twelve indigenous Fijian farmers in the Yaladro area. Every second Indian farm, starting from the northern end of the survey area was selected, to ensure that land quality and topographic differences were covered. A detailed questionnaire was used to gather relevant information on past practices, acreages under various crops, fallow and grazing land, and information on livestock. Farmers were asked to recall what and how much they had planted and the number of livestock they had reared. Information given in this way for previous years is unlikely to be as precise as current records, but given the large number of sample households it should at least provide a good basis for evaluating trends. Moreover, livestock, such as bullocks, cows, horses and goats, formed a very important component of the cane farming system and the cane farmers were able to provide quite reliable information regarding them for a number of years (Ali 1986b: 6-9, 174-192).

The period 1971-82 was chosen because it was a time of dramatic change in cane farming in terms of variations in ownership of sugar-milling assets and fluctuation in the price and production of sugarcane. First, the Australian-owned and operated Colonial Sugar Refining (CSR) Company withdrew from its Fijian operation in 1972, with the newly independent Fiji Government taking over all its assets. Secondly, from 1971 to 1974, annual sugar production declined from 2,505,013 to 2,117,325 tonnes. Thirdly, sugarcane prices fluctuated wildly during this period, with a dramatic rise beginning in 1974 and then, since 1981, a serious decline in world market sugar prices. In 1975, the Fiji Government and the government-owned Fiji Sugar Corporation (FSC) attempted to increase sugar production by 6 per cent per annum to take advantage of high world prices. As a result, by 1979, production had doubled, reaching over four million tonnes (Fiji Sugar Corporation 1981: 1).

This increasing emphasis on sugarcane can be seen as part of a world-wide trend towards specialisation by farms (Bull *et al.* 1984), in which Fiji sugarcane farmers increasingly have been caught up over the past fifteen years and which is apparent in Yaladro. Unfortunately, this specialisation has also encouraged the gradual dissociation of crop production from livestock raising. Whereas the tradition of keeping a range of farm animals became more prominent in the early 1970s (according to farmers interviewed) because of uncertainty in the sugar industry, with increasing emphasis on sugarcane monoculture as a result of high world sugar prices and government policy, this movement was reversed in the mid-1970s, with livestock rearing beginning to decrease in importance. Table 1 shows the number of livestock on the twenty-six sample farms between 1971 and 1982.

In 1971, every farm had at least one cow with some having as many as eight. Farmers took great pride in keeping healthy animals that gave plenty of milk and bred healthy bullocks. Some Hindu farmers attached great religious importance to cows, which were regarded as a symbol of prosperity, especially by older farmers. By 1982, however, the number of cows on the twenty-six sample farms had dropped from 69 to 27, a decrease of 61 per cent, with only eighteen farms having cows. The majority had only one, compared with the usual two or three ten years earlier. Only two farmers each had three cows.

During the same period, the number of goats showed an even greater decrease of 71 per cent. In 1971, twenty-one of the twenty-six farmers reared goats on their farms with numbers of animals ranging from two to forty per farm. By 1982, only fourteen farmers had goats, with numbers ranging from two to twelve. Poultry numbers showed a decrease of 37 per cent. Whereas prior to the sugar boom of 1975, all the farmers in the area kept chickens and ducks, with a mean of twenty-nine per farm and numbers ranging from three to sixty, by 1982, although twenty-four farms still had poultry, the average number per farm was just over twenty, with a range from three to thirty.

Table 1
Holdings of Livestock on 26 Sample Farms in the Yaladro Area, 1971 and 1982

Type	1971		1982	
	No. of animals	No. of farms	No. of animals	No. of farms
Dairy cows	69	26	27	18
Goats	232	21	67	14
Poultry	754	26	475	22
Bullocks/ Horses	77	26	42	20
Total	**1,132**	-	**611**	-

Source: Questionnaire surveys and field inventories, 1982.

Draught animals had decreased in number by approximately 45 per cent. Whereas in 1971 every farm had two to six bullocks or horses, by 1982 only twenty farmers had draught animals, with the number of individual farms ranging from two to four. Of the six farmers who had no draught animals in 1982, four had purchased their own tractors, the other two occasionally hiring tractors from other farmers. By 1982, there was a total of eight tractors on the twenty-six farms, thus reducing the need for draught animals. Many of these tractors were, however, grossly under-utilised because they were used only for land preparation prior to planting and for cultivation during early growth periods.

The main reasons stated for the reduction included: decreases in grazing and fallow lands; declining on-the-farm feed production; and labour shortages and animal damage to crops. All these reasons relate to the expansion of sugarcane monoculture in the mid-and late-1970s. Nearly all farmers named the shortage of grazing land and fodder, resulting from the extension of cane land into the grazing areas and river banks and the reduction of fallow land, as the major factors behind the reduction in livestock in the cane belt.

From the onset of the smallholder system in Yaladro, the CSR company made various provisions for farmers' housing and the tethering and grazing of farm animals, depending on whether farms were located at the foot of Yaladro Hills or along the banks of Nasivi Creek (Figure 1).

Those farms located at the foot of Yaladro Hills were allotted grazing land adjacent to their cane farms. Those located along the banks of Nasivi Creek had small patches of land (0.1 to 0.2 hectares) for building dwellings and tethering farm animals during the wet season allocated to them on the slopes of Yaladro Hills. Many of these farmers were also members of a co-operative grazing land scheme. In 1971, the total area of grazing land to which Yaladro farmers had access was approximately 34.5 hectares, with individual plots ranging from 0.4 to 6.5 hectares. By 1982 the total land under grazing, to which farmers had access, had decreased by 19.4 per cent to 27.8 hectares (Table 2). The rest had been brought under sugarcane or new homes. This expansion had been carried out primarily by those farmers whose cane farms were located adjacent to their grazing land at the foot of the Yaladro Hills (Figure 2). In fact, six farmers said that they had bulldozed part of their grazing land to plant cane. Others had allowed their relatives or farm labourers to build houses on their grazing land.

Although the decrease in available grazing land was only 19 per cent, other factors made it significant. According to farmers interviewed, the carrying capacity of the grazing land in the early 1970s was sufficient to accommodate larger numbers of farm animals, partly because of the greater amount of fallow land available at the time, but also due to an abundance of fodder grass on the river banks, farm edges, and adjacent farm drains and tramlines. During the dry season, animals were grazed on the fallow land and fed on the tops of freshly-harvested cane (Quartermain, 1980). The river banks between the cane crop and the edge of the river were normally covered with high quality fodder. These areas were also used for grazing draught animals after work. The moist farm drains had a fairly rich growth of fodder grass during the dry season as they were not then required to be kept clean and free of grass. Some farmers also grazed their livestock along the tramline.

Figure 1:
The Yaladro Cane Area

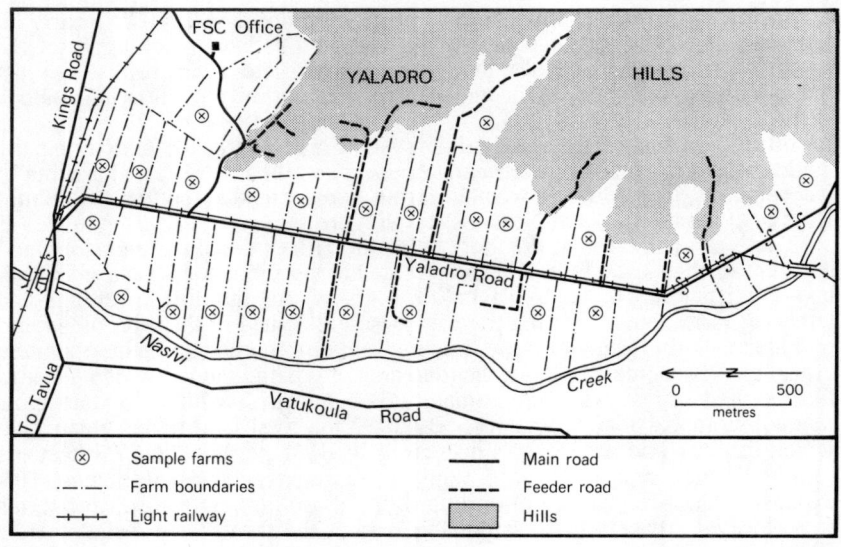

Consequently, the hilly grazing land was rarely used during the dry season as it had little grass on which animals could feed, and was generally reserved for grazing during the wet season when there was ample grass and when fallowed farm land was too wet and boggy. Many farmers also believed that

Table 2
Land Area on the 26 Sample Cane Farms
Under Sugarcane and Grazing in 1972 and 1982

	1971	1982
Sugarcane	78.8 hectares	107.6 hectares
Grazing	34.4 hectares	27.8 hectares

Source: Questionnaire surveys and field inventories, 1982.

Figure 2
Layouts of 'Typical' Farms at the Foot of the Yaladro Hills

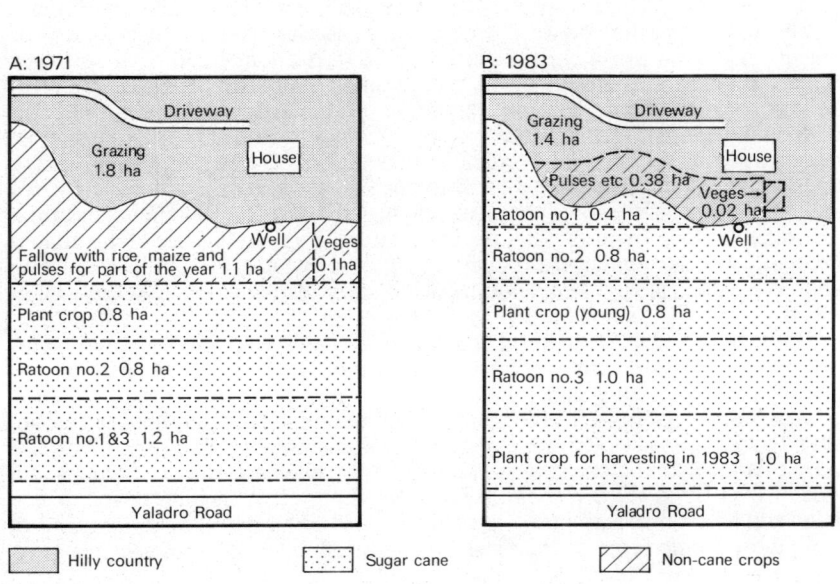

trampling of fallow land during the wet season made preparation of crop-land in the ensuing season difficult.

By 1982 there was little grazeable fallow land left on any of the farms since all available land was kept continuously under cane crops (Table 2). River banks were ploughed and planted in sugarcane to the very edges, farm drains were required by the FSC and the Drainage Board to be kept free of grass (often para grass or *Brachiaria mutica*, an excellent fodder grass), and herbicides were used increasingly to keep farms weed-free. As a result of these practices, there was little fodder on the cane farms proper, thus relegating animals to decreasing areas of grazing land throughout the year, including the dry season. Overgrazing on the diminishing grazing land resulted in further shortages of fodder in the dry season, and accelerated soil erosion.

In the case of poultry production, shortage of farm-produced feed, coupled with the high costs of purchased feed were major factors contributing to the reduction in birds. Before the sugarcane boom, nearly all farmers grew subsistence crops such as rice, sorghum and maize on their farms. The rice husks and dried maize were used as poultry feed, and little purchased feed was needed. With decreased planting of these crops, farmers experienced shortages of farm-produced poultry feed, and some began supplementing this with expensive purchased feed at $12 to $18 per 45-kilogram bag in 1982. Some farmers consequently considered it cheaper to buy frozen chicken from shops or even live chickens from poultry farmers than to rear their own.

Strong competition between crop production and livestock husbandry for household labour, as stated by Camoens (1985), is another contributing factor to the reduction in the number of farm animals. With higher sugar prices in the mid-1970s, labour became expensive in the cane farming areas. To reduce labour cost, farmers increasingly mechanized farm work. Instead of using draught animals and manual labour, many began labour-saving practices, such as using tractors, and intensified the use of artificial fertilisers and chemical pesticides. They also felt that the amount of labour and time previously spent in attending to farm animals could be more profitably directed towards sugarcane production. In other words, the farmers chose to make these changes under economic pressures to take advantage of high sugar prices.

Damage to sugarcane and other crops by animals was also seen as a factor leading to decreased animal production on cane farms. As mentioned earlier, the decrease in grazing and fallow land put more pressure on the cultivated areas as sources of food for the animals. Consequently, during the dry season, when fodder was short in grazing areas, animals escaped through fences and caused damage to the crops of both owners and their neighbours. Ducks and chickens ventured further afield in search of food, often causing havoc to rice fields and vegetable gardens. This led to conflicts among neighbours, and to avoid these, some farmers simply sold or reduced the number of animals.

EFFECTS OF A REDUCTION IN LIVESTOCK PRODUCTION ON SMALLHOLDER CANE FARMS

The figures for animal ownership show that prior to the sugarcane boom of the mid-1970s, more farmers kept cattle, goats and poultry than in 1983. Since the mid-1970s, and especially by 1982, the rearing of goats and chickens had declined (see Table 1), and purchased meat, such as imported mutton, goat, frozen chicken and tinned fish, had become more common sources of animal protein on cane farms.

Whereas in 1971 six out of the twenty-six farmers indicated that they were self-sufficient in meat production on their own farms, fifteen supplemented their supply commercially, and only five were fully dependent on shops, by 1982, none were self-sufficient, nine supplemented their supplies from shops, and seventeen depended entirely on shops for the supply of their meat (Table 3).

Table 3
Sources of Supply of Animal Protein for Farmers on the 26 Sample Farms in Yaladro, 1971 and 1982

	Own farm only 1971	1982	Farm & shop 1971	1982	Shop only 1971	1982
Milk	22	4	4	14	0	8
Poultry/Eggs	15	2	10	17	1	7
Meat	6	0	15	9	5	17

Source: Questionnaire survey, 1982.

Similarly, in the case of poultry and eggs, whereas fifteen farmers were self-sufficient in 1971, with ten supplementing their farm suppliers from shops, and one depending entirely on shops for his supplies, by 1982, only two farmers remained self-sufficient, seventeen supplemented their supplies from shops, and seven depended fully on shops.

Increasing dependency on imported dairy products could also be seen in the Yaladro area. Survey results show that while in 1971 twenty-two farmers produced all their own dairy supplies, only four having to supplement these from shops, by 1982, the situation was completely reversed, with only four farmers remaining self-sufficient, fourteen supplementing their supplies from shops, and eight having become fully dependent on shops.

These data collected in Yaladro area show that, in the early 1970s, farmers had integrated crop-livestock complexes which supplied most of their animal protein needs. Moreover, most of these products were produced on the farm and were consumed fresh with very little processing. In recent years, however, production of livestock has decreased considerably, with the majority of farmers having become increasingly dependent on purchased and processed meat, often imported fish and dairy products, as well as on chickens and eggs from local broiler and egg-laying establishments.

This reliance on off-the-farm supplies of animal protein has resulted in decreased consumption of these products. According to farmers interviewed, in the early 1970s chickens and goats were available on farms, and the frequency and quantity of consumption depended almost entirely on an individual family's wishes. By 1982, however, when chickens and goats became scarce on farms, consumption increasingly depended on the availability of cash, availability of the product in the village store, or on frequency of visits to towns.

Whereas in 1971 fresh meat was consumed about three times a week by all family members and fresh eggs nearly every day by working males, by 1982, most farm families consumed store-bought meat or poultry products on an average of only once a week. Fresh chicken and goat meat were eaten only on special occasions such as Christmas Day or when special visitors came.

Similarly, consumption of dairy products had also declined significantly by 1982. A number of farmers reported that in the early 1970s, most people had fresh milk at home, which was drunk by most family members. Nearly everyone drank tea with milk, infants were weaned on fresh milk, and most households consumed ghee (clarified butter) made at home. By 1982, however, the scarcity of fresh milk was widespread. Farm families frequently drank black tea, a large proportion of infants were weaned on store-bought baby formula, and imported ghee was purchased from shops and consumed less frequently. Home-made ghee was used only on special occasions, such as festivals, and in prayers.

There are also national-level economic implications of decreasing on-the-farm animal production. As Table 4 shows, imports of beef, mutton, and goat meat have increased significantly since 1974. Beef imports rose dramatically because of greater imports of boneless beef for canning in Fiji. Although much of this can be attributed to natural population growth and increasing urbanisation, the effect of decreasing livestock production on some 21,000 cane farms throughout Fiji must have had a significant effect on national self-sufficiency in animal protein. It should be pointed out, however, that, during the study period, Fiji almost achieved self-sufficiency in pork and poultry production (Table 4) at a national level because of wide-ranging government incentives to small-animal production. At the same time, there was a simultaneous reduction in on-the-farm poultry self-sufficiency in sugarcane growing areas. In addition the import content (grain feed) of locally produced pork and poultry production is considerable[2].

Table 4
Imports of Meat Products into Fiji, 1971-1982
(tonnes — fresh and canned combined)

Year	Beef	Pig	Sheep	Goat	Poultry
1971	234	156	165	78	638
1972	457	198	1,840	115	1,063
1973	319	193	1,971	75	929
1974	384	137	2,036	118	913
1976	2,258	98	3,390	na	451
1977	2,240	184	4,034	290	359
1978	2,284	104	4,634	285	341
1979	1,652	5	4,124	242	88
1980	976	47	3,510	230	9
1981	1,314	15	4,039	236	0.5
1982	2,296	21	3,128	247	2

na Data not available

Source: Adapted from Fiji Central Planning Office (1975: 83, 1980: 114-21); Fiji Ministry of Agriculture and Fisheries (1983: 23-33).

TOWARDS A REINTEGRATION OF CROPS AND LIVESTOCK

There are nutritional implications in such a dietary shift, for example, possible deleterious effects on the populations concerned, as emphasised by Johnson and Lambert (1982), Deo (1983), Thaman (1979, 1982b, 1983a, 1984), Baxter (1980) and Parkinson (1975, 1977). Imported processed foods are generally higher in fats, salt, and sugar and lower in vitamins, minerals

---

2 This dependence was underlined after Fiji's recent military coup when large commercial poultry producers, such as the Watties-owned Country Chicken, temporarily suspended production because of imported food shortages due to trade embargoes imposed by Australia and New Zealand.

and fibre than fresh farm foods. As stressed by Coyne (1984) and Thaman (1983b), such dietary shifts are seen to be major contributing factors in the alarming increase in cardiovascular disease, hypertension and stroke, diabetes, obesity, iron deficiency anaemia, and associated premature deaths in Fiji and other areas of the Pacific. Although these problems are more common among the sedentary urban dwellers, they are also likely to affect the affluent class of sugarcane farmers (and their families) whose farms are mechanised and where the bulk of farm work is done by hired labourers. Furthermore, as more and more farmers become increasingly dependent on force-fed chicken from poultry farms, there is a greater likelihood of growth hormones, antibiotics and other chemicals, which are concentrated in the animal fat, being passed on to consumers as cancer 'promoters' and other physiological pollutants (Thaman 1983b).

The reduction in the number of draught animals has resulted in a growing reliance on tractors and mechanisation of farms. Furthermore, some land initially used for grazing has been released for cultivation of sugarcane. This change was quite rational on the part of farmers during the mid- and late-1970s, when sugarcane prices were high. Since 1981, however, farmers have experienced difficulties. The grazing land brought under sugarcane cultivation has lost productivity due to poor farming practices. The price of sugar has declined on the world market, and the price of fuel, spare parts for farm machines and other farm inputs has continued to increase. As a result the profit margins of many farmers have been drastically reduced. The reduction in livestock has also resulted in a loss of organic fertilisation from animal waste. By depriving the soil of organic forms of nitrogen and by increasing use of inorganic nitrogen fertilisers, the natural processes of nitrogen fixation, which sustain the soil, are disrupted (Commoner 1971).

The livestock component of the integrated crop-livestock complex system of smallholder sugarcane farms contributed significantly towards the well-being of farm families. By providing meat, milk, eggs, and replacement bullocks, by saving the cost of fossil fuel through the provision of draught power, and by providing cash incomes from sales, it is estimated that livestock production in the early 1970s constituted from 20 to 25 per cent of total farm cash incomes, and possibly even a greater percentage of real cash and non-cash incomes and productivity.

In the face of the recent drop in world sugar prices and increasing costs of fossil fuel and animal protein, it is in the interests of the sugarcane farmers and the country as a whole to advocate the reincorporation of symbiotic livestock-cropping production systems on sugarcane farms in Fiji. It may even be possible, at this stage, to evolve, through applied and adaptive research, systems of crop-livestock combinations which will not necessarily reduce sugarcane acreages. This might be done by making more efficient use of resources such as the grazing land and the cane land itself. Serious consideration should be given to controlling overgrazing by setting aside limited areas for forage cropping and establishing forage banks and by the use of short-term planted pastures in crop rotations. This might be achieved by identifying suitable legumes which could serve the multiple purposes of human feed, fodder and nitrogen fixation. Hilly grazing land should be used for controlled grazing only during the wet season, and, in the dry cane-harvesting season, grass from forage cropping areas and cane tops could provide feed for livestock. Additional feed in the dry season could be obtained by utilising weeds and grass from cane farms and farm drains, thus also reducing the need for costly and environmentally hazardous herbicides. To feed poultry, there is a need to grow crops, such as rice, maize, sorghum, and legumes, as intercrops with sugarcane. These crops will help supplement human food needs, and waste by-products, plus surpluses, being used to feed poultry.

To make the cane farming agroecosystems less dependent on imported fossil fuel and fertiliser and to prevent further ecological degradation caused by extension of cane land into slopes of grazing land, there is a need to reunite livestock and crop production. The divorce of these two traditionally interrelated activities has taken its toll. In the face of lower sugar prices, increasing fossil fuel costs, imported inflation, and continued deterioration in terms of trade, plus further signs of food dependency, it is time to 'mend the fences' and remarry cropping and livestock production on smallholder sugarcane farms in Fiji.

Marginal cane land, Ra

12

DEVELOPMENT COMMUNICATION: A STUDY OF TWO BEEF CATTLE PROJECTS

Asesela Ravuvu

Development requires effective communication if the people to be assisted are to respond positively and participate fully in the process. Effective development communication depends on the ability of the communicator to deliver a development message efficiently and on the receiver's capacity to receive and understand the message in terms of his or her perceived development needs. Persons who deliver development messages can be termed 'change agents', whilst those to whom the development messages are directed are referred to as the 'target group' and generally include those at the lowest rung of the social and economic ladder. The active participation of these people at the 'grass roots' in the formulation and implementation of development projects has been seen as essential; yet being part of the development process does not necessarily mean controlling its outcome or receiving the most benefits.

For the past twenty years or so, Fijian villagers have been the main target of rural development efforts by 'change agents' of the Fiji Government and non-government organisations. Many villagers, however, still find it difficult to adhere to the kind of development process prescribed by such agents. Fijian people's success in development projects, particularly in commercial enterprises aimed at improving their standard of living, has been problematic. The initial success of a number of such development projects was seldom sustained, and most Fijian development projects have been overshadowed by failure and ultimately abandoned. There has been more demonstration of failure than of success.

Little has been written on development communication and grass roots participation in Fiji. Although a great deal has been said about their importance, particularly in national development plans, much remains to be done in practice. The general approach has been for change agents to investigate and initiate projects they think appropriate for those living in a subsistence economy, and which at the same time provide revenue to the government and lessen foreign imports. Even where it is claimed that villagers have been involved, their involvement has been mainly in implementing the advice of change agents. Lacking a power base for the mobilisation of financial and other resources essential for the implementation of any project, they have little say in the allocation of development resources and in the sharing of benefits. They generally accept suggestions from change agents in the hope of receiving some benefit. They are thus usually dependent upon the mercy and goodwill of those who control the resources.

Individual or communal needs and aspirations are frequently ignored unless they comply with national development plans and policies. More often they are left to individuals or village communities which have to mobilise their own meagre resources and receive little support from outside change agents who prefer to work within the national development plan. Thus, development communication in Fiji is still very much a one way affair, from the powerful to the powerless at the grass roots level. Because of this, people's participation is passive and token.

This study looks at some of the reasons for failure and partial success among Fijian beef cattle farmers of Tilivalevu and Verata communities. It aims to assist development change agents to understand better the participation of rural Fijian farmers in development projects. Such understanding should help provide new strategies for more effective development communication, and the attainment of sustained successful effort in rural development project.

HISTORICAL OVERVIEW

Long before the attainment of Independence in 1970, Fijians had been continually advised by government officials to use their land or it would be used by others to increase national income and earn foreign exchange. Following Independence, the reality of maintaining and expanding government services for Fiji's increasing population have pressured the independent government to exploit and develop all available natural resources. The acquisition of more foreign capital to finance its development needs through increased exports has become an important priority of the government, and indigenous Fijians, being the owners of large tracts of underdeveloped land, have been under constant pressure to use their land for market production and hopefully to benefit financially. The pressure to develop Fijian land commercially has also been an attempt by the government to reduce the increasing income disparities between the rural and urban sectors, and between the ethnic communities, as well as the need to expand agricultural production to provide for growing industrialisation and urbanisation.

Although generally reluctant to see their land exploited by others, especially as land which is leased may be lost for thirty years under the Agricultural Landlord and Tenant Act, Fijians now have much incentive to use their land for economic development. The fear of letting others use their land, coupled with their growing aspiration for more cash to meet their increasing wants, made Fijian landowners eager to be involved in commercial development projects involving their land. Although knowing little of how the market economy works, and being committed to some behaviour which in antithetical to it, they are under constant pressure to be involved in the system. Lacking the knowledge and skills to exploit the market to their own advantage, they have developed a sense of great dependence on those who advise them in implementing commercial projects. Within this general scenario the government established beef cattle projects to involve Fijian farmers in commercial production.

THE VERATA BEEF CATTLE SCHEME

In the early 1960s, commercial dairy and beef production was almost exclusively a European activity, though Indians were beginning to play a greater role. There was a significant political and economic need for Fijians to be involved if the economic gap between the three major races in this industry, as in most others, was not to become wider still. The first major effort at beef development on individually-owned Fijian farms on Fijian land, started in 1962, at Verata, on the initiative of the Veterinary Section of the Department of Agriculture. After twenty years of operation, it is still considered by officials as unsuccessful.

The beginnings of the Verata Scheme

Initially, the Verata Beef Cattle Scheme was intended to be a demonstration project to show the potential of Fijian cattle farming. It originally involved twelve Fijian men from villages in the locality. Participants were approached and encouraged by officers of the Veterinary Section and the Native Land Trust Board (NLTB). Personal knowledge of the abilities and motivation of those to be included in the project was an important factor in their selection. Six of them had been grazing some cattle on traditional land and had been known to the expatriate Veterinary Officer for the area.

Most of the prospective cattle farmers, had lived for some years away from their villages and had experienced the rigourous discipline of being employed as wage-earners. Their personal experiences in the monetised sector and their wish to control their own destinies, spurred them to return to their villages to use their *mataqali* land for cash cropping and, where possible, cattle grazing.

For example, Farmer A, who was sixty-nine years old at the time of this study (1987), had worked as a caretaker manager on a European cattle farm. From his earnings he bought twenty cattle and moved back to his village where he grazed his stock on his uncle's land. The land was acquired on an informal *kerekere* arrangement. Farmer B, aged fifty-nine years, first worked as a *galala* farmer after being away from his village for eighteen years. From his earnings he bought three cows which, by 1964, had grown to a herd of sixteen. These grazed on land used by the above farmer, also by informal customary arrangement[1]. Farmer C, now seventy-four, was once a teacher, then worked for thirty years in the Public Works Department boat-building shed in Suva. He returned to his village with $4000 he had saved, fenced an area borrowed from his relatives, and grazed twenty cattle. Farmer D, now fifty-nine, served in the army during the Second World War, and at demobilisation returned to his village but opted to become a *galala* farmer, raising pigs. From the proceeds of his pigs, he bought a cow which he left with farmer A to look after among his own. D returned to the village to look after his aging father until his death, and continued to raise pigs. He then sold the pigs and bought ten more cows. He and Farmer A often worked together. Farmer E, fifty-four, served in the army during the Malayan Campaign in the 1950s. He returned to his village and helped his father, who was then also a *galala* farmer. He and his father later returned to the village and, at the death of his father, he took over his gardening area and cultivated cassava and yams for subsistence and sale. From the profits, he purchased some cattle, which numbered twenty by the time the Verata cattle scheme started.

These five examples illustrate the motivation of the farmers starting in the scheme[2]. All were involved in the cash economy through commercial cropping and cattle grazing. The extent to which their interest is dominated by the acquisition of cash or by the achievement of social goals is impossible to discern, but it is apparent that both are important. In particular, cattle were seen as a way of satisfying both economic and social objectives. Cattle are looked upon as an investment not only for acquiring cash when needed, but also as a reserve for the 'rainy days' when life crises and other traditional demands and obligations need attention. In brief, cattle were more for the subsistence mode of living rather than the cash economy.

Through government concern to control cattle diseases and improve animal husbandry, both local and expatriate Veterinary Officers checked village herds regularly. During such visits in the early 1960s, the Verata locality was selected as the ideal place for a pilot beef cattle scheme to implement the policy of lessening beef imports by encouraging local production. Six Verata villagers who had already kept some cattle and had

---

1   Both farmers A and B are nephews of the landowners.

2   The other five farmers have had similar experiences. All lived away from the village at some stage but remained socially part of the village, all were able to acquire village land easily, all aspired to commercial farming, and all, but one, had some cattle before the Verata Scheme was established.

been the focus of such visits were first approached and encouraged to join. Since the land required did not belong to those who had been chosen to participate in the scheme, the inclusion of landowners was necessary in order to obtain their consent to leasing.

The twelve villagers recruited into the beef scheme were the first indigenous Fijians involved in commercial cattle production aimed entirely at regularly supplying beef for the urban markets. It was a major change in attitude from the idea of keeping some cattle only for the rainy days or to meet social commitments.

The land for the Verata Beef Scheme was acquired on behalf of the cattle farmers by the Department of Agriculture from the NLTB. The farmers were each allocated a block of 60 to 80 hectares. Those who had already established themselves in the area and had made some improvements to their pastures were shifted to new blocks in order to comply with the plan devised by the Department of Agriculture. Each farm lot was adjacent to another. The farmers had little say in the allocation of blocks and had to be content with the decision of the supervising officials. Loans from the Agricultural and Industrial Loans Board were acquired with the assistance of Veterinary Officers, who also arranged for the purchase of cattle from neighbouring European farms and, later, from coconut plantations on Taveuni. Fencing material, seeds, tools and weedicides were provided from the loan money. Each farmer had a loan account of $1200 to $2000 with the Development Bank. A condition of these loans was that the project would be supervised by the Veterinary Division of the Department of Agriculture.

The initial development work on the farm lots was done on a communal basis. All the farmers worked together and there was considerable cooperation between them and their supervising officials. Enthusiasm and interest were high as both the farmers and the officials strove to make this first Fijian beef scheme a success. Farmers and local supervising veterinary officers spent a great deal of time together on the farms and socially. Verata farmers, when interviewed, indicated that this was a time when they had a great deal of confidence and trust in the officials, particularly Messrs David Lornie and Ilisoni Cokanasiga. Both were said to have had a strong commitment to the project and David Lornie, apparently, had initiated the scheme.

Ilisoni Cokanasiga, Lornie's assistant, remembered this time with some satisfaction and spoke of the close cooperation between farmers and officials[3]:

> I worked with the farmers, ate and stayed with them even
> for weeks. I once spent Christmas with them on the farm. I
> invited them into to my home whenever they were in Suva.
> Sometimes we had annual social get-together at my house; I
> invited all the farmers regularly and noted problems that

---

3   Ilisoni Cokanasiga is now retired. He was interviewed in 1987.

needed attention; and then back in the office I prepared my
work programmes in relation to the farmers' I observed. I
submitted a monthly report to Headquarters. Detailed
reports of cattle inspection or routine inspection were
submitted to the office and comments were sent back to
field-officers. I was fortunate that I had a vehicle for my
use. It helped me to see the farmers regularly and even
helped transport fencing material for the farmers. I even
used it at times to transport farmers from one paddock to
another during group work on the farms. When I found a
farmer behind on his work, I went around and asked all the
other farmers to help.

Even with all the close supervision and support, though, progress was
slow. With the exception of transportation of stock and fencing material,
most of the work was done by hand. Also, as Ilisoni Cokanasiga recalled,
cattle and fencing material were not delivered on time and this distracted the
veterinary officers. The farmers, too, were often faced with other problems
of subsistence living which affected their overall performance. Thus one of
the agricultural supervisors wrote in his review a few years later:

Progress was slow. The farmers had lots of problems.
They were not used to a steady work rhythm; some still had
social obligations and the objective [of the beef scheme] in
many cases receded in the face of difficulties. The ravages
of wild pigs ... upon their gardens, the failure of crops, and
in some cases the damage to their houses in bad weather
had to be coped with. The saving grace was their
accessibility to a good road.

Yet, with tolerance, close supervision, and commitment on the part of
agricultural supervisors, some progress was made. At the end of the second
and third years of operation, some cattle were sold to urban butchers in good
fat condition and initial payments were made into the farmers trading
accounts with the bank.

Although the farmers expected to earn considerable profits when they
started, this expectation began to be dampened when most of the net proceeds
from sales went to loan repayments. In their eagerness to be involved in the
project, farmers received loans without realizing the extent to which
repayment of the principal and interest would diminish their returns in the
first few years. The Agriculture Department and the bank had agreed on a
six-year loan repayment schedule with 6 per cent interest. Interest was not
payable for the first two years but was allowed to accumulate until the third
year. The bank also paid the land rents for the initial years and this was
included in the farmer's debt. Although all this might have been explained
and agreed to by the farmers, it is doubtful that they fully understood the

financial implications. Most accepted the terms because they believed their leaders and trusted the supervisors. The supervisors, however, in preparing the loan repayment schedule, had estimated yearly income and expenditure based on assumptions about calving and mortality rates, sale prices and turn-off rates which over-estimated the yearly net revenues. As a result, loan repayments in accordance with the schedule, came to account for more than 70 per cent of net revenues.

The Governor-General of Fiji visited the scheme just after its establishment. The participants were presented to him at a public gathering. He congratulated them on their effort and told them that they would be the first Fijian millionaires if they worked hard and followed the advice of the supervisors. Six and a half years later, though, the Veterinary Officer in charge of the scheme reported:

> Progress was not as good as anticipated and new schedules of repayment were formulated — this time on a 12 year repayment basis. There were quite wide differences in progress as may have been expected but generally the original 'motivated farmers' were more satisfactory than the others ... Two farmers are on the point of repaying their entire loan, four will do so in the next two years and five farmers will require several years more. One farmer is likely to fail entirely and may soon leave his farm. However this man has suffered personal domestic tragedy and cannot really be considered a 'failure in terms of the scheme'.

Twenty years later the above comments could still be applied to the present state of the Verata Beef Scheme. Apart from one or two farmers who have just cleared their debts and another two who have left the scheme, the rest are still struggling to pay their loan debts. One of them is on the verge of leaving the scheme. His cattle have broken fences and gone wild. He has now resorted to planting *yaqona* to help meet his debts and, hopefully, repair the fences and re-establish his cattle holding.

A change of policy

One of the main reasons for the continued failure of the scheme was a change in management practices brought about by a wider shift in policy towards the beef industry. However, this change only came after an initial phase of herd and pasture development at Verata.

Pasture improvement and upgrading the stock were two main priorities for the supervisors once the individual cattle holdings were established. Women and children of the nearby villages were employed to plant Batiki Blue Grass on paddocks. Initial stock were from the farmers' own herds or neighbouring dairy farms and these were used for breeding and to keep the pastures in good condition. In an effort to acquire better quality stock, Santa and Brahmin cross-breed bulls were introduced to improve some of the existing herds. Farmers who did not have initial breeding stock were provided directly with SG and Brahmin store steers from European farmers in other regions.

After some time, a new scheme for supplying stock was introduced. Farmers were advised that their local breeding cattle and some heifers from the newly-improved herds, had to be sold to make room for more steers raised on the drier side of Viti Levu. The Agriculture Department wanted to pursue a new policy of beef-raising, whereby areas in the drier western side of Viti Levu, such as Tilivalevu, were to be used for breeding and the better pasture areas of southeastern Viti Levu, including Verata, were to be involved only in fattening. It meant that store steers, one to two years old, had to be transported from the west to the east, closer to the slaughterhouses and the main market of Suva.

The effects of this change in policy are still well-remembered by Verata farmers:

> At the start of the scheme I already had more than twenty cattle all of mild temperament because I used to milk some of them. Then SG bulls were brought in to mate with the local cows. New beautiful SG crosses were produced. I was just beginning to admire them and appreciated my new improved stock when I was told that all the young new heifers had to be taken to Niue and Kadavu. I could not say anything to the veterinary officer but just kept quiet. I was in tears and sad to see my fine heifers being taken away. Later on we were told that we had to sell all our bulls and cows and to get steers from Tilivalevu cattle farmers in Nadroga. Because at times Tilivalevu farmers could not supply us with steers we needed, we had to be given steers from Vanua Levu, most of which were wild and soon took to the bush as soon as we unloaded them from the truck. Before that our cattle had were quite tame. We used to take some of them to the Agricultural show in Suva and we won prizes[4]. At times we could not get steers at all and our paddocks were almost empty. In fact my paddock was almost without cattle for three years. It was fortunate that a Peace Corps volunteer by the name of Max saw the problem and encouraged us to have our own breeding stock again. It was hard to get cows at that time, but through this fellow's effort and his local assistants we were given some cows bought from dairy farms in Navua and Korovou, Tailevu.

---

[4] The author was shown some of the ribbons won, which had become proud mementoes for the farmers.

Almost half of the cows given to each of us died after a short period in our paddocks. I lost twelve of the twenty-two I received. They were old dairy cows. We did not get any compensation for the lost cows. Some time later we approached the Minister for Agriculture about this and he was kind enough to act on it. We were given a bull each from the hurricane relief gift of the Australian Government.

The new policy had been adopted to resolve the problems arising from having small beef ranches, averaging 50 hectares and with a carrying capacity of only fifty to sixty cattle. The officials believed that it was not viable to breed and fatten at the same time on these small holdings and they thought that Verata farmers, being on the wetter side of the island with luxuriant grass growth would do well fattening steers, while others on the drier side would breed store steers for fattening. But the reasons for the change were not understood by the farmers and they believed that they had been used by the Department as an experiment. Also, apart from being already dependent on the assistance and advice of the agricultural supervisors, Verata farmers were made further so by having to rely on outside breeders for their stock steers. When store steers from breeders were not available, Verata farmers found their paddocks almost empty. This was the situation for several years. Although their paddocks were empty, interest on loans accumulated.

Faced with the difficulties of acquiring store steers, farmers were again encouraged to have their own breeding cattle. Being in a desperate situation, they accepted whatever cattle were acquired for them by the officials from neighbouring dairy farmers. Farmers claimed that old dairy cows were acquired because they seemed to cost less ($60-$90) but this was because they were in poor condition. Almost half of the new stock died shortly after being placed in their paddocks. None of the farmers interviewed knew exactly the financial aspects of this transaction — whether the cattle were paid for in cash or bought from loan money and debited to the farmers' bank accounts. All they knew was that a number of cows were given to them to build up their stock again.

Despite the problems associated with the change in policy, the farmers mentioned how appreciative they were of the efforts of a number of veterinary supervisors. Mr. Lornie and his local assistants were frequently mentioned as was the Peace Corps volunteer named Max (above). Apart from recouping breeder herds and his work in arranging and establishing individual accounts for Verata farmers, Max conducted negotiations with a commercial bank in Suva. Most felt that if he had stayed longer with them, they would have cleared their debts by now and been 'freed'. Unfortunately, like Mr. Lornie, Max left after his term and the farmers came under other supervisors in whom they had less confidence, and were not able to work closely. In the farmers' words, they were 'advisers' and not 'workers' with farmers. Farmers' requests were not promptly attended to.

The farmers and their present situation

With the exception of one young farmer who took over his father's holding and debts with the Bank, the other beef farmers of Verata are well beyond their fifties and sixties. The oldest is seventy-four. Apart from the help of their wives, the farmers maintain their farms generally with their own labour. Village labour is occasionally available, but only when a head of cattle is needed for a ceremonial occasion and this is only possible with the approval of the Livestock Officer and the Bank. With no working capital for the hiring of additional labour, Verata farmers have to depend a great deal on personal effort. As most of them are now becoming elderly and less active, the state of their holdings is declining. Fences are not fully repaired and weeds have spread over the pastures which the aging farmers try to control manually.

With old age slowing down work on the farm, some have begun to draw back to the security of their villages. Five have already built permanent-material houses in their respective villages and spend a great deal of time on village affairs. They also have a good house on their farm, though the better one is in the village. The quiet aspiration of each farmer is to build a well-constructed house of imported materials for retirement in his village. This is considered an achievement in life. According to most, the farm house is only a temporary base until a much better dwelling is built in one's village.

It is important to understand that these people are members of village communities and will continue to be, because each farmer's personal worth is evaluated in terms of his contributions to his kin and village affairs. Although made to settle on farms for the sake of concentrating their efforts on beef farming and isolating themselves from village social activities, Verata farmers continue to be affected by community expectations. This is psychologically important to the farmers if they are to continue to be accepted and their worthiness to be recognised and publicly acclaimed by those with whom they are closely identified. Thus the village setting continues to be very influential in their lives.

To be useful to one's village community requires public acceptance and approbation, and provides personal satisfaction. Verata farmers continue to be part of a number of inter-related social entities to which they have to contribute if they are to be considered worthy of membership. Their success in the beef project is going to be greatly determined by how each farmer compromises between development project demands on the one hand and personal and communal needs and expectations on the other. Although a farmer may like to ignore some of his traditional communal links to free himself from the 'burden' of tradition, he will never be totally free from other forms of harassment that will continue to frustrate his work.

Lacking the appropriate technology to assist them in their labour, farmers continue to depend a great deal on their own efforts and on locally available village labour which can only be acquired through maintaining favourable social relationships with their village communities. For instance, a farmer of

Verata who opted out of involvement in his village affairs now finds it difficult to acquire assistance from his village people. He thus changed his church affiliation and has become an adherent of a new sect, to whose members he has now turned for help. It is noteworthy that that particular farmer is one of the two with the largest debts with the Fiji Development Bank (FDB). The two farmers who have paid up their debts continue to maintain strong links with their villages and involve themselves in village affairs.

The need to maintain the beef scheme as a viable economic enterprise and to provide a continuous supply of beef animals to urban butchers can no longer be left entirely to the efforts of the original aging farmers. Little thought was given at the initial planning of the scheme to the need for maintaining continuity. Transfer of holdings to young able-bodied and enterprising successors has been long overdue, and the need to do this as soon as possible is important if the beef scheme is to be revived and continued.

Of the twelve farmers originally involved in the Verata scheme, nine remain and three are no longer part of the project. Those who have left the scheme generally have found other sources of income which give them much more control and freedom in the use of their earnings. One farmer who left the scheme in 1975, did so after he had paid his debts by selling logs to timber millers. Although he still has fifteen cattle, he does not want to be involved in the scheme again. He said he left the scheme because he had little control over the funds acquired through sales of his cattle. He claimed that the FDB controlled all revenue and that he used to receive only about $10 at a time, which was not adequate even for subsistence. He has built four timber houses with iron roofs for his sons in his village through cash from sales of timber from his clan land, and from his sons' wage earnings, he intends to purchase an electric generator to light the family homes. He has also repaired the fences on his already well-pastured paddock and is hoping to increase the number of his cattle which, according to him, are a stand-by to be disposed of when needed. Another farmer is now employed as a prison farm manager. He is trying to pay his FDB loan from his wages. Although his farm still exists, fences are falling down and cattle are straying.

Those that remain within the Verata Scheme are concentrating on freeing their debts to the FDB and to gaining greater control over their farms. However, to achieve these objectives, there are a number of serious obstacles to be faced. These include:

Indebtedness. Debts are increasing while proceeds from sales have not kept up with the yearly scheduled loan repayments. Farmers worry that their farms may be taken over by the FDB.

Lack of information. There are difficulties in getting information about sales and proceeds. Farmers claim that their statements for cattle sales and expenses incurred are not usually given to them unless they ask for them and that they often have to wait for as long as two weeks before they receive their shares of the sale of their cattle. Also, deductions are often made from farmers' accounts during the course of commercial transactions, but these are not usually explained to them.

Lack of diversification. Farmers are not encouraged to diversify their grazing activities to include other small ruminants, such as goats, which might augment their low incomes. No explanation has been given.

Lack of credit. Getting supplementary loans from the FDB to improve pastures, repair falling fences and employ labour is difficult because of unpaid balances on existing loans.

Farmers also complain that official control over their activities is too heavy. For example, disposal of cattle for traditional obligations has been rigidly controlled by the FDB and the veterinary supervisors. Thus the private sale of cattle occurs infrequently. Other sales are very restricted and depend on the effectiveness of the Livestock Officer in arranging sales. Also, farm management procedures generally are biased towards improving the quality of stock rather than producing enough cattle to allow for frequent and regular sales to help farmers clear their debts and provide them with some take-home cash. The Verata farmers continue to be disillusioned by their experience. The scheme promised them a financially better future, yet after twenty-one years of operation, most are still in debt.

Problems of management and communication

All of the complaints are administrative or management problems which could have been resolved through better communication and efficient management. Farmers interviewed complained about the long period they usually endured before any response to a request for help was received, in contrast to the early days of the project when their problems were quickly identified and resolved, and when they said they were frequently visited and worked hand in hand with veterinary supervisors.

Initially, loan requests were channelled through the local Veterinary Officer who supported or rejected them before passing them direct to the bank for action. Now, the local Livestock Officer sends farmers' requests for loans (and other representations) to the district Agricultural Officer at Korovou, thence to the Divisional Veterinary Officer for approval (or not), and finally the FDB. The FDB, if approval is given, grants supplementary loans for the purchase of cattle, fencing material and so on. At present the Bank is reluctant to grant supplementary loans to those who have not kept up their stipulated annual repayments. In 1985 only two farmers out of eight in debt were allowed supplementary loans. Although officials of the Veterinary Division are again now closely supervising the Verata Beef Scheme, farmers' debts with the FDB continue to increase. Between 1984 and 1985, debt increases were between $1000 and $2000 for each farmer.

Verata cattle farmers have long suffered from over-dependence and ineffective management. The over-dependence has been due to their being made to adopt a beef farming technology of which they have little knowledge or confidence to handle on their own. Their situation has been made worse by inconsistent farm management policies initiated by successive agricultural supervisors and which often do not take a hard look at the commercial implications. The farmers' initiatives to resolve their own problems have been stunted and they continue to be dependent upon agricultural officials.

It is unfortunate that the task of freeing farmers from an increasing debt burden is entrusted to the already over-committed livestock officers. Although generally competent in animal husbandry and some aspects of farm management, the livestock extension officers lack business acumen[5]. If extension officers are to be expected to make beef cattle farms commercially profitable they need specialist skills and experience in the business side of the meat industry.

Whereas in the early stages of the project the farmers received considerable assistance from the local officials, now this is much less forthcoming. The present Livestock Officer and his stockman have inherited problems which they are unable to resolve on their own. Although professionally equipped to help farmers, the local Livestock Officer has felt inadequate when confronting Verata farmers who are more senior in age to him and have worked under other more experienced livestock officers. Being his first post after graduating from the Fiji College of Agriculture and with little experience in practical farm management and budgeting, he has had little alternative but to concentrate on routine veterinary activities such as tuberculosis testing, and attending to clinical and surgical cases. In addition, he has had to handle other nearby beef projects such as the Naitutu/Sote scheme with eleven further smallholders on the Verata model[6]. The time and resources once spent on Verata farmers have been diminished and farmers complain that they are not visited regularly and their problems are not discussed or attended to as before. As a result, they have not developed important work plans in association with the local Livestock Officer.

There is an obvious lack of cooperation and communication between the local officer and the farmers and also between that officer and his superiors[7]. Such communication, to explain a particular course of action, share in decision-making or air problems, is both highly informative and encourages

---

5   Interestingly, the Commercial Undertaking section of MPI is also managed by an animal husbandry specialist rather than a business expert.

6   The Livestock Officer finds it easier to work with the new farmers who are generally younger and more enthusiastic than the more senior farmers of Verata whose productive efforts have declined with age.

7   Not only has the local officer not developed a systematic record of how he and his stockman spend time with the farmers, but also there seems to have been little supervision or encouragement from his superiors over the past six years.

cooperation and trust between all ranks. A concern with the problems of the workers and not just those of the work is thus enhanced and maintained.

It is encouraging, however, that since mid-1985, senior veterinary officers of the MPI have again begun to be concerned with the problems faced by Verata beef farmers and their extension officer. This renewal of effort partly came about after the villagers of Verata complained to the Governor-General of Fiji, during one of his visits, about stray cattle from the beef scheme damaging their gardens. All involved in the Verata project have now held amicable meetings, and farmers, livestock officers and bank officials are again being encouraged to discuss their respective problems and ways of resolving them together. This move has been very effective, and the farmers and the Livestock Officer are again demonstrating enthusiasm and confidence.

Although some effort has already been made at improving communication and cooperation, a great deal more is needed. Other problems continue to frustrate such efforts at regular contact and supervision. The Livestock Officer and his stockhand cannot regularly visit and help the farmers without the use of a safe and well-maintained four-wheel drive vehicle. The use of such a vehicle was very effective during the early years of the scheme but the small 100cc motorcycle presently used by the Livestock Officer is inefficient and unsafe for the rough roads in the area, let alone for carrying materials required for work with the farmers. Frequently, the motorcycle is awaiting repair, or idle because of bad road conditions or insufficient funds for running it. Vehicles that might be available for other staff suffer from lack of maintenance or drivers and extension officers cannot visit farms as regularly as they would wish.

The present practice of expanding cattle projects in rural areas without related expansion of infrastructural support results from attempts to satisfy the political demand of expanding economic development projects in rural areas. It is important that expansion be considered in relation to available infrastructure. Aid donors often provide vehicles or other machinery for development projects, but care must be taken in accepting such donations if support is not available to operate and maintain them.

THE TILIVALEVU CATTLE SCHEME

The Tilivalevu Beef Scheme started in 1966. It consists of thirteen individually-owned small ranches on the Verata model. Being on the drier southwestern side of Viti Levu, Tilivalevu farmers initially were engaged in breeding store steers for the better pastures of southeastern Viti Levu, including Verata, in accord with the Department of Agriculture's policy of using the drier areas to breed store cattle and the well-watered pastures of the southeast to fatten them. Tilivalevu farmers were thus to sell store steers, surplus heifers and cull cows to Verata farmers and others, transactions being conducted through the Commercial Undertaking unit of the Department of Agriculture.

Motivated by news of the early progress at Verata, and encouraged by the Agricultural Department and the district administration, landowners of Tilivalevu village and other neighbouring communities were prompted to become involved in beef cattle farming. With over 4000 hectares then in possession, there was a great deal of potential. With the advice and assistance of the Department of Agriculture, thirteen Fijian cattle farmers were each allocated an average of 200 hectares of leased land. They were required to settle on their ranches away from their villages and to establish subsistence gardens within their individual blocks before financial loans could be obtained from the FDB.

Encouraged by the possibility of loans, Tilivalevu farmers worked hard during the initial stages. With the guidance and encouragement of local Livestock Officers, who also owned ranches within the scheme, Tilivalevu farmers put in a great deal of work before any substantial assistance was received from the government. Rugged, and inaccessible by road, the land area covered by the scheme was difficult to develop without motor transport and machinery. Thus much of the initial clearing of fence lines, and obtaining fence posts from surrounding bush, was done by hand or using bullocks and horses. With one of the livestock officers acting as a farm manager, the farmers and their wives toiled as a group putting up fences, subdividing farm lots, and establishing pastures of Nadi Bluegrass.

One livestock officer, Joeli Lesavua[8], worked with the farmers at the initial stage:

> Managing Tilivalevu at the beginning was a difficult task. I had to sleep and work with the farmers and discussed with them what to do next. I impressed upon them the difficult nature of the project and its long-term benefits for the sake of their future generations. I also encouraged the close involvement of their wives in farm activities and often spoke to them of the importance of supporting and caring for their husbands if they were to achieve their goals. Every week I visited the farmers and spent two to three days with each of them. I did not impose my ideas but I tried to also listen to them and reached some agreement. I encouraged them to talk and mention their problems. Each family's problems were taken into account when planning our work. Friday and Saturday were set aside as free days for farmers

---

8   He had been one of the junior Veterinary Officers who worked with David Lomie and Ilisoni Cokanasiga at the initial stage of the Verata Scheme. That experience equipped him well.

to do their own things. Team work was encouraged and the farmers assisted one another.

At the beginning of the Tilivalevu Scheme only one of the thirteen farmers possessed any cattle. Because of the interest in raising cattle, the others were nominated by the members of the landowning *mataqali* or *bito* to participate. All farmers were advised from the start that they were to breed store cattle to be sold to Verata and other beef schemes.

Because of the desire to emulate the progress being made at Verata which had been widely publicised, and the need to acquire some cattle and a leasehold, Tilivalevu farmers were very highly motivated. They worked hard to attain this goal of owning a cattle ranch, as a source of regular income. It also accorded with the Government policy of encouraging income-generating projects in rural communities, and of mobilising undeveloped land. Thus, Tilivalevu farmers saw themselves as contributing to the national need for more beef cattle for local markets.

Changing the initial policy

Due to the rugged and dry nature of Tilivalevu, larger holdings of 120 to 200 hectares were established, providing a stocking rate of one animal to 1.5 to 2 hectares. Once all the holdings were fenced and pastures established, SG or Brahman cross-breed stock were obtained.

The original plan had been to breed store cattle to be sold for fattening elsewhere. However, the establishment of improved pastures, coupled with the reluctance of the Tilivalevu farmers to sell their store steers of one or two years old for only $70 or $80 a head, prompted them to change the earlier policy. They realised that Verata farmers only bought the best store steers and left the rejected ones with the Commercial Undertaking which would try to sell them to other buyers and they felt cheated. They also felt that the Commercial Undertaking was selling their cattle too cheaply and was too slow in paying them the proceeds. Thus, they decided to fatten and market their cattle on their own[9], a move which disadvantaged Verata and other fattening schemes.

The government policy of separating breeding and fattening therefore failed because it was not adopted successfully in either scheme. The assumption that two sets of Fijian cattle farmers geographically distant from one another could work in close cooperation, with control and supervision by veterinary supervisors, demonstrated the paternalism and short-sightedness of those who created the policy.

---

9   With other cattle farmers in the neighbourhood, they even took the bold step of establishing their own butchery, though it was closed later through mismanagement.

New initiatives and diversification

Tilivalevu farmers displayed a greater sense of independence than their Verata contemporaries. In trying to resolve their numerous difficulties, the farmers initiated group meetings where common problems were discussed and ways of overcoming these sought. Farmers' meetings have become regular events, providing a forum where Tilivalevu farmers are encouraged to talk about their problems which are then conveyed to their veterinary supervisors for attention. In this way farmers' inhibitions are discouraged, and group spirit and solidarity are enhanced. Work groups to attend to major tasks involving individual cattle holdings are also an important feature of work organisation at Tilivalevu. Bullocks and horses are also harnessed to help farmers in heavy and difficult tasks.

Tilivalevu farmers are encouraged to use their initiative and have become very resourceful. Diversification has occurred. Knowing that they cannot get a quick cash flow from cattle only, some farmers have turned to rearing goats for sale, others produce peanuts and maize for the local markets, and some plant sugar cane. Cash from such sales is used for the farmer's family sustenance and other monetary obligations. At times, cash is used as working capital to help the farmer develop his cattle holding, such as acquiring treated pine posts, clearing, repairing fences and improving pastures. Although initially, supervisory officials did not directly encourage diversification, pragmatism and sensitivity to the numerous difficulties facing the farmers led to some flexibility[10].

The Tilivalevu farmers

With the exception of two or three in their forties, most Tilivalevu cattle farmers are in their mid-fifties and are beginning to be less active. Some fences have fallen down and weeds and bushes are evident in pastures.

Like their Verata contemporaries, the farmers of Tilivalevu are still very strongly tied to their village and other customary obligations. A number of them were not on their farms during this study — they were either attending to village activities or bedridden with sickness and some were working on their sugar cane plantations.

One of the few progressive farmers of Tilivalevu was met at his home, a well-built concrete and iron building close to his wife's village. His house on the farm was a 'lean-to' temporary shelter. Two other farmers who had built concrete and iron buildings on their farms were determined to live on their farms. Both believed in helping themselves and not depending on others such as relatives in their villages. When they required the assistance of village

---

10   Also, the presence amongst them of professionally qualified veterinary officers on the scheme is a source of additional confidence and advice, not always available from the scheme's official supervisors. They act as a check on advice and suggestions which are not in the best interest of the cattle farmers.

workers they usually paid them in kind. Another farmer had built a wood and iron house on his lot. He too was determined to live on the farm, but complained of the theft of his cattle.

All the farmers are assisted in their work by their wives and children. Other assistance normally comes from the village communities nearby who sometimes require one or two cattle for payment. Organised group work among the farmers themselves is also utilised for major tasks such as clearing fence lines and paddocks, or putting up fence posts.

One major problem faced by most farmers is the inaccessibility to an all-weather road. The existing access roads are only usable during dry weather and by four-wheel drive vehicles. Thus, work on the farms has to depend a great deal on human and animal energy. All Tilivalevu farmers, but one, have a pair of working bullocks. Without all-weather roads, sales of cattle are greatly limited and generally take place during the dry season from June to September.

The Extension Officers

Tilivalevu farmers speak very highly of the local Livestock Officer who has been working closely with them. They display a great deal of trust and confidence in him, and do not hesitate to express their concerns to him as he is very receptive and helpful, and avoids bureaucratic procedures to get things done for the farmers. Through constant and regular visits he has acquired a better understanding of the farmers' problems and established rapport and warm relationships with them. This puts him in a strong position to negotiate with his superiors and development bank officials to resolve farmers' problems.

The above close relationship does not hold, however, with the more senior officers who, according to some farmers, hardly visit them. A number of farmers showed indignation at the way the sale of their cattle was handled, and the rather autocratic manner in which their requests were dealt with. The Area Livestock Officer is seen as inflexible, particularly regarding FDB requirements on loans and repayments, and communication is poor.

Statistical success as a delusion of reality

The Tilivalevu Cattle Scheme has been generally considered by senior agricultural officials as a success. It is important, however, to view such an evaluation not only quantitatively but also qualitatively. Senior officers of the MPI have based their evaluation of the success of the project on reports by supervising Veterinary Officers and financial statements from the FDB. Although such reports are statistically impressive, they are generally misleading regarding the realities faced by farmers.

In the summary report of sales for 1985, the total allocation for personal expenses for each of the twelve farmers of Tilivalevu was $1204, and their operating account was $402 for the year. Payments to the bank averaged $1012. When loan repayments and operating costs were deducted from each farmer's earnings from cattle sales, only two farms could be regarded as being successful (farmers 1 and 11). Table 1 shows the actual personal expenses for farmers after loan repayments and operating costs have been accounted for.

Table 1
Tilivalevu Farmers: Gross and Net Income, 1985
($)

Farmers	Proceeds from Sales	Loan repayments & operating costs	Balance of personal income earned
1	8,124.00	1,414.00	6,710.00
2	4,045.00	1,414.00	2,631.00
3	2,425.00	1,414.00	1,011.00
4	2,030.67	1,414.00	616.67
5	1,232.00	1,232.00	-
6	2,855.22	1,414.00	1,441.22
7	1,261.40	1,261.00	-
8	686.90	687.00	-
9	1,339.94	1,340.00	-
10	3,271.70	1,414.00	1,857.70
11	5,454.94	1,414.00	4,040.94
12	no sale	-	-

Source: MPI Annual Beef Farm Extension Report, South West Division (unpublished).

According to these data, five of the twelve farmers did not get any 'take home' money at all. Another five received only $2600 or less for the whole year's toil[11]. Even with these net incomes, the picture is still misleading because the actual stipulated amount paid by each farmer to the FDB was not shown on the record, nor the real operating cost due to each. In fact, most farmers have complained about the lack of money to pay operating costs, and the difficulty of getting additional loans because annual stipulated repayments

---

[11] Assuming that households average seven people, the income *per capita* ranges from $376 to as low as $88 per annum.

to the bank have not been met for one reason or another. Unforeseen shortfalls in the number of cattle to be sold, due to low calving rates, cattle thefts, irregular sales, or the fluctuating and unstable market price for beef, were not taken into account in projecting the amount to be received by each farmer from any projected sale.

Lacking income to cover many operating costs, they find it difficult to maintain their properties by keeping the fences and pastures in good order, or buying new stock. This financial constraint has meant that stocking rates are below what is possible. At present, the rate is only one beast to 2.9 hectares of grazing land, but with improved pastures, this could increase significantly. Also, the low rate has meant that pastures are deteriorating, with stock unable to control weeds and scrub. Poor fences have led to cattle 'going bush'. With inadequate income to cover maintenance, this situation is likely to worsen.

Statements of debts at the end of 1985 show that unpaid debts are, for many, standing at 69 per cent of the total amount borrowed from the bank. The average debt was $11,038.75, while that of Verata was $7402.25. At Tilivalevu, this represented between 27 per cent and 96 per cent of the total debt and, after almost twenty years of operation, hardly any farmer has cleared his debts with the bank. The most successful farmer still owes 60 per cent of the total amount loaned, although he received an additional loan for the construction of a concrete and iron house, for farm improvements and for purchasing more cattle.

All Tilivalevu farmers interviewed indicated that if it was not for their other cash-earning activities, such as rearing goats for sale and cash cropping, they would have found it much more difficult to meet their daily living expenses and to provide some working capital for the maintenance and improvement of their farms. One farmer praised the effectiveness of rearing goats among his cattle. He said he did not have to look for markets, but buyers came to his farm and usually paid $70 to $90 a head.

All Tilivalevu farmers have stockyards, eleven permanent and one temporary, whereas those at Verata have only two permanent stockyards and the rest are temporary. Tilivalevu also has a communal loading yard which Verata farmers do not have. Record keeping and farm management at Tilivalevu is ahead of Verata. There have also been some technical achievements at Tilivalevu. Calving percentages range from 45 per cent to 65 per cent, with an average of 53 per cent. This is very high for Fiji. Tilivalevu farmers each have a large farm which allows flexibility to graze goats and grow cash crops, whereas the smallholdings allocated to Verata farmers do not allow such diversification. Further, by way of contrast, the Tilivalevu group have enjoyed good leadership and supervision from their energetic local Livestock Officer. Yet both are still dependent on the local officer for many tasks, such as the castration of bull calves, segregation of stock and even the mustering of cattle.

It is unfortunate, however, that such effective supervision has been often frustrated by other factors similar to those found among Verata farmers. Absence of farmers from their farms for village customary activities and other traditional obligations usually upset pre-planned work schedules[12]. Sickness is another problem and old age means that many cannot work as hard. Uncontrolled stock continues to restrict those who cannot apply suggested stock management techniques, whilst unofficial sales of cattle, and cattle thefts, have been a menace. Lack of capital for farm maintenance and improvement and for the purchase of additional stock to meet debt obligations and other expenses is a major problem. And, as in Verata, regular supervision by MPI officials is often hindered by inadequate funds to run departmental vehicles[13]. Finally, the lack of an all-weather road connecting each farm means that the rugged terrain makes it more difficult, even during dry weather, to traverse the area by foot or vehicle.

DIFFERENT YARDSTICKS FOR SUCCESS

Often, development projects are best evaluated in terms of the goals and aspirations of participants. When farmers were asked whether they were happy with their performance, all answered in the affirmative and qualified their statements by itemising what they had achieved during their involvement in the beef scheme. Some said that they had managed to pay school fees regularly and provide bus fares for their children, and that they had also managed to build improved houses for their families. With a number of cattle at hand on the farm, most also found it easier to meet traditional contributions which were required of them every now and then. Even though the demands made upon them to contribute beef animals for ceremonial feasts were not frequent, they displayed a sense of satisfaction in contributing in one form or another to ceremonial affairs. The fact that each farmer was identified with a leased cattle holding which is considered as his possession, irrespective of it being still under mortgage, is seen as a substantial achievement. Having rights to a piece of land to oneself for the purpose of economic development in the market sense is not often accessible to many villagers, who normally hold land rights in groups. Thus, the establishment of a cattle holding in itself, which, in turn, provides for the satisfaction of some basic needs for daily living is a mark of success. As long as the farm exists with some cattle on it, the farmer is generally pleased with his effort and that he has an economic resource which he can turn to in times of crisis. His main worry has been to clear his debts with the FDB.

In terms of the supervisory veterinary officer's evaluation, the best and most successful farmer is he who practices good animal husbandry, has the

---

12 Tilivalevu farmers, unlike those in Verata, have work schedules prepared in consultation with the local Livestock Officer.

13 As in Verata, the local Livestock officer has only a small 100cc motorcycle, which is not suitable for his job or the terrain.

best farm management plan, has a permanent stockyard and maintains full control over his stock. He practices stock segregation and carries out breeding improvement through better selection of breeders and the use of quality bulls. He keeps good records of his stock and diversifies his farm activities to cater for immediate financial needs. It is interesting to note that the best Verata farmer, according to these criteria, is one of the two with the highest bank debts. According to the FDB, the best farmer is he who has paid his stipulated annual repayments regularly, and better still has cleared his debts and is thus in a better position to be encouraged to apply for another loan.

The adequate satisfaction of these three competing interests — the farmer's desire to satisfy his basic and traditional needs, the professional aspiration of the supervising officers to produce better quality beef cattle, and the FDB loan repayment requirements — has been a major inherent management problem throughout the history of the schemes. The compromising of these three interests demands the services of a good manager who is adept at both farm and commercial management. This basic problem must be addressed if beef farming is to become a success among Fijian farmers.

THE PROBLEM OF SUCCESSION AND INTER-GENERATIONAL COMMUNICATION

There is an expressed wish among Verata and Tilivalevu farmers that their children will continue their efforts and inherit their farms. This is understandable but it may prove unworkable. For some farmers, most of their children are still attending primary and secondary schools which continue to emphasise academic achievement and the hope of gaining a professional career or white collar jobs. Although children assist their parents on the farm every now and then, there is little assurance that they will stay on the farm and take over from their parents. In fact, most farmers send their children to school not because they wish them to be on the farm, but to enable them to get better wage employment elsewhere. The farm is used as a source of income for school fees, school bus fares, and other educational needs. Farm work is looked upon not as an end in itself but as means to other 'higher' goals, the most important of which is that children acquire good salaried employment. Only those children who did not succeed in school and find it hard to get a paid job would be prepared, as a last resort, to work on the farm. Wage employment is more lucrative than farming.

Although a small number of older farmers have transferred their farms to one of their sons or a married daughter, the continuity and success of the cattle projects are very doubtful. Successors are not selected for their strong commitment and experience in beef farming, but on the basis of close kinship and other social reasons. For instance, a younger married son who had been a casual wage worker in town, but returned to live in the village, was selected over his elder brothers who still are working in towns. Since he is the only one living in the village with his father, and with no paid employment, he is the logical choice as far as the old man is concerned.

Another farmer, who has no son, is planning to transfer his cattle farm to his daughter, who is married to a church minister officiating in another locality. Yet another with no son is also in the process of transferring his cattle farm to a nephew in the police force. Whether these relatives with regular employment would abandon their jobs to live on the farm is problematic. Some aging farmers are reluctant to release completely the control of their farms to their children or other relatives and some still wish to exert some influence in order to ensure provision for old age. This often creates doubt and insecurity for the young successor who consequently will not work whole-heartedly and commit himself to maintaining and improving the farm.

Because of the inherent cultural make-up of the successors, and their continuing association with their kinsmen and other villagers, they are unlikely to do better than their fathers. They inherit a number of socio-economic problems even before they start. Thus, inheritance is too narrow a base for continued successful commercial farming. It is necessary that provision be made for transfer to other Fijians (not necessarily one's own kinsmen) with high motivation and appropriate skills. Such people are likely to achieve success in commercial farming and maintain continuity in the projects.

CONCLUSION

The study shows two major categories of communication problems, each of them complex. The first is bureaucratic where the main difficulties lie in appropriate training of staff in effective dialogue with farmers and between headquarters and the field staff. The second category is cultural, translating the needs of national economic policy to village-based, subsistence-oriented rural communities whose first priorities are local socio-cultural commitments. This requires tolerance, understanding and compromise, and thus the careful development of a new *modus vivendi* for both. The process is in motion in Fiji, but it is inevitably slow, often frustrating, and sometimes painful.

In general both the Verata and Tilivalevu Schemes have suffered from the absence of an effective beef farming policy suitable for smallholders still living largely at the subsistence level. Both schemes also involved a beef farming management policy which greatly increased farmers' dependence rather than independence. Such a management policy also posed a commercial risk to both schemes. Lessening this depends on the professional expertise and business acumen of supervising veterinary officials, yet both have been guided by veterinary officers who, though professionally qualified in animal husbandry and to some extent in farm management, are in most cases not skilled in business management, nor sufficiently aware of the commercial nature of the meat industry. Thus, they sometimes unduly emphasise the professional part of their work to the detriment of the commercial. The schemes have suffered: from a $2000 initial debt, each farmer now averages eight times this amount. After twenty years of operation, only two farmers on the Verata scheme have cleared their debts with the bank, but this was only possible because of financial support from their wage or salaried relatives, their children in the army and police forces.

Yet ineffective communication has not been the only cause of slow progress. A major difficulty has been the introduction of a commercial farming technology among Fijian smallholders who hardly have any previous experience or knowledge of it. Because of this, farmers have to depend a great deal on the expertise of the veterinary supervising officers. Political decisions to involve rural Fijians in economic development projects to attenuate income disparities between Fijians and other ethnic groups often ignore the problems of introducing business enterprises among those who are still largely dependent on a subsistence mode of living and a different ideology. The realities of life facing each farm family must be well understood and fully assessed in planning and implementation if progress is to be achieved. Failing to do this will only increase frustration for each farm family as they try to keep up with the demands of the project and meet their expected obligations in life. To satisfy these basic and social needs is the very essence of the farmers' initial interest and enthusiasm to participate in any economic development project. The two schemes have only survived because many farmers have been able to find alternative sources of income to meet their social obligations and basic household needs. Development planners and project directors have not given enough consideration to incorporating the way of life of the people they wish to develop. Often rules and conditions which work contrary to the wishes and aspirations of those to be 'developed' are imposed.

To date, cattle farming, or any commercial farming for that matter, has been unsuited to the personality of most Fijian farmers and the tempo of village life of which they are a part. More regular effort will have to be made by local extension officers in educating the farmers for self reliance and in farm and business management skills. Good supervision involves encouraging farmers to do things themselves: to work with farmers rather than for them. It is easy to blame the farmer for the failures, but the manager or supervisor must also reflect on their effectiveness in developing commercial beef farming among those with little experience. Differences in personality and effectiveness of supervising veterinary officers have been important factors in the fluctuating fortunes of the Verata and Tilivalevu schemes.

Planners of these two beef projects also failed to consider long-term infrastructure requirements. The schemes have not been provided with adequate staff training or transport facilities. Recurrent expenses should have supported the projects at least until their income equalled their operating and overhead costs. To establish and maintain any new project, which policy-makers think appropriate to their political and economic objectives, project implementers should be forced to run on a shoe string budget. Many projects start well, but either fail after the initial financial support ends, or absorb an unacceptable amount of local and foreign aid resources.

The poor performance of many of the smallholders is a function of the dual impact of socio-cultural constraints and inadequate effective management and supervision. Nevertheless, the cattle owners themselves do not all consider their farms as failures. They are generally still enthusiastic about keeping their cattle which give them status and recognition, and are quietly looking forward to clearing their debts and freeing themselves from the control of the FDB and the supervising officers. Farmers see some veterinary officers as working for the bank, rather than for them, and, thus, their confidence in the officials is diminished. The reconciliation of the interests of the FDB, the MPI and the farmers themselves must be addressed if the beef projects are to benefit all participants.

Thus, effective development communication and grass-roots participation are not by themselves a panacea for success and economic development. Although they can facilitate the development process, they cannot alone guarantee its success. Political, social and cultural factors are strong impediments to effective development communication and thus to the realisation of the project objectives. Change agents in positions of power often become so arrogant and paternalistic that they impose what they think is right upon those in a subordinate position who, in turn, often accept this willingly, through lack of knowledge or confidence. Failure to appreciate these factors has led to resistance to change, loss of capital investment in agricultural projects, and the failure of many technical assistance programmes. Unless these constraints are well understood in the planning and implementation stages, economic development projects among Fijians will continue to fail even in the face of effective communication.

NOTES ON AUTHORS

Imam Ali is a lecturer in geography at the University of the South Pacific. After spending a number of years as a high school teacher he returned to university where his research on Yaladro cane farmers formed the basis of his MA thesis at USP. He is due to begin PhD research at the Australian National University.

Tim Bayliss-Smith is a lecturer in geography at the University of Cambridge. He has had a long record of research in Fiji, including participation in the UNESCO/UNFPA project on the Eastern Islands and, more recently, was a consultant with the Atkins' team on the regional plan for Western Vanua Levu.

Joseph Chung is a former Principal Agricultural Officer in Fiji and his extensive experience of Fijian agriculture has led to a number of publications on the subject. Recently, he has acted as a consultant on several projects including communication in rural development and a comparison of the Hawaiian and Fijian ginger industries. He has a long-standing interest in indigenous agricultural systems and disaster rehabilitation.

Margaret Chung is currently a PhD student at the Australian National University and is conducting research on fertility change in Fiji. She lived and worked in Fiji for many years prior to completing an MA programme at the University of Hawaii in 1986. Her studies and research on the impact of the new Monasavu road in Wainimala were supported by the Population Institute, East-West Center, Honolulu.

Setareki Delana is Principal of Nabua Secondary School. After teaching throughout Fiji, he returned to university to complete his degree in 1985. As the leader of a student research group on small-scale commercial fishing during course work, he is principal author of the chapter on this topic.

Charles Eaton presently is manager of the Southern Development Company Ltd in Fiji, which is involved in the production of tobacco. His long involvement in this and other rural industries in Fiji led him to undertake research for an MPhil degree at the University of the South Pacific, which he completed in 1988.

Patrick Haynes is Chief Agronomist for Atkins Land and Water Management Company, Cambridge. As well as working on the Atkins Western Vanua Levu plan, he participated in the UNESCO/UNFPA project on the Eastern Islands of Fiji and his knowledge of Pacific agricultural systems is extensive.

Jiten Mangal, when he wrote his paper on *yaqona*, was an undergraduate student at the University of the South Pacific. A resident of Ovalau, he had first-hand experience of the marketing networks for this crop.

John Overton, a Research Fellow at the Australian National University, was a lecturer in geography at the University of the South Pacific in 1985. Then, and after, he conducted research in a number of villages and settlement schemes, examining changes in agriculture and processes of socio-economic differentiation.

Asesela Ravuvu is Professor and Director of the Institute of Pacific Studies at the University of the South Pacific. He completed his doctorate in anthropology at the University of Auckland and his books *Vaka i Taukei* and *Fijian Ethos* have become standard references on Fijian culture. His intimate knowledge of rural Fiji and research projects have led him to many parts of the country.

Randy Thaman is a lecturer in geography at the University of the South Pacific. He has researched and written widely on Pacific agriculture but has had a particular interest in agricultural systems, nutrition, and environmental issues. His energy and enthusiasm have stimulated many USP geography students and fostered a recent growth in postgraduate research in applied rural geography.

Mesake Tukai completed his BA degree at the University of the South Pacific in 1985 and is now a teacher at Queen Victoria School, Tailevu North. From Cautata village in Tailevu, he has been able to note some of the profound changes occurring in village society as the result of economic pressures.

GLOSSARY

bele	'bush spinach' (*Abelmoschus manihot*), a common green leaf vegetable
bili ni koro	the outskirts of a village
bito	(see *i tokatoka*) sub-lineage of a *mataqali*, term used in western Viti Levu
bure	a thatched house
dalo	taro (*Colocasia esculenta*)
duruka	'Fiji asparagus', cane inflorescence (*Saccharum edule*)
galala	a person who is independent of the village and free of, or exempted from, communal obligations
i cavuti	a sacred totem, often a plant or tree associated with a particular *mataqali*
kakana dina	root crop food
kerekere	to request in the traditional manner
koro	village
kumala	sweet potato (*Ipomoea batatas*)
lali	a wooden gong or drum
lawena	the stem of the *yaqona* plant
leqa	a problem
masi	tapa, bark-cloth made from the bark of the mulberry tree
mata-ni-vanua	a herald, usually the spokesman of the chief
mataqali	an agnatically related unit, usually a lineage of a *yavusa* descent group. It is exogamous, patrilineal and the main recognised land-owning unit
ota	fern, used as a green vegetable
qele ni teitei	garden, agricultural land
raki	fallow areas
rourou	leaves of the *dalo* plant used as spinach

sevusevu	ceremonial offering, usually of *yaqona*, between guest and host in respect and recognition of the other
soli	a collection
tabua	whale's tooth, used for ceremonial exchange
talasiga	high-laterised grasslands common on the drier western parts of the main islands
tikina	an administrative unit, below the level of the province
tokatoka	(*i tokatoka*) sub-lineage of a *mataqali*, an 'extended family'
vakavanua	in the customary manner, the way of the land
vanua	the land, the people, custom. Also an association of *yavusa*
vei delana	uplands
vei were	active gardens
veikau	bush or forest
vudi	cooking bananas (*Musa* cultivars), often called plantain
waka	the root of the *yaqona* plant
wasewase	division, sometimes used to mean the process of dividing (land), and that which is divided in the traditional manner to members of the landowning descent group
yaqona	kava, *Piper methysticum.*
yasa	an absentee from a village, a migrant
yavusa	agnatically related clan, comprised of a number of *mataqali* and sharing a common male ancestor

---

Source: Nayacakalou 1978, Ravuvu 1983. A. Capell *A new Fijian dictionary* (Government Printer, Suva, 1968) was also consulted.

For further crop and tree names, see Appendix 1 of chapter 4.

BIBLIOGRAPHY

Airey, A., 1984. 'The role of feeder roads in promoting rural change in eastern Sierra Leone', *Tijdschrift voor Economische en Sociale Geografie* 76(3) 192-201.

Ali, I., 1986a. 'Increasing technological and food dependency on small-holder sugar cane farms in Fiji: a case study of dediversification and increasing vulnerability from 1975 to 1983'. Paper presented to Commonwealth Geographical Bureau, Workshop on Small-Scale Agriculture, Australian National University, Canberra, December.

————, 1986b. 'Polyculture to monoculture: a case study of changing agriculture in the Yaladro cane sector, Ba Province, Viti Levu, Fiji'. M.A. thesis, University of the South Pacific, Suva.

Anderson, A.G., 1969. 'Duality in Indo-Fijian small-farming', in I.G. Bassett (ed.) *Pacific Peasantry*. Manawatu Branch, New Zealand Geographical Society, Palmerston North, pp. 23-47.

————, 1974. *Indo-Fijian Smallfarming: Profiles of a Peasantry*. University of Auckland Press, Auckland.

Atkins Land and Water Management Ltd, 1983. *Western Vanua Levu Regional Plan* (5 vols). Ministry of Economic Planning and Development, Suva.

Australian Agricultural Consulting and Management Company Pty. Ltd., n.d. 'Fiji: Hurricane Flood Rehabilitation Project - Agricultural Development Programme. Unpublished report, Australian Agricultural Consulting and Marketing Company Pty. Ltd., Adelaide.

————, 1982. Fiji Rice Development Study. Unpublished report, Australian Development Assistance Bureau, Canberra.

Barrau, J., 1958. *Subsistence Agriculture in Melanesia*. Bulletin no.219, Bernice P. Bishop Museum, Honolulu.

————, 1961. *Subsistence Agriculture in Polynesia and Micronesia*. Bulletin no.223, Bernice P. Bishop Museum, Honolulu.

Baxter, M.W.P. 1980. *Food in Fiji: the Produce and Processed Foods Distribution Systems*. Monograph no.22, Development Studies Centre, Australian National University, Canberra.

Bayliss-Smith, T.P., 1983, 'A household survey of villages in Bua Province'. Technical Paper 1, *Western Vanua Levu Regional Plan*, Vol. 4, Ministry of Economic Planning and Development, Suva.

Bayliss-Smith, T.P.; Bedford, R.D.; Brookfield, H.C. and Latham, M., 1988, *Islands, Islanders and the World: the Colonial and Post-Colonial Experience of Eastern Fiji*. Cambridge University Press, Cambridge.

Bedford, R.D. 1981. 'Melanesian internal migration: recent evidence from Eastern Fiji', *New Zealand Journal of Geography* 71, 2-6.

Belshaw, C.S., 1964. *Under the Ivi Tree: Society and Economic Growth in Rural Fiji*. Routledge and Kegan Paul, London.

Belshaw, D.G.R., 1984. 'Planning and agrarian change in East Africa: appropriate and inappropriate models for land settlement schemes', in T.P. Bayliss-Smith and S. Wanmali (eds), *Understanding Green Revolutions*. Cambridge University Press, Cambridge, pp. 270-279.

Bienefeld, M., 1984. *Work and Income for the People of Fiji: a Strategy for More Than Just Survival. The Final Report of the Fiji Employment and Development Mission*. Government Printer, Suva.

Blaikie, P.M., 1980. *Nepal in Crisis: Growth and Stagnation at the Periphery*, Oxford University Press, New Delhi.

Blaikie, P.M., Cameron, J., Seddon, D., 1977. *The Effects of Roads in West Central Nepal*. Overseas Development Group, University of East Anglia, Norwich.

Borgstrom, G., 1980. 'The need for appropriate animal production systems'. Paper presented to the conference called by the International Foundation for Science, Aborian, Palawan, Philippines, May 17-21.

Bouchard, J.F., 1972. *The Impact of Roads on the Monetary Activities of Subsistence Economies in the Ikapa Region of Papua New Guinea*. Occasional paper no.4, Department of Geography, University of Papua New Guinea, Port Moresby.

Britton, S.G., 1980. 'The evolution of a colonial space-economy: the case of Fiji', *Journal of Historical Geography* 6(3), 251-274.

_____, 1983. *Tourism and Underdevelopment in Fiji*. Monograph no. 31, Development Studies Centre, Australian National University, Canberra.

Brookfield, H.C., 1976. 'The Taveuni farmers'. Working paper no.5, UNESCO/UNFPA Population and Environment Project in the Eastern islands of Fiji. Development Studies Centre, Australian National University, Canberra, for UNESCO\UNFPA.

_____, 1977. 'Constraints to agrarian change', pp. 133-138 in J.H. Winslow (ed.), *The Melanesian Environment*, Australian National University Press, Canberra.

_____, 1979. 'Land reform, efficiency and rural income distribution: contributions to an argument', *Pacific Viewpoint* 20(1) 35-52.

_____, 1985. 'An historical and prospective analysis of the coconut economy and the coconut districts of Fiji', in H.C. Brookfield, F. Ellis and R.G. Ward, *Land, Cane and Coconuts*. Department of Human Geography Monograph HG/17, Research School of Pacific Studies, Australian National University, Canberra, pp. 91-215.

_____, 1987. 'Export or perish: commercial agriculture in Fiji', in M.J. Taylor (ed.) *Fiji: Future Imperfect?* Allen and Unwin, Sydney, pp. 46-57.

Brookfield, H.C.; Ellis, F.; and Ward, R.G., 1985. *Land, Cane and Coconuts*. Department of Human Geography Monograph HG/17, Research School of Pacific Studies, Australian National University, Canberra.

Bull, C., Daniel, P. and Hopkinson, M., 1984. *The Geography of Rural Resources: Conceptual Frameworks in Geography*. Oliver and Boyd, Edinburgh.

Burns, A., Watson, T.Y., and Peacock, A.T., 1960. *Report of the Commission of Enquiry into the Natural Resources and Population Trends of the Colony of Fiji*. Parliamentary paper no.1, Government Printer, Suva.

Camoens, J.K. (ed.), 1985. *Regional Workshop on Livestock Production Management: The Proceedings*. Asian Development Bank, Manila.

Campbell, J.R. and Chung, J., 1986. *Post-Disaster Assessment   A: Management; Post-Disaster Assessment B: Field Survey.* Pacific Islands Development Program, East-West Center, Honolulu.

Chambers, R., 1969. *Settlement Schemes in Tropical Africa: a Study of Organisation and Development.* Routledge and Kegan Paul, London.

————, 1983. *Rural Development: Putting the Last First.* Longmans, London.

Chandra, R., 1980. *Maro: Rural Indians of Fiji.* South Pacific Social Sciences Association, University of the South Pacific, Suva.

Chandra, R., and Gunasekera, H.M., 1984. 'Regional planning and policy in Fiji', in B. Prantilla (ed.), *Regional Development.* United Nations Centre for Regional Development, Nagoya, pp. 281-339.

Chandra, S., 1981. *Energetics and Subsistence Affluence in Traditional Agriculture.* Occasional paper no. 24, Development Studies Centre, Australian National University, Canberra.

————, 1983. *Agricultural Development in Fiji.* Australian Universities International Development Programme, Canberra.

Chapelle, T., 1978. 'Customary land tenure in Fiji: old truths and middle-aged myths', *Journal of the Polynesian Society* 87(2), 71-88.

Chung, M., 1987. 'Structural change and population mobility: the impact of a road in rural Fiji'. M.A. thesis, University of Hawaii, Honolulu.

Clarke, W.C., 1965. 'From extensive to intensive shifting cultivation: a succession from New Guinea', *Ethnology* 5, 347-359.

————, 1977. 'The structure of permanence: the relevance of self-subsistence communities for world ecosystem management', in T.P. Bayliss-Smith and R. Feacham (eds), *Subsistence and Survival: Rural Ecology in the Pacific.* Academic Press, New York, pp.363-384.

Clarke, W.C., and Morrison, J., 1987. 'Land mismanagement and the development imperative in Fiji', in P. Blaikie and H.C. Brookfield (eds), *Land Degradation and Society.* Methuen, London, pp.176-185.

Clay, G., 1955. *A Report by Sir Geoffrey Clay, Advisor on Agriculture to the Secretary of State for the Colonies, on his Visit to Fiji in 1954.* Parliamentary paper no. 31, Government Printer, Suva.

Commoner, B., 1971. 'Evaluating the biosphere', in T. Detwyler (ed.), *Man's Impact on the Environment.* McGraw-Hill, New York, pp. 50-60.

Connell, J., 1985. *Migration, Employment and Development in the South Pacific - Country Report No. 4, Fiji,* South Pacific Commission/ILO, Noumea.

Coyne, T., 1984. 'The effect of urbanization and Western diet on the health of Pacific populations', in J. Badcock and R. Taylor (eds), Technical paper no.186, South Pacific Commission, Noumea.

Crocombe, R.G., 1971. 'Review article: R.F. Watters: Koro: economic development and social change in Fiji', *Journal of the Polynesian Society,* 80(4) 505-520.

Deo, I., 1983. 'Food cropping: the vital link', *Fiji Food and Nutrition Newsletter* 493, 1-2.

Derrick, R.A., 1965. *The Fiji Islands: a Geographical Handbook.* Government Printer, Suva.

Doulman, D.J., 1976. 'Benefit cost analysis and income distribution in developing countries: a review of the Rigo Road appraisal'. Unpublished seminar paper, Simon Frazer University, Vancouver.

Duve, R.N., 1980. 'Food adulteration trends in Fiji', *Fiji Agricultural Journal* 42(2), 15-18.

Duve, R.N. and Prasad, J., 1981. 'Quality evaluation of yaqona (*Piper methysticum*) in Fiji', *Fiji Agricultural Journal* 43(1), 1-8.

Eaton, C.S., 1986. 'Directed smallholder agriculture in Fiji: present status and future potential', Paper presented to Commonwealth Geographical Bureau, Workshop on Small-Scale Agriculture, Australian National University, Canberra, December.

————, 1988. 'Directed smallholder farming in Fiji: a case study of Virginia tobacco farming', M.Phil thesis, University of the South Pacific, Suva.

Eckholm, E., 1980. 'Land reform and development', *Dialogue* 13(1), 54-64.

Ellis, F., 1983a. 'Employment and incomes in the Fiji sugar industry', Discussion paper no.146, School of Development Studies, University of East Anglia, Norwich.

————, 1983b. 'An overview of employment in agriculture, forestry and fisheries: past trends and current policy issues', Discussion paper no.147, School of Development Studies, University of East Anglia, Norwich.

Evans, D.B. 1982a. 'The Seaqaqa sugar cane development project: a study of farmer commitment with some implications for the selection of settlers', *Fiji Agricultural Journal* 44(1), 1-8.

————, 1982b. 'Plantations and the plantation mode of production', in R.J. May and H. Nelson (eds) *Melanesia: Beyond Diversity*, Vol 2. Research School of Pacific Studies, Australian National University, Canberra, pp. 340-349.

Farmer, B.H., 1957. *Pioneer Peasant Colonisation in Ceylon.* Oxford University Press, London.

————, 1974. *Agricultural Colonisation in India Since Independence.* Oxford University Press for Royal Institute of International Affairs, London.

Fiji Bureau of Statistics, 1983a. *Current Economic Statistics.* Bureau of Statistics, Suva.

————, 1983b. *Overseas Trade Report for the Year 1982.* Parliamentary paper no.48, Government Printer, Suva.

————, 1984. *Overseas Trade Report for the Year 1983.* Parliamentary paper no.40, Government Printer, Suva.

————, 1985. *Overseas Trade Report for the Year 1984.* Parliamentary paper no.77, Government Printer, Suva.

Fiji Central Planning Office, 1975. *Fiji's Seventh Development Plan 1976-1980.* CPO, Suva.

————, 1980. *Fiji's Eighth Development Plan 1981-1985.* CPO, Suva.

—————, 1985. *Fiji's Ninth Development Plan 1986-1990*. CPO, Suva.

Fiji Electricity Authority, n.d. *Monasavu Power Three: From the Water and the Rock*. Government Printer, Suva.

Fiji Institute of Agricultural Science, 1984. Proceedings of workshop on Land Use, September 24-26, Lautoka.

Fiji Ministry of Agriculture and Fisheries, Fisheries Division, 1982. 'Fish marketing and distribution in Fiji', paper presented at the workshop on fish marketing and distribution, Hong Kong, 17-27 May.

Fiji Ministry of Agriculture and Fisheries, 1983. *Annual Report for the Year 1982*. Parliamentary paper no.66, Government Printer, Suva.

Fiji Ministry of Co-operatives, 1983. *Report for the Year 1981*. Parliamentary paper no.42, Government Printer, Suva.

Fiji Ministry of Primary Industries, Agricultural Commodities Committee, 1985. *Rice Profile: a Programme for Future Development of Rice Industry*. Ministry of Primary Industries, Suva.

Fiji Sugar Corporation, 1981. *Sugar in Fiji*. FSC, Suva.

Fisk, E.K., 1970. *The Political Economy of Independent Fiji*. ANU Press, Canberra.

Flenley, J.R. and King, S.M., 1984. 'Late Quaternary pollen records from Easter Island', *Nature* 307, 47-50.

France, P., 1969, *The Charter of the Land: Custom and Colonization in Fiji*. Oxford University Press, Melbourne.

Frazer, R.M., 1961. 'Land use and population in Ra Province, Fiji', PhD thesis, Australian National University, Canberra.

—————, 1964. 'Changing Fijian agriculture', *Australian Geographer* 9(3), 148-155.

—————, 1973. 'The Fijian village and the independent farmer', in H.C. Brookfield (ed.) *The Pacific in Transition*. Edward Arnold, London, pp. 75-96.

Funnell, D.C., 1976. 'The role of the small service centers in regional and rural development with special reference to Eastern Africa', in A. Gilbert (ed.) *Development Planning and Spatial Structure*. John Wiley, London, pp. 77-112.

Gould, P.R., 1970. 'Tanzania 1920-63: the spatial impress of the modernization process', *World Politics* 22(2), 151-170.

Griffin, C. and Davis, M.M. (eds), 1986. *Fijians in Town*. Institute of Pacific Studies, University of the South Pacific, Suva.

Griffin, V., 1978. 'Namosi: an area undergoing the impact of change'. Mimeo, Pacific Women's Resource Centre, Suva.

Groome, J.G. and Associates, 1981. *Namosi Provincial Forest Development*. Report prepared for the Fiji Government under the New Zealand Government's Bilateral Aid Programme. Groome and Associates, Wellington.

Gunasekera, H.M., 1982. 'Trends in regional planning in the South Pacific', in B. Higgins (ed.) *Regional Development in Small Island Nations*. United Nations Centre for Regional Development, Nagoya, pp. 31-48.

Gunasekera, H.M.; Tabakaucoro, F.; Waymark, D.; and Young, J., 1983, 'Seaqaqa sugar cane farmers and Fijian villagers in the Seaqaqa periphery', Technical Paper 2, *Western Vanua Levu Regional Plan*, Vol. 4. Ministry of Economic Planning and Development, Suva.

Hardaker, J.B.; Fleming, E.M.; and Harris, G.T., 1984. 'Smallholder modes of agricultural production in the South Pacific: prospects for development', *Pacific Viewpoint* 25(2), 196-211.

Harriss, J.C., 1984. 'Social organisation and irrigation: ideology, planning and practice in Sri Lanka's settlement schemes', in T.P. Bayliss-Smith and S. Wanmali (eds), *Understanding Green Revolutions*. Cambridge University Press, Cambridge, pp. 315-338.

Hugo, G., 1981. 'Road transport, population mobility and development in Indonesia', in G.W. Jones and J.V. Richter (eds) *Population Mobility and Development: Southeast Asia and the Pacific*, Monograph no.27, Development Studies Centre, Australian National University, Canberra, pp. 355-386.

Jayawardena, C., 1971. 'The disintegration of castes in Fiji Indian rural society', in L.R. Hiatt and C. Jayawardena (eds) *Anthropology in Oceania*. Angus and Robertson, Sydney, pp. 89-120.

Johannes, R.C., 1982. 'Traditional conservation methods and protected marine areas in Oceania', *Ambio* 11(5), 258-261.

Johnson, J.S. and Lambert, J.N. 1982. ' The National Food and Nutrition Survey of Fiji'. Field Document no.6, National Food and Nutrition Development Programme (FIJ/79/004), National Food and Nutrition Committee, Suva.

Jones, S.; P.C. Joshi; and M. Murmis (eds), 1982, *Rural Poverty and Agrarian Reform*. Allied Publishers, New Delhi, for ENDA, Dakar.

Kerr, G.J.A. and Donnelly, T.A., 1969. *Fiji in the Pacific: a History and Geography of Fiji*. The Jacaranda Press, Melbourne.

Kirch, P.V., 1982. 'Ecology and adaptation of Polynesian agricultural systems', *Archaeology in Oceania* 17(1), 1-6.

Klee, G.A., 1980. 'Oceania', in G.A. Klee (ed.), *World Systems of Traditional Resource Management*. Edward Arnold, London, pp.245-281.

Knapman, B., 1976. 'Indigenous involvement in the cash economy of Lau, Fiji, 1840-1946', *Journal of Pacific History* 11(3), 167-188.

————, 1987. *Fiji's Economic History 1874-1939: Studies of Capitalist Colonial Development*. Pacific Research Monograph no. 15, National Centre for Development Studies, Australian National University, Canberra.

Lehmann, D. (ed.), 1974. *Agrarian Reform and Agrarian Reformism*. Faber and Faber, London.

Leinbach, T.R., 1983. 'Rural transport and population mobility in Indonesia', *Journal of Developing Areas* 17(3) 349-364.

Lloyd, D.T., 1982. *Land Policy in Fiji*. Department of Land Economy, University of Cambridge, Cambridge.

Low, J., 1985. *Factors Affecting Off-farm Labour Supply: a Case Study of Fiji Sugar Cane Farmers.* Islands/Australia working paper no.85/5, National Centre for Development Studies, Australian National University, Canberra.

Massal, E. and Barrau, J., 1956. *Food Plants of the South Sea Islands.* Technical paper no.94, South Pacific Commission, Noumea.

Mayer, A.C., 1961, *Peasants in the Pacific: a Study of Fiji Indian Rural Society.* Routledge and Kegan Paul, London.

McCall, M.K., 1977. 'Political economy and rural transport: a reappraisal of transportation impacts', *Antipode* 9(1), 56-67.

McCoy, P.C., 1976. *Easter Island Settlement Patterns in the Late Prehistoric and Protohistoric Periods.* Bulletin no.5, Easter Island Committee, International Fund for Monuments, New York.

McGee, T.G., 1975. *Food Dependency in the Pacific: a Preliminary Statement.* Occasional paper no. 2, Development Studies Centre, Australian National University, Canberra.

McLennan Magasanik Associates, 1984. *Vunidawa Integrated Regional Development Scheme.* McLennan Magasanik, Albert Park, Victoria, for Australian Development Assistance Bureau, Canberra.

Narokobi, C.S.N., 1984. 'The law of the sea in the South Pacific', *Ambio* 13(5/6), 372-376.

Native Land Trust Board, 1984. Annual report. NLTB, Suva.

_____, 1986. *The Native Land Trust Board. 40 years of Service to Fiji and its people.* Fiji Times, Suva.

Narayan, J., 1984. *The Political Economy of Fiji.* South Pacific Review Press, Suva.

Nayacakalou, R.R., 1975. *Leadership in Fiji.* Oxford University Press, Melbourne.

_____, 1978. *Tradition and Change in the Fijian Village.* South Pacific Social Sciences Association, University of the South Pacific, Suva.

Oedekoven, K.H., 1962. 'Saving our vanishing forests', *Unasylva* 16, 55-58.

Overton, J.D., 1986. 'Resettlement re-examined: accumulation and differentiation in Waibau and Lomaivuna, Fiji', Paper presented to Commonwealth Geographical Bureau, Workshop on Small-Scale Agriculture, Australian National University, Canberra, December.

————, 1987. 'Fijian land: pressing problems, possible tenure solutions'. *Singapore Journal of Tropical Geography* 8(2), 139-151.

————, 1988. 'A Fijian peasantry: *Galala* and villagers', *Oceania* 58(3), 193-211.

Parham, J.W., 1972. *Plants of the Fiji Islands.* Government Printer, Suva.

Parkinson, S.V., 1975. 'Some observations on the cause of malnutrition in Pacific Islands urban communities', in J. Harré and C. Knapman (eds) *Living in Town.* South Pacific Social Sciences Association and University of the South Pacific, Suva, pp. 69-75.

————, 1977. *The South Pacific Handbook of Nutrition.* YWCA, Suva.

————, 1982. 'Nutrition in the South Pacific: past and present', *Journal of Food and Nutrition*, 39(3), 121-125.

Patridge, I.J., 1979. 'Improvement of Nadi blue grass (*Dichanthium caricosium*) pasture on hill land in Fiji with superphosphate and sirato: effects of stocking rate of beef production and botanical composition. *Tropical Grasslands* 3(2), 157-164.

Powell, J.M., 1976. 'Ethnobotany', in K. Paijmans (ed.) *New Guinea Vegetation.* Australian National University Press, Canberra, pp.106-183.

Quartermain, A.R., 1980. 'Livestock', in R.G. Ward and A. Proctor (eds) *South Pacific Agriculture: Choices and Constraints.* Asian Development Bank, Manila, pp. 261-292.

Ravuvu, A., 1983. *Vaka i Taukei: the Fijian Way of Life.* Institute of Pacific Studies, University of the South Pacific, Suva.

————, 1987. *The Fijian Ethos.* Institute of Pacific Studies, University of the South Pacific, Suva.

Richardson, D., 1981. *Forestry and the Environment in the South Pacific.* Topic review paper, South Pacific Regional Environmnetal Programme (SPREP), South Pacific Commission, Noumea.

Riddell, J.B., 1968. *The Spatial Dynamics of Modernization in Sierra Leone.* Syracuse University Press, Syracuse.

Rizer, J.P.; Lin, J.; Waqavonovono, M.; Saumatua, S.; and Marjoram, A.G., 1982. *The Potential Impacts of a Namosi Copper Mine: a Case Study of Assimilation Planning.* Centre for Applied Studies in Development, University of the South Pacific, Suva.

Roth, G.K., 1953. *Fijian Way of Life.* Oxford University Press, London.

Rothfield, R. and Kumar, B., 1980. *Report on the Census of Agriculture 1978.* Parliamentary paper no.28, Government Printer, Suva.

Rutz, H.J., 1976. 'The efficiency of traditional agriculture, phases of development and induced economic change in the Waidina Valley, Fiji', in D.C. Pitt (ed.) *Development from Below: Anthropologists and Development Situations.* Mouton, The Hague, pp. 167-188.

_____, 1977. 'Individual decisions and functional systems: economic rationality and environmental adaptation in the Waidina Valley, Fiji', *American Ethnologist* 4(1), 156-174.

_____, 1978a. 'Ceremonial exchange and economic development in village Fiji', *Economic Development and Cultural Change* 26(4), 777-805.

_____, 1978b. 'Fijian land tenure and agricultural growth', *Oceania* 49(1), 20-34.

_____, 1987. 'Capitalizing on culture: moral ironies in urban Fiji', *Comparative Studies of Society and History* 29(3), 533-557.

Sahlins, M.D., 1962. *Moala: Nature and Culture on a Fijian Island.* University of Michigan Press, Ann Arbor.

Samarasinghe, V., and Samarasinghe, S.W.R.de A., 1984, 'Income and wealth disparities in a land settlement of the Sri Lanka Dry Zone', in T.P. Bayliss-Smith and S. Wanmali (eds), *Understanding Green Revolutions.* Cambridge University Press, Cambridge, pp. 173-193.

Sharma, P., 1985. 'Issues and implications of rising food imports: the case of Fiji', *South Pacific Forum* 2(1), 47-58.

————, 1986. 'Pricing policy in Fijian agriculture', *Review* 13, 34-39.

Shephard, C.Y., 1944. *Report on Agricultural Policy for Fiji and the Western Pacific High Commission Territories.* Parliamentary paper no. 24, Government Printer, Suva.

————, 1945. *The Sugar Industry in Fiji.* Colonial no.188, HMSO, London.

Smith, C.T., 1984. 'Land reform as a pre-condition for Green Revolution in Latin America', in T.P. Bayliss-Smith and S. Wanmali (eds), *Understanding Green Revolutions.* Cambridge University Press, Cambridge, pp. 18-36.

Sofer, M., 1985. 'Yaqona and peripheral economy', *Pacific Viewpoint* 26(2), 415-436.

————, 1987. 'Progress through transformation: a Fijian village', *Pacific Viewpoint* 28(1), 1-19.

Soja, E.W., 1968. *The Geography of Modernization in Kenya.* Syracuse University Press, Syracuse.

Southern, R., 1973. 'Road Transport in the New Guinea Highlands', Occasional paper no.6, Department of Geography, University of Papua New Guinea, Port Moresby.

Sovasova, J.R., 1980. 'Seaqaqa Sugar Development Project, Annual Report 1980'. Unpublished, Fiji Development Bank, Seaqaqa.

Spate, O.H.K., 1959. *The Fijian People: Economic Problems and Prospects.* Parliamentary paper no. 13, Government Printer, Suva.

Standal, B.R.; Street, J.M.; and Warner R.M., 1974. 'Tasty, protein rich, and easy to grow: the new edible 'sunset' hibiscus', *Hawaii Farm Science*, Second Quarter, 2-3.

Stannar, W.E.H., 1953. *The South Seas in Transition.* Australian Publishing Company, Sydney.

Sutherland, W.M., 1984. 'The state and capitalist development in Fiji', PhD thesis, University of Canterbury, Christchurch.

Thaman, R.R., 1976. *The Tongan Agricultural System: With Special Emphasis on Plant Assemblages*. University of the South Pacific, Suva.

————, 1976/77. 'Plant resources of the Suva Municipal Market, Fiji', *Ethnomedicine*, 4(1/2), 23-62.

————, 1979. 'Food scarcity, food dependency and nutrition deterioration in small Pacific Island communities', in W. Moran, P. Hosking and G. Aitken (eds) *Proceedings of the Tenth New Zealand Geographical Conference and Forty-Ninth ANZAAS Congress (Geographical Science)*. New Zealand Geographical Society, Auckland, pp. 191-197.

————, 1982a. 'The foods that came first', *Alafua Agricultural Bulletin*, 7(3), 105-116.

————, 1982b. 'Deterioration of traditional food systems, increasing malnutrition and food dependency in the Pacific Islands. *Journal of Food and Nutrition* 39(3), 109-121.

————, 1983a. 'Food and national development in the Pacific Islands: an introduction', in R.R. Thaman and W.C. Clarke,(eds), *Food and National Development in the Pacific Islands*. University of the South Pacific, Suva, pp. 1-16.

————, 1983b. 'Food for urbanizing Polynesian people'. *Proceedings of the Nutrition Society of New Zealand* 8, 1-22.

————, 1984. 'Food dependency and malnutrition: deterioration of traditional Pacific food systems', pp. 67-117 in E. Utrecht (ed.), *Fiji: Client State of Australasia?*. Transnational Corporations Research Project, University of Sydney, Sydney.

————, 1985. 'Pacific islands health and nutrition: trends and areas for action', in *Development and Change: Issue Papers*, Pacific Islands Conference, Rarotonga, Cook Islands, August. Pacific Islands Development Program, East-West Ceter, Honolulu, pp.III-A.1-27.

————, 1986. 'Trees, conflict resolution and peace: the preservation of trees as a precondition for environmental and social stability', in J. Maas and R.A.C. Stewart (eds) *Toward a World of Peace: People Create Alternatives*, University of the South Pacific, Suva, pp.379-396.

————, 1987. 'Urban agroforestry: the Pacific islands and beyond', *Unasylva*, 39(155), 2-13.

Thaman, R.R. and Ba, T., 1979. 'Energy needs and forest resources of small islands', in W. Moran, P. Hosking and G. Aitken (eds) *Proceedings of the Tenth New Zealand Geographical Conference and Forty-Ninth ANZAAS Congress (Geographical Science)*. New Zealand Geographical Society, Auckland, pp.198-204.

Thaman, R.R. and Clarke, W.C., 1983. 'Pacific island agrosilviculture: systems for cultural and ecological stability', paper presented to the Fifteenth Pacific Science Congress, Dunedin, 1-11 February.

Thaman, R.R. and Thomas, P.M., 1982. 'The cassava invasion: the cultural, nutritional and ecological impact of cassava on Pacific island food systems', in R.M. Bourke and V. Kesavan (eds) *Proceedings of the Second Papua New Guinea Food Crops Conference: Part Two*. Department of Primary Industries, Port Moresby, pp.330-350.

————, 1985. 'Cassava and change in the Pacific island food systems', in D.J. Cattle and K.H. Schwerin (eds) *Food Energy in Tropical Ecosystems*. Gordon and Breach, New York, pp.191-228.

Thompson, L.M., 1940. *Fijian Frontier*. American Council Institute of Pacific Relations, New York, San Francisco and Honolulu.

Titley, A.L., 1976. 'Regional planning and rural development in Fiji', mimeo, United Nations Regional Planning Project, Suva.

Tubuna, S., 1985. 'Patterns of Fijian return migration in the Wainibuka River valley, Viti Levu, Fiji', in M. Chapman and R.M. Prothero (eds) *Circulation in Population Movement*. Routledge and Kegan Paul, London, pp. 213-224.

Tudge, C., 1977. *The Famine Business*. Penguin, Harmondsworth.

Twyford, I.T., and Wright, A.C.S., 1965. *The Soil Resources of the Fiji Islands*. Government Printer, Suva.

UNESCO/UNFPA, 1977. *Population, Resources and Development in the Eastern Islands of Fiji: Information for Decision-Making*. Australian National University Press, Canberra, for UNESCO.

UNFAO/ Fiji Ministry of Agriculture and Fisheries, 1982. 'The rice industry of Fiji: an analysis of the rice industry with recommendations for its improvement'. Unpublished report, UNFAO, Suva.

Ward, M.W., 1970. *The Rigo Road: a Study of the Economic Effects of New Road Construction.* New Guinea Research Bulletin, no.33, Australian National University, Canberra.

_____, 1975. *Roads and Development in South-West Bougainville.* New Guinea Research Bulletin no.62, Australian National University, Canberra.

_____, 1982. 'Roads', in R.J. May and H. Nelson (eds), *Melanesia: Beyond Diversity*, Vol 2. Research School of Pacific Studies, Australian National University, Canberra, pp. 415-433.

Ward, R.G., 1960. 'Village agriculture in Viti Levu, Fiji', *New Zealand Geographer* 16(1), 33-56.

_____, 1964. 'Cash cropping and the Fijian village', *Geographical Journal* 130(4), 484-506.

_____, 1965. *Land Use and Population in Fiji: a Geographical Study.* HMSO, London.

_____, 1980a. 'Migration, myth and magic in Papua New Guinea', *Australian Geographical Studies* 18(2), 119-134.

_____, 1980b, *'Plus ça change ...* plantations, tenants, proletarians or peasants in Fiji', in J.N. Jennings and G.J.R. Linge (eds), *Of Time and Place.* Australian National University Press, Canberra, pp. 134-152.

_____, 1985. 'Land, land use and land availability', in H.C.Brookfield; F. Ellis; and R.G. Ward, *Land, Cane and Coconuts.* Department of Human Geography Monograph HG/17, Research School of Pacific Studies, Australian National University, Canberra, pp. 15-64.

_____, 1986. 'Change in land use and villages - Fiji: 1958-1983', *Travaux et Documents de Geographie Tropicale CEGET* 55(1), 109-120.

_____, 1987. 'Native Fijian villages: a questionable future?', in M.J. Taylor (ed.). *Fiji: Future Imperfect?* Allen and Unwin, Sydney, pp. 33-45.

Ward, R.G. and A. Proctor (eds), 1980. *South Pacific Agriculture: Choices and Constraints.* Asian Development Bank, Manila and Australian National University Press, Canberra.

Watters, R.F., 1969a. *Koro: Economic Development and Social Change in Fiji.* Clarendon Press, Oxford.

————, 1969b. 'Tribesman or peasant? The evolution of rural society in Fiji', in I.G. Bassett (ed.) *Pacific Peasantry.* Manawatu Branch, New Zealand Geographical Society, Palmerston North, pp. 7-21.

Weiner, M.A., 1984. *Secrets of Fijian Medicine.* University of California, Berkeley.

Wilson, W.A., 1984. 'Pacific trade in livestock products since 1965'. Agricultural policy discussion paper no.5, Centre for Agricultural Policy Studies, Massey University, Palmerston North.

World Bank, 1976. *Fiji: Appraisal of the Sugar Development Project.* Report no.986a - FIJ, World Bank, New York.

Yarrow, R.H., 1986. 'Crop development, livestock and fisheries projections for the DP9 period', paper presented to the Fiji Institute of Agricultural Science, Lautoka 23 March.

Yen, D.E., 1980a. 'Pacific production systems', in R.G. Ward and A. Proctor (eds), *South Pacific Agriculture: Choices and Constraints.* Asian Development Bank, Manila and Australian National University Press, Canberra, pp.73-106.

————, 1980b. 'Food crops', in R.G. Ward and A. Proctor (eds), *South Pacific Agriculture: Choices and Constraints.* Asian Development Bank, Manila and Australian National University Press, Canberra, pp. 197-234.

INDEX